HARRY AGGANIS
"THE GOLDEN GREEK"
AN ALL AMERICAN STORY

Harry Agganis
"THE GOLDEN GREEK"
An All American Story

Nick Tsiotos
Andy Dabilis

with a Foreword by
George Sullivan
and Epilogue by
Steve Kiorpes Bulpett

Hellenic College Press
Brookline, Massachusetts 02146

© 1995 Nick Tsiotos and Andy Dabilis
Published by Hellenic College Press
50 Goddard Avenue
Brookline, MA 02146

Library of Congress Cataloging-in-Publication Data
Tsiotos, Nick.
Harry Agganis, the Golden Greek: an All-American story/by Nick Tsiotos and Andy
Dabilis; foreword by George Sullivan; post-script by Steve Kiorpes Bulpett
    p.   cm.
Includes bibliographical references and index.
ISBN 0-917653046-7
    1. Agganis, Harry. 2. Baseball players—United States—Biography. 3. Boston
Red Sox (Baseball team) 4. Football players—United States—Biography. 5. Boston
University—Football. I. Dabilis, Andy. II. Title.
GV865.A28T75 1995
796.357'092—dc20
[B]   95-14294
                                                                    CIP

For my father, Vasilios, who first told me of the legend of Harry Agganis, "The Golden Greek."
For my mother, Margaret, who taught me about the value of love and family, and who, like Harry, was selfless, kind and thought of others first.

Andy Dabilis

To my father, Constantinos, and my mother, Polixeni, who instilled in their children their example of selflessness, education, work, and family, as the way to attain the American dream.

Nick Tsiotos

And in the hope American youths will learn from the example of Harry Agganis and from the oath taken by Athenian youths in Ancient Greece: "We will transmit this city not less, but greater, better and more beautiful than it was transmitted to us."

◆ CONTENTS ◆

◆ ACKNOWLEDGMENTS ◆

The authors wish to thank all the members of the Agganis family for giving their trust, unfettered support and authorization for this exhaustive project, especially Phil and Helen Agganis for their words, and fine meals where we discussed Harry and his life. Also, Jimmy, Demo, Constantina, and Paul Agganis and his wife, Bess, for their remembrances.

And special thanks to Tony Raimo and his family for continuing to keep the voluminous record of Harry's life that was begun by his sister, Mary, who died in 1991.

To my wife, Margaret, and my daughter, Catherine Dabilis, for the many nights when we were away researching and writing and interviewing, to my sisters Kim and Debbie, and brother John, for listening to me talk about Harry, and to my cousin, Nick Gavriel, for coming through to enable us to keep working on this book, my uncle, George Dabilis, and to my *Boston Globe* colleagues, especially editors Dick Powers, John Burke and Marvin Pave, and workmates Jerry Taylor, John Vellante, Julie Kersh, Dan Caples, Deborah Canzater, Karen Keough, Kevin Horrigan and Ben Greene, there is much appreciation from Andy Dabilis.

For my brothers, Chris and John Tsiotos, my sister Elaine Mallios, Chris Zikos, Mike Condakes, George Kalogeris; and my Greek school teachers, relatives and teammates, my aunt Sophia Speliakos, whose understanding of the nuances of Greek was invaluable, and the finest educators I've worked with, my colleagues in the Boston Public Schools, great thanks from Nick Tsiotos.

We also are very grateful to Kathy McCabe of *The Boston Globe* for the use of her laptop computer and her patient understanding, and to Themis Stoumbelis, whose loving collection of letters and memorabilia was a treasure trove for research. And to Nick Spiliotis and Effie Orgettas for the use of their beautiful house on a pond for some tranquility.

George Sullivan, who wrote the foreword for this book, almost single-handedly kept alive the legend of Harry Agganis with his constant writings over the years that convinced the unbelieving of the Golden Greek's exploits. And to *Boston Herald* Sports Columnist Steve Kiorpes Bulpett for his epilogue.

And there were Harry's best friends, who were unswerving in their devotion to this cause: Jimmy Andrews, Jimmy Orphanos, Nick Sentas, Mike and Charlie Frangos, and the inimitable singer, Jimmy Kirios Kerr, former Boston Celtic Lou Tsioropoulos, Harry Zingus, Louis Thallasites, Andy and Jimmy Vrees, and Tommy McGee. And to Joan Fitzgerald, Jim O'Brien, and Jean Dallaire for their time and patience in recalling Harry.

To Harry's Lynn Classical teammates, including George Bullard, who, with

Harry, helped comprise the greatest backfield in the history of New England high school football, and Nils Strom, George Pike, and Dave Warden.

Ed Carpenter, the sports information director at Boston University and Rick Young of the B.U. Photo Services, Harry's B.U. teammates and friends, who never forgot him: Bobby Whelan, Dick Fecteau, John Simpson, Len D'Errico, Harry Botsford, Joe Stoico, George Winkler, Charlie Kent, Tom Oates, John Nunziato, Frank Giuliano, Joe Terrasi, John Toner, George Spaneas, assistant coach Steve Sinko, Silvio Cella, Frank Luciano, Titus Plomaritis, and Irv Heller.

The rivals who admired him: Mel Massucco, Paul Millerick, Andy Konovalchik, Arthur Drivas, Joe Regis, Charley St. Paul, Jack Scarbath, Ed and Dick Modzelewski, Chuck Stobbs, and Johnny Unitas.

His Red Sox teammates Ted Lepcio, Norm Zauchin, Dick Gernert, Frank Sullivan, Johnny Pesky, Billy Consolo, Ike DeLock, Sam Mele, and Ted Williams, and former general manager Dick O'Connell and his secretary, Mary Trank, and Mary Jane Ryan of the publicity department, and former General Manager Lou Gorman.

Those who passed away before this book was written, but whose words lived on: Tom and Jean Yawkey, Harry's former Lynn Classical coach Bill Joyce, Lynn Item Sports Editor Red Hoffman, former B.U. coach Buff Donelli, Telly Savalas, Harold Zimman, and former B.U. President Harold Case.

There were countless others who provided information in interviews or through their resources, including Nancy Agris, editor of *The Hellenic Chronicle*, her mother, Anne, whose late husband, Peter, who founded the newspaper, knew and admired Harry.

And leaders of the Church and Hellenic College Press, including Archbishop Iakovos, Bishop Methodios, our editor Father N. Michael Vaporis, Tony Vrame, Rev. Steven Anthony, who was at Harry's side after he died and helped console his family, Rev. Charles Mihos and John Mihos of St.George's Greek Orthodox Church in Lynn, Massachusetts, and Sophia Nibi of the Greek Orthodox Diocese of Boston.

Former B.U. marketing professor and baseball adminstrator John Alevizos, WEEI Sports Radio talk show hosts Eddie Andelman and Teddy Sarandis, Athan and Maria Anagnostopoulos of the Greek Institute in Cambridge, philanthropists Mike Demoulas and George Behrakis, George Zaroulis, and all those who donated to the Harry Agganis Team Fund which erected a statue in his memory. And to Bob Costas, who lent his great good name as honorary chairman, broadcasters Ken Coleman and Curt Gowdy, who called many of Harry's games at B.U. and with the Red Sox.

The great Columbia All-American Gene Rossides, New York Congressman Gerald Solomon, Angelo "Junior" Dagres, Bob and Marty Goldman, George Gonis, Art Fiste, Peter Kostopoulos, Peter Mazareas, Elaine Demakis Grevelis, Stella Agganis Spyropoulos, Pericles Panos, Mel Palumbo, National AHEPA President Charles Georgeson, George Stephanos, Marine Gunnery Sgt. Sylvia Gethicker of Camp LeJeune, North Carolina, Dick Johnson, curator of the Sports Museum of New England, 1951 Heisman Trophy winner Dick Kazmaier, Harry's basketball coach Jim Twohig, John Galaris, Dr. Timothy Lamphier, Peter Stamas, Louis Pappas, Nick Kladis, Louis Manesiotes, Tom Demakes, Fred Smerlas, former Lynn Mayor Tom Costin, leaders of the Logganiko Society, including Spiro Makris and Bill Markos; John Chipouras, Harry Demeter, Nick Condakes, Leo Condakes, and Harris Jameson, Leon Stavrou of the American-Hellenic Institute, Jim and Kay Pappas, Charles Pappas, Melissa Bassett, Thor Jourgensen and Judy Johnson of *The Lynn Item*, Bob Keaney of *The Lynn Post*, Cleo Sophios, Diane Shepherd and Ken Turino of the Lynn Historical Society, Andy Coburn, Bill Ferguson, Julia Thacker, Amy Blumenthal, and Mike Eruzione of Boston University's Alumni Office.

And to the New England sports community, the friends and admirers of Harry Agganis, and to the Greek-American media and Greek-American community, whose chorus in unison for four decades made sure Harry would stay alive, and that, finally, this book would be done.

MYTHOS ◆ **MYTH** ◆ ΜΥΘΟΣ
by George Sullivan

Long ago I quit telling younger people about Harry Agganis. I'd start reciting the litany of a legend, and their eyes would glaze over with increasing disbelief. And I understood.

How could they believe me? You had to have seen Harry Agganis to have believed him. Even then you sometimes had difficulty trusting your eyes. He was one of a kind, and there has never been another like him.

Agganis was the corny Merriwell hero come to life in the American dream come true — the son of immigrant parents who fights his way from the wrong side of the tracks to fame and fortune. And, in an instant, he was the Homeric hero, dead at barely twenty-six.

In life he was the ideal model for the great American sports novel. In death he was the ironic portrait of a Greek tragedy.

Can it really be forty years since that stunning transition — like a bolt of lightning crackling across the Boston skyline — numbed and bewildered us all in disbelief? Four decades?

Significantly, over all that time — one generation melting into another —

the Agganis legend has prospered. Parents telling children — and grandchildren. Passing the torch. Yet, until now, there has been no book to fully spell out that story, assembling all the facts once and for all — the complete painting, from unlikely beginning to incredible end, documented by the records and recalled by those of us fortunate to have known Harry and witnessed his magic.

Such a book is long overdue, and I had despaired it would ever be written. So I was thrilled when Andy Dabilis and Nick Tsiotos, two men I admire as diligent researchers and talented writers, told me they were tackling the task. Clearly, they were dedicated to the project.

Later came more good news: fittingly, the book would be published by Hellenic College Press — a beacon in maintaining the light of the Greek Orthodox religion and heritage that Harry treasured.

And I was delighted once again when I saw the manuscript. Even for one who had been there, the book was mesmerizing. Coming alive again were Agganis' magnetic heroics, from Manning Bowl, to Fenway Park, from the Orange Bowl to Yankee Stadium, and beyond. And not just those who say it all will revel in this replay. So should those not as fortunate, who must settle for reading about Harry Agganis. They'll be spellbound, too — if they can believe it.

It's a cynical time, when little seems genuine any more. It's an age when counterfeit is common, when some legends are inflated, if not wholly artificial.

Worry not about the Agganis Legend. This in one hero whose statue does not have feet of clay. Harry was the real thing, an ideal off the playing fields as well as on them.

So the saga of the Golden Greek requires no exaggeration. It need not be enlarged beyond all that Agganis created on the gridiron and diamond, where he spun dazzling excitement — whether it be foiling the University of Miami's powerhouse Hurricanes or the world champion New York Yankees. The man was electric. Graceful, he made things happen — often with drama, always with style.

A game-winning touchdown was needed? Bingo — Number 33 spiraled a picture pass to an open receiver (and booted the point after for extra measure). The enemy was storming back? No problem — here's a leaping interception or a coffin-corner punt. The Red Sox are trailing? No sweat — there's Number 6 slamming an extra-base hit.

Drama spiced Agganis' extraordinary career. Like late one memorable Sunday afternoon in early June 1954 — the favorite among all my mental snapshots of Harry.

Boston University commencement awaited its most famous graduating senior, but the Red Sox were locked in a tie game with the Detroit Tigers at Fenway Park. So Agganis smashed a two-run, game-winning home run, grabbed cap and gown from his locker, and rushed up Commonwealth Avenue in his red and black '53 Mercury hardtop to collect his diploma at old Braves Field — thus making two ballparks echo with thunder. Take that Hollywood!

And so the Agganis legend goes — on and on. It's all here, in all its triumph before being concluded by tragedy.

I frequently wonder what might have been — what further mountains Agganis would have scaled, how many more lives he would have enriched. I wondered that on a warm late-June night in 1955 as I saw Harry for the last time, on the altar of St. George's Church, and forty years later I still wonder.

I also still marvel at all the man accomplished during his twenty-six years. There is enough to fill a book. And here it is.

I can think of only one person who might not enjoy reading it. Harry Agganis. Not because it isn't the definitive recounting of his life, but because it is — in all its glory. And Agganis was not a glory boy. Fame and the spotlight almost embarrassed him. He was the ultimate team player, and I can't recall Harry ever talking about his contribution except as it related to the team. Or in answer to a reporter's question.

Harry Agganis let his actions speak for themselves, and did they ever. Eloquently.

So for all these reasons I thank the Lord a book finally has been written about the Golden Greek — and not just a book, but the book, thanks to the dedication and talents of Andy Dabilis and Nick Tsiotos.

Besides all the obvious reasons, I also am grateful for a selfish motive. It means I no longer need worry about what to tell younger generations about Harry Agganis. Now I can simply give them a copy of this book.

It's all here — all the celebrations of an athlete who, while extraordinarily gifted, was not too good to be true. It's a story for the ages. Enjoy.

PSYCHE ◆ **SOUL** ◆ ΨYXH

The story of Harry Agganis, the greatest New England-born athlete, has passed from legend into mythology. It would be unbelievable — except that it's true. They called him "The Golden Greek," because of the shining way he played sports and lived his life, and Harry Agganis left an indelible mark on everyone who knew him.

Trying to document his incredible life, especially the glorious decade from 1945-55 when he dominated sports headlines in New England, and became one of the country's best known athletes, was an arduous labor of love that required reading and surveying nearly 3,000 news stories, magazine articles, and personal letters, and interviewing nearly one hundred people, trying to get a representation of friends, family and teammates and those he had touched, or those who just knew of him and his exploits.

This book was authorized by Harry's family who said they waited almost forty years for it because they saw, every day, how he was a role model as a son and brother and athlete and friend. He was The Real Natural, a perfect gentleman and athlete to whom sports came easily, but who nonetheless worked hard to perfect his craft and hone his abilities. And where many athletes have little regard, and even contempt, for their fans, Harry loved his and especially idolized children who followed his career. There was no cost for a Harry Agganis autograph and no cold shoulder when you wanted to talk to him.

After his mother's death, Harry was closest to his sister Mary Raimo. She and her family kept a scrapbook of virtually every story ever written about him. She spent countless hours with her husband, Tony, keeping two newspaper-sized scrap books which contained the hundreds of stories which provided a base of resources for research. The authors spent hundreds of hours there and at Boston University library's special collections division, poring over microfilm, newspapers and videotape, and listening to scores of hours of audio tapes.

There have been too many tragedies in sports. Among native New Englanders, there was the death in 1990, at age forty-five, of former Red Sox star Tony Conigliaro, who grew up in a town near Harry and played his high school baseball in Lynn, Harry's hometown. Conigliaro, the youngest player ever to hit 100 home runs, sustained a serious eye injury in a game in 1967, but returned to struggle through adversity before his tragic death. And there was the death of Boston Celtics star Reggie Lewis in 1994.

Except for Lou Gehrig, there has never been a sports tragedy like that of Harry Agganis. His death was paralleled in the minds of fans and admirers only by that of President John F. Kennedy in its impact.

The real story of Harry Agganis, who seemed to be in perpetual motion, isn't his All-American career as a quarterback at Boston University or his burgeoning stardom as a first baseman for the Boston Red Sox. It wasn't his peerless high school career at Lynn Classical, where he became regarded as the best amateur football and baseball player in the country while still a teenager, when he was also an all-star basketball player.

It is of the humanity and generosity, the spirit of compassion and selflessness he exhibited, and how he put his family, friends and church above all else, even sports. His tragic death, some friends still insist, came because he returned to his teammates on the Red Sox too soon after a hospitalization because he wanted to help the club. He was, as the tribute on his headstone suggests, a role model for the youth of America.

Today, more than ever.

George Sullivan, his former baseball teammate at B.U, and the premier chronicler of Harry's life, put it best when he wrote: "Long ago, I quit telling younger generations about Harry Agganis. I'd start reciting the litany of a legend, and the young eyes would glaze over with increasing disbelief, and I would understand. How could they believe me? You had to have seen him to have believed him."

Perhaps not. Thanks to the dedication of people like George Sullivan and those who did know Harry, we have tried to compile, finally—in one place—the anecdotes, stories, myths and truths of a man who was called "perfect" by one of his admirers. This then, is a love story, of the love and admiration in which he was held, and which he gave back.

Writers have tried before to put together a biography on Harry, but gave up, either because it was such an overwhelming task or because there was no scandal, nothing tawdry or lascivious or corrupt. And that is the essence of why this book was done, to perpetuate his memory for the next generations.

There's another reason. In an age of avarice, selfishness, drug abuse, the breakdown of the family and moral values, Harry Agganis epitomized the best attributes of a human being. He had plenty of reason to become arrogant or aloof. He was the most celebrated schoolboy athlete in America and had to survive the pressures of almost impossible expectations wherever he went or played. What he left behind was more than records — it was the legacy of love and respect and how he has never been forgotten.

He was the Golden Greek in the Golden Era of high school sports, and brought B.U. its greatest years in football.

The Greek writer Nikos Kazantzakis once wrote of a character who felt his life a failure that, "He had weighed up his life and come out wanting." Harry's life was too short, but he never came out wanting.

Nor did those who knew him.

EMPNEUSIS ◆ **INSPIRATION** ◆ ΕΜΠΝΕΥΣΙΣ
June 19, 1956

Ｉt had been a long plane ride from Boston to Camp LeJeune, North Carolina for Mrs. Georgia Agganis. She was seventy-one-years old now, dressed in black on a warm summer day. She was heading for a ceremony where her son, Harry, was going to have the baseball stadium at the Marine training center named for him. Oh, how she wished he could have been here to see it.

Mrs. Agganis had been transported on a Navy plan and had her daughter, Mrs. Mary Raimo, by her side. Tom Costin, the mayor of Lynn, Massachusetts, where Harry had starred as a football, baseball and basketball player for Lynn Classical, was there also. So was Harry's old football coach at Boston University, Aldo "Buff" Donelli, and Tom McGee, one of Harry's best friends at B.U., who had been a Marine too. Harry's boyhood friend Mike Frangos, who now owned a restaurant in Beverly, Massachusetts, and Harry's godmother, Connie Visvis, made the trip.

So did Tom Dowd, the traveling secretary of the Boston Red Sox, for whom Harry had played in 1954 and 1955, showing promise he would be one of the rising stars of major league baseball for years to come. Dowd had delivered to the team the sad news about Harry, just a year before.

It was a bittersweet time. Harry Agganis was the youngest son of seven children of a Greek immigrant family that struggled through poverty and saw him become one of the most acclaimed athletes of his time in New England and the United States. And now his mother was coming to see him honored.

But she would rather have had him there, still swinging for the fences and dropping back in the electrifying zig-zag scrambles that made him famous, flashing the wide, bright smile that made him stand out in a room or a photograph, bouncing into a room he would fill with his presence, jumping in joy at the sight of an old friend, bending to talk to children, for whom he was a hero.

Mrs. Agganis was amazed at the sight of so many prominent Marine officers there to greet her. Maj. Gen. J.C. Burger, the camp's commanding general, was there, as was an even higher-ranking officer, Lt. Gen. E.A. Pollock, commandant of the Marine Corps station at Quantico, Virginia, where officers trained. Harry had been stationed at Camp LeJeune in 1950, called up while a student at B.U. during the Korean War build-up, one of only a small number of reservists pressed into duty.

He led the camp's football team to the Sixth Naval District championship and took the baseball team to the national service title. He was named the best amateur player in the country at a national tournament where he took the Marine team to fourth place against the best teams in the United States. He hit .347 and brought out crowds just to watch him swing for the Marines.

Mrs. Agganis was a quiet, dignified woman for whom stoicism was a traditional demeanor. The daughter of Spartan parents, she had married a Spartan man, and raised a Spartan family of five sons and two daughters who were devoted to each other. As she had since her husband died in 1946, she was dressed totally in black, broken only by a festoon of white embroidery circling her flat, black hat.

Harry's fame as the country's most celebrated high school athlete, as an All-American at B.U., and as a major league player for his home town Boston Red Sox, didn't diminish his sense of humility or dedication to his family, friends and church. He would rather have been with his friends than starring on a football or baseball field, they often said.

His skill, nobility, proud stance and poise, coolness on the field, and the regal way he carried himself, and an imminent sense of fair play, had him being called "The Golden Greek," by sportswriters who elevated him to a pantheon reserved for the greatest athletes.

But Harry's position, he felt himself, was better suited to sitting down to dinner at his mother's modest home at 118 Waterhill St. in Lynn, or riding around with his friends like Frangos and Jimmy Kirios, brothers Socrates and George Maravelias and Harry's nephew, Jimmy Orphanos, who was his age because Harry's brothers were so much older.

2

Mrs. Agganis carried herself proudly too, walking slowly through a frame of trees while Marine dignitaries marched solemnly in front of her as they headed to the field where a plaque with her son's name on it was waiting.

The Marines were naming the field after Harry, over war heroes like Gen. Chesty Puller, and it was a proud moment indeed for his family, although Mrs. Agganis was still a little puzzled why her little boy, who had grown into such a warm man and famous athlete, had been chosen.

There were a lot of sports figures and civic officials because Harry's name was still famous in the area around Camp LeJeune where his play had attracted civilian crowds too. They loved to watch the elusive Number 33 get out of harm's way in a football backfield. His baseball prowess made a lot of Marines give up their time off to come by the field to watch him play.

For Costin, who had just been elected mayor of his home town the year before, and McGee, the return had a double-meaning. They had both gone through Camp LeJeune as Marines and were struggling with those emotions as well as their thoughts of Harry.

Costin, dressed in a light-weight light-colored suit to be comfortable in the tropical climate, said there was as much melancholia in the air as celebration. "Everybody still had a sense of loss," he sighed. "He had such potential and had done so much in his young life." He marveled at how Harry's mother was holding up in the heat and emotion. He had known her and Harry's family for a long time and had served as a ward councilor in the Lynn neighborhood where the family lived.

Costin's family had grown up in that ethnically-mixed working-class neighborhood too, where people walked over to work at the General Electric plant or leather factories. His brother, Dick, had played in the same backfield with Harry at Classical in 1947, on a team that was acclaimed as one of the greatest in New England history. Classical's 1946 team may have been even better.

As he walked to the field, where 2,000 Marines were waiting, Costin thought of the irony. "We realized that we were honoring someone we had grown up with, and all admired because of his athletic ability, but he had a great sense of people power. He was able to relate to people. He never gave you the impression he was better than you or that he could overpower you," said Costin.

The entourage walked to the field where a large, bronze plaque was covered with a drape. Marines stood at attention at the sight of commanding officers. Costin stepped up to a microphone and looked out at the soldiers who had come to honor one of their own. "This ceremony," he said, "proves the statement—once a Marine, always a Marine." It was the Marine Corps code, *Semper Fidelis*, "Always Faithful." That's how Harry was to his friends.

Donelli, a short, tough man who had an imperial dignity about him, came up and said of the man he had loved like a son. "He had those qualities of which all Marines are so proud, loyalty and esprit de corps."

Dowd reached back into Greek history, of which Harry was so proud, to compare him to Pheidippides, the Greek soldier who had run from the battlefield of Marathon to Athens in ancient times to let the people of Greece know what was happening in an epic struggle against Persian invaders.

"NIKE!" Pheidippides had shouted before collapsing dead from his grueling run. It was the Greek word for victory.

Helped by the generals, as an honor guard snapped to attention, Mrs. Agganis stepped forward to take hold of a corner of the white drape, and pulled it down slowly.

As they were riding to the ceremony in the open staff car reserved for high-ranking officers and dignitaries, Mrs. Agganis leaned over and said to General Burger, in broken English, "So many boys die in war, why you name this field for my son?"

General Burger smiled back. It was an easy question to answer.

AXIOS ◆ WORTHY ◆ ΑΞΙΟΣ
June 25, 1955

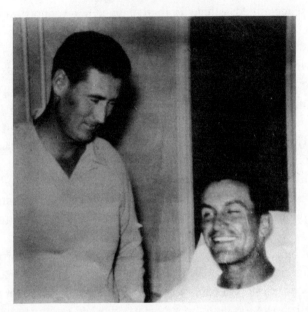

He was the most famous figure in baseball, and no one was going to keep Ted Williams from seeing his Boston Red Sox teammate, Harry Agganis, who was in bed at Sancta Maria Hospital in Cambridge, struggling to recover from a second bout of pneumonia that put him on the disabled list. Heads turned when Williams strode through the halls of the small hospital, which sat along the banks of the Charles River just across from Boston. It was within sight of Fenway Park, where they played together.

The "No Visitors" sign was up. But this was Ted Williams. He was larger than life, a regal man with a slighty aloof air who always seemed to be in a private, ethereal conversation with his own thoughts or a different set of gods, and when he walked by, even the air moved aside.

Harry had been so ill the past few weeks that few visitors, except his family and a few close friends, had been allowed to see him. It was a dispiriting sight. Harry had been called "The Golden Greek" since his high school days at Lynn Classical, because of his shining nobility, and because of the Greek God-like body, a perfect physique fit for a statue on the Acropolis. But the illness was taking its toll on even him, and he looked wan, with his usual slight beard a little darker, and his eyes were weary.

Even teammates, like Norm Zauchin, who was battling for the first base job with him for the Red Sox, had been kept away and his teammates were worried about the twenty-six-year-old rising star they called "Aggie." Left-handed first basemen were unusual in the league, and Harry had earned the respect of his teammates by not being a prima donna, although he had come to baseball as one of the most acclaimed college football players in the country, an All-American at Boston University, at quarterback and safety.

This was Teddy Ballgame. He loved Harry, and he was going to see him. No nurses, no officials, no security guards stopped him. Ted had his own troubles to think about too. Because of a complicated divorce proceeding, he had not joined the team until the middle of May, a few days before Harry first took ill. After a 10-day stay in the hospital, Harry had come back to join his teammates, but played only one game before becoming ill again and rushed back to Boston from Kansas City early in June.

Ted hadn't seen much of Harry that year, but he was glad to have him on the team. Harry was a fleet running left-handed slugger hitting ahead of Ted, and that kept pitchers at bay. They had to worry about a combination of Harry-and-Ted. It gave Ted, also left-handed, better pitches to look over.

When he became ill, Harry was hitting .313 and showing promise of becoming the American League's All-Star first baseman for the next decade, although he was only in his second year with the team. Ted had loved the work ethic Harry had shown too, and the way Harry worked as hard at baseball as he had in football. When he was only fourteen, Harry had been declared by many sportswriters the best high school football and baseball player in the country. He told friends he loved baseball, and Ted Williams.

Mary Trank, a Red Sox secretary, loved Harry too because he and another football and baseball teammate at Boston University, Tom Gastall, used to come over to Fenway Park to talk to her. One of the team's business managers, Dick O'Connell, had to laughingly shoo them out of her office, although he had known Harry for years too. Harry had played some high school all-star games at Fenway, and his college football games had been played there too, often to capacity crowds of more than 30,000, most of whom had come just to see him. He was well known and well-liked by Red Sox officials, who had scouts watching him since he was a teenager playing semi-pro baseball under an assumed name.

Williams, a decade older than Harry, used to talk with Trank about him. Harry had an electric smile and same kind of presence as Williams. Harry, she said, had a way of making you instantly like him. "When he walked into a room, it was like an aura. He didn't have to say anything," she said.

"Ted admired this kid. He played with the same kind of intensity Williams did and that made a difference with Ted. He couldn't tolerate anyone who put a half effort into anything." And Harry never did. He was immensely strong at 6'2" and 200 pounds and his body rippled with power and beauty. He had been called an "Adonis," and an "Apollo," but had never become conceited, although there were many female admirers.

Since his days at Classical, Harry had dominated sports headlines with his stardom in football, baseball, and basketball. He had captured the imagination of sports fans as an amateur in the same way Williams had as a pro. For the last glorious decade, their names had been the most talked about in sports in New England. Harry's football legerdermain had fans talking about him across the United States.

But something was terribly wrong now. Harry had been back in the hospital for several weeks and there had been a frustrating lack of progress. The pneumonia had been complicated by phlebitis, a swelling in Harry's right leg, which had been packed in ice to relieve the swelling. There was worry about a potential blood clotting.

Harry had been worthy enough to make it to the major leagues, and had told his brother, Phil, that the Baltimore Colts were going to offer him a contract to play quarterback in the offseason, which could make Harry a star in pro baseball and football. The Cleveland Browns had drafted him number one three years earlier, when he was still a junior at B.U., but had given up trying to convince him to play football, and traded his rights to the Colts.

Harry's name and exploits as an athlete were legendary. He had led Classical to national high school football prominence, had taken B.U. to stunning upsets of national powers who had better teams. Everything he touched or done had been golden for him. What made it even better, his friends said, was that there was no arrogance or imperiality about him. He was still Harry to them, still the friendly, engaging down-to-earth man who would always introduce a friend and think of others first. He was warm, generous, kind and loving, and it was returned measure for measure by those who knew him.

That included Williams, who usually kept a professional distance from most people. But he too took an instant liking to Harry, and this day he wanted to see how his friend was doing. The first time Harry was ill, back in mid-May, Ted had come to see him then, striding into the room where Harry was sitting up in bed talking to his boyhood friend, Mike Frangos, who had just opened a restaurant in Beverly, next to Lynn.

The air went out of the room. It was like the collision of two super-novas to have Harry and Ted in the same small space. There was gawking in the halls and people casually walked by just to peek inside. Frangos was there with his

7

brother, Charlie. A photo was taken showing Ted, looking ill at ease and his face fraught with worry through a forced smile, standing next to the bed and looking down at Harry, his famous smile struggling for joy, his eyes hooded with pain.

Ted took over. "Here, you big Greek, I hope you enjoy this," he smiled, tossing a magazine about Davey Crockett on the bed. The Davey Crockett saga, about the frontiersman who had died at the Alamo, was a national sensation on television, in a Walt Disney series that featured Fess Parker as Crockett. Boys and girls everywhere were running around in coonskin caps.

Then Ted got serious. "Harry, you're going to be fine. We're waiting for you. You're going to be fine. We want you back. You're going to be allright, take your time, take your time," he said, a sense of wish in his voice. And then he said, "We need you back, you big Greek. Get back on your feet." The way he had hundreds of times before, after pileups in football.

The Frangos brothers got up to leave and give the two friends their privacy. They closed the door softly on their way out, walking into a crowd of people outside the door.

Today was different. There weren't any visitors waiting in Harry's room, although he was expecting his family to come by later that afternoon. He hadn't seen any teammates in a while, including the only athlete he idolized.

Then the door opened.

AGAPE ◆ **LOVE** ◆ ΑΓΑΠΗ
1904 – 1943

Shortly after the turn of the 20th century, Lynn, Massachusetts was a destination for thousands of immigrants lured by the promise of the American dream, work in the city's leather and manufacturing factories and accessibility to Boston, only a dozen miles south. It was a working-class city of ethnic neighborhoods, some of which lay along the easy, curving coastline of the Atlantic Ocean.

Lynn had become known as one of the premier shoe manufacturing cities, and the downtown area was dotted with large brick buildings, much like those of the textile mills in Lowell and Lawrence, further north and inland, which had been the center of the industrial revolution in the United States.

Lynn boasted the huge plant of the General Electric company in the west section of the city, and it was there that thousands of immigrants found work, although there was a smaller, but equally famous business, the Lydia Pinkham Vegetable Compound, a medicinal product originally aimed at women.

There were neighborhoods of Irish, Polish, Jewish, and Italian families, and a growing influx of Greeks, who found company in their countrymen in the city and adjoining communities like Peabody, and, further away, Ipswich.

They came to America seeking a better future for their families. They were a people of laws, who worked hard to learn the language and become citizens of the United States, their new land. They brought with them their language and customs and family values, but they were Americans.

Two of these Greek immigrants had come from the same village of Logganiko, Sparta. George Agganis and Georgia Pappalimberis shared the same sense of homeland, a village that was where the Parnon and Taïgettos mountains met. Logganiko was built on the flat eastern side of the Taïgettos, at a height of nearly 800 feet, next to a plain where waters flowed and slopes were planted with olive trees, vineyards and fruitbearing trees.

It was a ruggedly beautiful place. But Lynn offered work and a future of economic hope in a new country, and there were so many friends and family from Logganiko that they could form their own society.

George Agganis was a small man, standing barely 5'4", but strong and athletic, and his face looked filled with light and wonderment, his eyes deep and cross-examining his surroundings, searching for the soul of life. He had tried out for the Greek Olympic team in the hop, step and jump, the forerunner of the modern triple jump, and it was an activity he loved. He served in the Greek military, too.

He was born March 15, 1875, and when he left Greece as a young man he came to Lowell. He spoke, French, Greek, Turkish, Albanian and, eventually, English. He moved to Lynn in 1904. There he met John Pappalimberis, who had a younger sister, a tall, stately woman named Georgia. She was five inches taller than George, but her brother arranged for them to be married, which was customary at the time.

Georgia, born June 16, 1885, was ten years younger than her husband-to-be. She spoke only Greek when they met and could not read or write. They were married on October 14, 1906. He was dressed in a traditional Greek outfit of the *Evzones*, a white skirt with 420 pleats called a *foustanella*, part of the uniform worn by fierce warriors whose fighting in the Greek War of Independence brought victory over the Ottoman Empire in a long battle that began March 25, 1821.

And that's how he was pictured in their wedding photograph, standing proud, while his new wife towered next to him, her lower lip pursed, her eyes locked on something only she could see.

They were both from big families. He had four brothers, George, Nikola, John and Epiminondas. Her parents, Michael and Chrisoula, lived in Ipswich, and she had four brothers, Louis, George, John, and Nicholas, and three sisters, Thanasia, Panayiota and Aphrodite. Nicholas and Panayiota lived in Greece.

The Agganis' first lived in apartments on Kirtland Street and Abbott Street.

George Agganis worked in the Benz-Kid leather factory and was an interpreter and aide for many Greeks going to take their citizenship tests.

It was an odd sight to see George speaking Greek to his compatriots and English to two lawyers named Shanahan and Coughlin, who were helping the immigrants.

George Agganis was present many times to hear the words, "Raise your right hand after me," as another Greek immigrant took the oath of allegiance for someone to become a naturalized American citizen. It was one of the proudest moments in their lives.

Their first daughter, Constantina, called Dena, was born in 1907. Demetrios, called Jimmy, was born two years later, and Demosthenes, called Demo, was born in 1911. George Agganis was a friendly man who liked to bounce his children on his knee, and he liked to talk and joke.

Shortly after Demo was born, war broke out in the Balkans. George Agganis went back to his homeland to fight against the Turks. He was an American citizen, and his wife, anxious to bring him home, packed up her three young children and took a boat to Greece, back to the village of Logganiko, where her children were cared for by relatives from both sides of their families.

Mrs. Agganis went to the Greek authorities to plead for his release. She said he had already served in the army, was now an American citizen and had three young children.

Her husband had two bullets in his right arm from being shot in combat against the Turks, she said. He wasn't even as big as his rifle when the bayonet was attached, but he was fearless. She wanted him back, and she was an insistent woman.

She didn't know where he was stationed or located, but she kept badgering authorities until he was found and released. It took two years. George Agganis was not alone in leaving the United States to come back to Greece. Thousands of Greek-Americans came back, leaving their families and hopes, and spent many years fighting Turkey in the Balkan Wars.

When they came back to Lynn, George Agganis worked again in a leather factory and saved his money until he could buy a modest three-story, two-family wooden home at 118 Waterhill Street, about a block from a big playground called Barry Park, and near a little Greek grocery store owned by Efthemios Demakis, and his wife, Yianoula.

The store had opened in 1914 and had a good clientele because West Lynn was full of Greek families, although living next to the Agganis family were the Mileskiewicz and Andriopoulis and Kirvan and Carbone and Booras families.

The Kanellas family lived a few doors away and had eleven children, and the streets in the summer were a symphony of sound, of neighbors and children and friends delighting in conversation. Despite their differences, most of the ethnic groups got along because they were striving for the same thing.

Going to the Demakis store was a social time too, but Yianoula Demakis had a recipe that brought in a lot of customers. It was for the Greek sausage called *lokaniko*.

The Demakis' would go into a back room and cure pork in salt and saltpeter for several days, and mix it with salt and pepper and spices, and add red wine and rind from thick orange peels, giving away the oranges to their help.

The Agganis' had another child, Phil, in 1919, and Paul a year later. It was about that time that Efthemios had his sons, Peter, Louis, Nick, and Charlie get up at 5:30 a.m., take trolleys in different directions, to Lowell, Lawrence, and Boston, and take orders from stores for their family's *lokanico*.

They would come back by 8 a.m., place their orders and go to school. After school, they would come back to the store, pick up the *lokaniko*, get back on the trolleys and deliver it. It was a good business that put their children through schools like M.I.T. and Harvard.

George Agganis would shop there, and he also liked to go to the Greek *kafeneea*, coffee shops in the neighborhood. He would savor time over small cups of thick Greek coffee in a cup called a *flijani*. He would talk with his friends, and his wife at home, about the Fates, tipping over the cup and letting the coffee residue settle, study it and try to tell their fortunes.

He worked hard and, by now, his oldest children were also working to help make ends meet. It was prohibition, when the sale of liquor was outlawed, and many familes bootlegged liquor too. For a short time, George Agganis made wine and sold it.

He was extroverted and joking and would question his friends and family to name all the politicians in the area because he knew the answers.

When he woke up in the morning, he would have a shot of Metaxa, a Greek brandy, after washing up and combing his wet black hair. The shot glass would be waiting on a curved shelf by the sink, left there by his wife, who ran the household.

The small, gray-shingled house had its bathroom in the cellar, where an overhead chain was used to flush the toilet, and the bathing was done in a huge tub called a *kazani*.

Sunday was family day, with dinner for all the relatives who'd visit. Jimmy liked to play baseball, and, as he grew older, played with the Con-A's, a semi-pro team, as a centerfielder and pitcher. But he had to work to help the family. He went to shine shoes at Joe Milo's, a shoe shine parlor on Exchange Street.

"*To bolo then vgazi psomee,*" his father would say. "The ball won't make bread, " it meant. They all had to work. The Greeks also would say, "*Fasouli*

fasouli, yameezee to sakouli," which means, "Bean by bean, the sack will fill." If they saved their money, little by little, it would grow.

Demo played catcher for the Con-A's too. He was a catcher but never used a mask because he couldn't afford one. Barry Park would be filled by people watching the games, a social setting on lazy Summer days.

By now, family life was the fulcrum for the Agganis'. They had a dirt driveway next to the house and there the children liked to play games and learn the hop, step and jump their father was teaching them.

The family, including George's nephew, Polichronis Agganis, would go to church together every Sunday, and the children looked forward to the days when their father would roast a lamb outside in the backyard, the succulent smells of garlic and basted meat wafting through the neighborhood, making everyone's mouth water with a spice taste on the tongue. He would baste the meat with olive oil and lemon juice, and sprinkle it with oregano. There would be potatoes roasting too and a savory rice with the reddened sauce of cooking.

Their mother would bake her own bread and cultivate vegetables in a back-yard garden, growing beans, and tomatoes and cucumbers for Greek salads with feta cheese and olive oil and vinegar, with a little oregano on top.

She liked to cook chicken and potatoes and make yogurt in a big sack, and a homemade pasta called *trahana*. She would also make desserts, little sweet braided cookies called *koulourakia*, butter cookies with powdered sugar called *kourambiethes*, and a syrupy cookie with walnuts called *melamakarona*.

Sometimes, when she wasn't cooking, Georgia Agganis would go to the next town of Salem to visit a Greek monastery.

On Sundays, three brothers who lived downstairs and who worked in a leather factory would come upstairs and eat with the family. Kostas, Andreas and Niko were musicians and, after dinner, they would take out a clarinet, the string instrument called a *bouzouki*, which produced a high-pitched joyous sound that would make you want to dance, and a *santouri*, similar to a hammered dulcimer with a softer, sweeter air that produced more melancholy notes.

There wasn't much money, but there was a lot of love. Greek music filled the room and everyone would want to dance, especially George Agganis, who loved the rousing steps of the *tsamiko*, where the leader would hold on to a handkerchief held by the next person in line.

He would leap high like an acrobat, kicking the front of his foot with one hand while the next person in line held him by a handkerchief, his other foot high and proud as he exulted loudly, "OPA!" while airborne.

These were the same songs and dances performed by Greek revolutionary war heroes a century earlier, and which would stir the blood of Greeks with militarism and urgent fervor for freedom. When they danced, they seemed to feel the spirit of their ancestors. George Agganis liked to sing *"O Stratiotis,"* the soldier, or *"O Aetos,"* the eagle. When he wasn't dancing or singing, George Agganis would play the bouzouki.

The women would dance more dignified line dances like the *kalamatiano* and sing folk songs that talked of poverty, war, love, courage and living in a foreign land, or described what it was like living in a small village.

There was one called *"To Papakee,"* about a swan going to a lake, and *"Pos To Treevoun To Peperee"* which is called "How Do You Grind The Pepper." Mrs. Agganis' favorite song was *"Panayoteetsa,"* the story of a young girl named Panayiota. The women were modest as they danced, and looked as delicate and fragile as the figures on an ancient Greek vase. And then, the men and women would come together and dance in a common circle.

The men would be whistling and hissing and laughing passionately, saying *"Yia Sou, Palikaree,"* which means "To your health, brave young warrior," and hugging each other. At the end of the night, a clarinet player would sound a song of Klephtic mountain warriors that could be sung alone or in a group. One of the favorites was named for the fighter Katsandonis.

Mrs. Agganis kept a *baoulo,* a big chest in which keepsakes were put, and she collected and sent clothes back to her relatives in her village in Greece. She would take them down to Greek liners which had docked in Boston Harbor, and watch them sail back to her homeland.

KOMODIA ◆ COMEDY ◆ ΚΩΜΩΔΙΑ

Every morning, George Agganis would come out from his room, meticulously groomed, and sit down for a shot of Metaxa. One morning though, he didn't know that Phil had put vinegar into the glass sitting on the curved shelf.

His mother saw him do it, and she waved her *koutala,* a wooden ladle, which she would, when needed, swing menancingly like a wand, warning her children with a reprimand.

George raised the glass to his lips and drank. He coughed and spit it out, and looked at his wife.

"Ti ekanes, yeeneka?" "What did you do, my wife?" he said sharply.

She said Phil had done it. He thought a moment as Phil sheepishly stayed away. But then George Agganis, who would always defend his boys, laughed and said "See how smart my boys are!" holding his sides, his face broadening proudly. The *koutala* was put away.

Although she was occasionally stern with her children, she was a woman full of compassion and a genuine and abiding love for them. They were adored by her, and she was respected by them.

It was a family of fun and jokesters and kissing and hugging. And always there was music and dancing. One day, Paul put out a plate for his older brother, Demo. "You never let me feed you, I want to feed you," Paul said impishly.

Feta cheese was a pure white goat's cheese cured in brine that was an irresistible staple on the tables of Greek homes, and Demo loved it. "Alright,you can feed me," he said.

Paul had put out a block of white Ivory Snow soap he had sliced to look just like a block of feta cheese, especially since he had sprinkled some real feta on top to make it look and smell like the cheese. Paul put a fork into the soap and handed it to Demo, who took a big bite, savoring it for a moment, until he gagged on the soap taste in his mouth. The whole family was at the table and they broke out in laughter, including Demo.

In 1923, Mary Agganis was born and it seemed the family was complete. George Agganis was 48 years old now, and his wife was 38, and they had six children and were a hardworking, close family where love was the most important commodity.

On April 20, 1929, George and Georgia Agganis had another child.

Aristotle Agganis, the youngest of seven children, and more than 20 years younger than his oldest brother, was born. He was called "*O mikros*," the little one. His mother adored him, and Mary, who was closest to him in age, began doting over him. His mother, shortening his name, called him Aristo, or, sometimes, Ari, which sounded a lot like Harry. The godparents were Aristotle and Connie Visvis. He, too, was called Harry.

The children used to take turns babysitting for Harry, and playing with him in their back yard. They would go to church every Sunday, and religious holidays were observed faithfully. There were icons of saints in the house, next to Mrs. Agganis' wedding crowns. Little Harry was getting a lot of attention as the youngest. The family especially enjoyed the Logganiko Society picnics.

He seemed slightly frail, and was growing into a gangly youngster. Like his oldest brother, Jimmy, he was naturally left-handed. His arm was strong and, as he grew, he liked to throw rocks in a field in Ipswich where he would play with his cousins.

Soon, his brothers taught him how to play baseball in the backyard, putting down rocks for bases and shortening their swings so they wouldn't break any windows in their house, or their neighbors homes. Harry was skinny, but cute, and already was showing a broad smile and tangly hair. Although the oldest brothers were working, the family was still poor. Mrs. Agganis had briefly worked for General Electric, but was needed at home, and returned.

In the 1930s, when the Depression hit, George Agganis went to work for the Works Project Administration, a federal program to put people to work on capital projects, building and repairing. Lynn was changing now too, struggling with the economic decline.

In 1931, the house of Mary Baker Eddy, the Mother of Christian Science, on Broad Street was opened to the public, and Lynn English's football team went to the White House where the players were greeted by President Herbert Hoover.

But foreign shoe imports increased 400 percent and there was worry about jobs in a city which depended on footwear. Lynn Classical, which had been designed as a college preparatory school, became more open and comprehensive. When the Warren Theater advertised an opening for a doorman, more than 150 applicants showed up.

By the next year, the city's unemployment bureau registered 6000 jobless, but a new Hotel Edison was built to replace the Hotel Lenox, which had burned down the year earlier. Times were tough everywhere, as a "bonus army" of veterans marched on Washington and sympathy hunger marchers passed through Lynn on their way to the state Capitol too. In 1933, there were bank collapses,and some reopened with limits of $10 per worker, but liquor stores offered credit to keep customers coming.

Bank withdrawals were allowed only for necessities, and after 10 days of uncertainty, banks reopened. In Boston, leather strikers rioted and were dispersed with tear gas. By the next year, there was a strike too in Lynn, of tanners and leather workers, and those in some shoe unions.

In 1936, Mayor Manning began his fourth term, and construction of the Manning Bowl was begun, a football stadium that would seat 20,000. It was built with federal funds. There was an upsurge in the business economy.

Manning lobbied for protective shoe tariffs as foreign imports began cutting deeply into the city's major industry. The depression had been referred to as the "unemployment crisis." Manning Bowl opened the next year for the annual Thanksgiving game pitting Lynn English against Lynn Classical.

By the time he was nine years old, Harry began heading for Barry Park to play baseball. He would spend all day there, taking a brown bag lunch. His mother didn't want him traveling with his friends to a river in nearby Saugus, where boys would go swimming, because he couldn't swim. So he would just play ball all day.

At first, he seemed an unlikely athlete. Nona Kirvan, a neighbor, said, "An athlete was about the last thing you'd figure Harry to be. Oh he'd try his best, always, but he was so skinny and frail. But Harry lived for sports, right from the start. He couldn't wait for our little games (touch football) And that intense desire never left him."

While he was playing, his mother would cook on a big black stove. On cold nights, the boys would sleep together in their attic bedrooms and talk about sports and family. And Harry loved to play with the family dog, a German Shepherd named Prince.

Mrs. Agganis would sometimes drive around Lynn in a jeep with a Catholic priest named Father Coffey, of Sacred Heard Church. She knew all the poor families, including those who weren't Greek, and she would point out to him those who needed help. They would do it from a distance, so no one would be embarrassed. On holidays, they would receive turkeys and clothing and other goods.

She would still send goods back to Logganiko, including glasses for her brother, Nikola and clothing for relatives.

Just as Jimmy and the other boys had done when they were Harry's age, Harry's mother wanted him to work, shining shoes in downtown Lynn. Harry went reluctantly, and then worked briefly in a bakery. But Phil, seeing how important sports were to his kid brother, and knowing how much he had missed playing, intervened. Phil loved sports too and had played football for Classical while his brother, Paul, was a middleweight boxer.

"Ma, I'll give you the money Harry would make shining shoes. Let him play." Phil gave her $5 a week, and Harry kept playing ball, never knowing what his brother had done.

And Harry was already developing a reputation as a precocious athlete. He had a long, loping running style that belied his speed, and he was becoming strong and powerful. He met a lot of friends at Barry Park, including a rapid runner and slick fielder named George Bullard, and Billy Porter.

All the parks in Lynn had their own neighborhood teams and rivalries developed quickly. Harry was already playing with older boys because of his ability. Nils Strom, who played for a team at another field, said the Barry Park team came over one day and the captain asked if Harry could kick off from the 50-yard line instead of the 40-yard line because he was so young.

The ball sailed over the heads of the receivers, past the end zone.

Harry went to Burrall Elementary School. One day, he and a couple of his friends were spotted taking apples off a tree, a harmless pastime for young boys. But a neighbor took their picture. Harry looked surprised, his coltish figure bolting, his eyes fixed suddenly on the camera. His friends, Ray Symanski and Fran McInerney, looked left and right, afraid.

Like the other Greek-American children, he attended Greek School to learn the Greek language. His teacher was Penelope Mazis, who said, "He was a good student and a good boy."

Times were changing fast in Lynn and the United States, as war broke out in Europe when the Nazis invaded Poland, and there were alternating cries for the United States to become involved, or to stay out. Harry was still playing

17

ball, or playing with Prince.

In 1938, President Franklin D. Roosevelt and first lady Eleanor Roosevelt had come through the city to Nahant for the wedding of their son, John, to Anne Lindsey Clark. There were layoffs of 200 persons working on WPA projects, and the Golden Seal Shoe Company left Lynn for Boston, a portent of a changing industrial base. In 1939, four Lynn shoe union leaders were sentenced to five-month sentences for strike activities in Maine factories.

With the war in Europe, America's industries would soon be called upon to produce the machinery of warfare for America too. Rearmament efforts meant many General Electric workers would forego their vacations. The company's more than 10,000 workers were photographed and fingerprinted as a security measure, and a mock bombing was held in Manning Bowl.

In 1940, Republican Presidential nominee Wendell Wilkie came to Lynn and spoke on the steps of city hall, but FDR carried the city by 6000 votes anyway, perhaps because he spent some time sailing off Nahant and Lynn as part of this visit to his grandchildren. Lynn was declared the best-fed city in the nation.

Harry was eleven then, and baseball was his passion, although he was taking a liking to football, as his brothers were tossing a football around to him in the backyard. He had an uncanny knack for not being able to be tagged during touch football because he was so elusive and shifty.

By 1941, Lynn payrolls were the highest in the city's history, with more than 17,000 workers receiving an average of $36.89 weekly, and there were signs of increasing war-fed prosperity. GE built a new $2 million gear plant as the defense industry boomed.

Hundreds left WPA projects for private industry, and relief rolls were cut in half. And then came Pearl Harbor on December 7, 1941, and America's entry into World War II. His older brothers were working and married now, and his brother, Phil, went into the Army in 1943.

With men at war, many women began working in jobs only men had held. Production records were broken. Worker enthusiasm and swing shifts kept factories going around the clock. There was an unprecedented business boom. Even the city's mayor, Albert Cole, was drafted into the service. Lynn, by Presidential proclamation, became the 16th most important defense area in the nation, and GE expanded again.

There was still some anti-Greek sentiment, despite the hard work and successes of the Greek immigrant families. In Lowell, where there were many Greeks, and where George Agganis had first come to the United States, two ten-year-old boys, Pericles Panos and Manny Voulgaropoulos, went to the YMCA one day and were talking to each other in Greek when the the director, Wilfred

Pearson, snapped at them.

"This is America," he yelled. "You don't speak Greek!" He threw them out of the club.

The boys were depressed. For two weeks they did not go to the "Y." But then they swallowed their pride, went back and apologized. But they never forgot the affront.

Harry was growing fast now, beginning to reach almost six feet tall when he was barely fourteen. His reputation as a baseball player was known not only in Lynn, where he was always called upon to play with older boys, but among established teams like the semi-pro Lynn Frasers. A Lynn Classical assistant coach named Mel Palumbo was the first to spot him at Barry Park.

When he entered Breed Junior High in September of 1942, Harry was in gym class doing warm up drills when he caught the eye of teacher Elmo Benedetto. "His movements were graceful, fluid-like and agile. This boy is a true, coordinated athlete," Benedetto said.

Benedetto spoke to him after class, and was shaken by Harry's maturity and enthusiasm. There was a bright sparkle in his eyes, lighting up his face over a shy smile, and his curly brown hair was tangled over his forehead.

"I'm Harry Agganis," he said softly.

In 1943, Harry played with the Frasers under the name of Ted Casey. The Frasers were well known and played against service teams. One night, the young Harry whacked three doubles off Walt Masterson, who had played for the Red Sox and Senators, and in another game he hit well off Doyle Lade, who had played for the Chicago Cubs. Harry hit .342 for the Frasers. Also playing in the league were catchers Yogi Berra and Jim Hegan.

But that same summer, while playing for the Connery Post American Legion team, Harry broke his right leg while trying to score from third base. He hesitated just a moment and crashed into the catcher, flipping and landing on his leg. In the stands watching was another young friend he had made, Mike Frangos, who said he could hear the snap across the field.

In Italy, where he was serving with the Army's 5th Battalion, 2nd Corps Engineers, Harry's brother Phil received a letter from his mother, written in English by a family member, blaming him for the accident. If he hadn't let Harry play ball, he wouldn't have gotten hurt, she said.

Phil went to his commander, who told him not to worry, that Harry's leg would be stronger after it healed. And it did. When he got better that Fall, as he entered Breed Junior High, he would sometimes leave the house with his books under his arm, and head instead to Barry Park where'd meet Bullard or Nipper Clancy, and they'd play ball.

He didn't want his mother knowing he had missed school that day and would have to sneak back along adjacent Cottage Street.

In every city, young men from many ethnic backgrounds had gone to war to fight for their country, America. But World War II in Europe had a special poignancy for Greek-Americans, who had many relatives in Greece, resisting Hitler's armies. They were hearing of atrocities, including the massacre of the male population, from ages twelve to eighty-five, in the village of Kalavrita.

More than 1000 were killed in an open field, when machine guns popped up from opposite ends, mowing them down. Their village was burned, and the Germans went to a nearby monastery called Agia Lavra, where the Greek revolution had begun, and killed sixteen priests.

In West Lynn, word came back to the Waterhill Street neighborhood that one of its sons, Ted Booras, had been killed in England by a German buzz-bomb. His brother, John, went on to fight in the hedgerows of France, where he won the Silver Star for bravery, and the British military medal from the King of England.

In the Agganis household, Harry was hearing of the fighting because his mother's brother, Nikola, and sister, Panayiota, were still in Logganiko, and Phil was fighting in Italy.

In February of 1945, U.S. Marines took the island of Iwo Jima near Japan in fighting so fierce that more than 6800 were killed taking the dusty, volcanic outcrop. It helped speed the end of the war, that came in the Summer with the ushering in of the Atomic Age and the nuclear bombs dropped on Hiroshima and Nagasaki.

For Harry though, the summer of 1945 was spent playing baseball and looking forward to September, when he would become a high school student. The coaches there were waiting too. By now, just about everyone in Lynn had heard of Harry Agganis.

ETHOS ◆ CHARACTER ◆ HΘΟΣ
1943 – 1948

Harry came into Lynn Classical High School in the fall of 1945 a strapping sophomore, at a time when the high school had three upper grades. He was already well known for starring as a baseball and football player on the sandlots and for organized teams, including with the Lynn Frasers baseball team.

He wouldn't play quarterback though, at least not to start. Classical, a school with a reputation for great quarterbacks, such as Boley Dancewicz a few years earlier, had the strong Don Miosky to run the team and pass. Wearing Number 20, Harry was placed at halfback by coach Bill Joyce, who recognized Harry's elusiveness and speed, and especially his size for a young man. And Harry wouldn't be starting there either. He would be behind an upperclassman, Dick Dooley, a pounding runner.

Harry spent virtually all his out-of-school time playing sports, running home to grab an apple or a sandwich and then to Barry Park, or on the basketball team at St. George's Church. But Harry was quickly becoming popular with girls too, who recognized his maturing handsomeness. Even a pitting of his cheeks in his teenage years gave him a rugged, masculine appeal.

There was a soaring sense of optimism and relief in the United States, with the end of World War II after the United States dropped the atomic bombs on Hiroshima and Nagasaki, and veterans were starting to come home, causing a housing shortage. General Douglas MacArthur was overseeing the American occupation of Japan, and the backorders of defense-related business at General Electric's Lynn plant equalled a year of peace-time business.

Classical opened with a win over Winthrop in football, before losing 6-0 to the Eastern Mass. champions of the previous year, Peabody, which was led by Hercules Harris and Jimmy Smyrnios. In the fourth game, Harry scored his first touchdown, on a pass from Miosky, as Classical beat Arlington, 13-6. He played some quarterback in the sixth game, against powerhouse Everett, but lost, 21-7 before 10,000 fans.

The next game, against Salem, gave Harry one of his biggest thrills. He ran 55 yards for a touchdown in the fourth quarter, swiveling around would-be tacklers, to help his team to a 26-14 win. He was attracting attention with his sensational style now. The next game, he had a scintillating 45-yard kickoff return against Saugus, which beat Classical, 14-12. In the stands watching was Dancewicz, who was heralded as Classical's greatest star five years earlier before he became an All-American at Notre Dame.

Harry had two touchdowns against Lowell in the next game, and Joyce was already thinking of grooming him to be his quarterback the next season, as Classical finished with an 8-3 record. Boston sportswriters were starting to write and talk about Harry too, and the buzz was growing about the sensational athlete on the North Shore, a sandlot legend.

That Fall, Harry went to a dance at Playland on Market Street, a ballroom for teenagers, where they could listen to the swing music of the 40s, have a few Coca-Colas, dance and talk with their friends. While Harry was chatting with his friends, he looked across the floor and noticed a winsome blond, with a tantalizingly shy look who was looking at him.

He walked over and said, "Would you like to dance?"

Joan Fitzgerald said yes.

"He was the nicest, kindest person you could ever meet," she said. Harry was handsome, with that dark, curly hair dangling a little on his forehead, the smile that was a beacon, and the muscles rippling through his suit. And, she thought, he was so tender and gentle, for all his strength. They danced, and he asked her to go to an upcoming prom.

Before long, she was wearing his Classical sweater on her way to school as she walked from her home on Washington Street, not far from Harry's neighborhood. After school, she would see Harry and some of his teammates, Chippy Chipouras and George Pike, walking over to the practice field in their uniforms, bouncing with the glee of boys on the brink of becoming men.

Lunch was the time the students most anticipated because they could leave school to go to a malt shop nearby, Sam Binder's. Joan brought her lunch every day, sandwiches and fruit and chips and pickles, and she sat with Harry and their friends and listened to the jukebox. Harry played one song over and over. It was "To Each His Own," a gentle ballad by Eddie Howard, with the Dick Jurgens band. They would smile at each other a lot.

Harry used to take her over to the three-story house on Ashland Street of his sister, Mary Raimo's, where they would walk up two flights in the back and go in for spaghetti dinners. Mary gave her the recipe she used for the sauce Harry liked. Mary's husband, Tony, was often there too. Sometimes, Joan and Harry would go up to see his other sister, Constantina Orphanos, who was living in Ipswich. Harry was good friends with his nephew, Jimmy.

There was strong reverence for the family, and for school, where authority was generally respected and where teachers were held in high esteem. There were few incidents of trouble because students were as fearful of being repri-manded by their parents and peers as by their teachers. If you were caught chewing gum, the teacher would make you put it on your nose and you'd have to stand in a corner, an embarrassing moment that was not often repeated.

Harry had learned that athletics and teamwork, and academics, helped build character. But when he talked with Mary, they didn't often discuss sports. He was still shy at speaking publicly, although he was the nucelus of his group of friends, which was growing.

Harry met one of his best friends at Classical. He was a slightly-built shy boy with a penchant for singing and entertaining, and who loved to play basketball. His name was Jimmy Kirios, and he was called "Jeep" because of the rapid way he used to putter around.

Kirios had first met Harry when they were both in the eighth grade, in different junior high schools. Kirios was a second baseman on his sandlot team, and one day Harry hit a double and wound up on second base. He was wearing chinos and a white T-shirt and was a lot bigger than the other boys.

They were in the same Boy Scout group together, Troop 40, made up of Greek-American boys like Harry's other close friend, Mike Frangos, who was also a star basketball player. Even if they went to different schools, the Greek boys played together for St. George's church basketball team. It was in a meeting room of the church that Kirios first had a chance to talk with Harry, who came in wearing a pencil-striped suit that belonged on an older man. They took a liking to each other, the shy Kirios, whose laugh was so reticent Harry used to kid him about it, and the sports star.

That winter, Harry showed his versatility by starring for Classical's basketball team, as a center and guard who handled the ball, was one of the leading scorers in the Essex County League, and was often called upon by coach Art Rogers to shut down the team's leading scorer. The stands were just as filled as they were at the football games because Harry was electrifying as a basketball player too. It seemed nothing could go wrong.

But tragedy came that winter, in the middle of a cold night when Harry was ill with pneumonia. On January 8, 1946, his father, George, went around to greet all his friends. He had taken his grandaughter, Georgette, his son Phil's daughter. After, he took her home to Phil's house.

He said one word, in Greek, to his son. "*Fevgo*." It was an odd and chilling recitation. It meant "I'm going," a way to say "I'm going to pass away."

Phil was alarmed. "Pa, don't talk like that," he said.

The next morning at 2:00 a.m., Phil received a call from his brother Paul that his father had died. Mrs. Agganis and her oldest daughter, Constantina, were in the house on Waterhill Street that night. As he was being taken out of the house to an ambulance, he turned to his wife and said "*Yeeneka, fevgo*." "Wife, I'm going."

Harry was in the house and so ill he couldn't get out of bed, but he wanted to go to the funeral parlor to see his father before the wake would be held. The doctors were in the house taking care of Harry, and Phil was there with other family members. Harry said, "I want to go see my father." The doctors said he couldn't go.

Harry, with tears in his eyes, insisted. He turned to Phil and said "I want to go see pa." Phil turned to the doctors. "We have to do something here." The doctors said they couldn't, but Phil suggested putting Harry on a stretcher, bundled up and bring the hearse to the back door to transport him.

The doctors said they would relent, but that he had to be brought back immediately after the visit. Harry's brothers took him to the funeral home on Boston Street, and carried him in. He was wrapped in blankets, like a mummy, on the stretcher. They held him up to the casket and Harry, crying softly, leaned down, braced by his brother's arms, and kissed his father goodbye.

It was a tough month in Lynn for a lot of people. A strike of 8000 workers at GE idled workers and lasted until mid-March, causing a disruption in the city's business climate at a time when there was still adjustment to the return of veterans and a shift in the nation's economy too. Harry was struggling to recover from the grief of his father's loss, using his family's support and basketball to help him get through the winter.

On Patriot's Day, the Boston Marathon gave Greek-American families another reason to cheer. Many of them had relatives in Greece, which was being wracked by a violent Civil War that pitted Communist sympathizers against loyalists, and there was widespread famine and poverty in the country following World War II, where the Greeks had refused to relent to the Nazis, and had resisted fiercely.

It was the 50th running of the world's most famous marathon. Greek runner Stylianos Kyriakides came with a message, to tell the world and Americans about the plight of his people and his country, where more than 7,000,000 were facing starvation.

Before he left, Kyriakides, who had run in the 1938 Olympic marathon in Berlin, told his family and friends he would win, or die trying. He was following the edict of Spartan mothers who, before sending their sons off to battle, would hand them a shield as they headed for battle and say, *"Ee Tan Ee Epi Tas."* It meant, "Come home with your shield or on it."

For Greeks, competition was a serious business. When the Nazis occupied Athens, a Greek soldier was ordered by a Wehrmacht officer to bring down the brilliant blue-and-white Greek flag from the Acropolis. The soldier complied, wrapping himself in the flag, stepping off the edge and plunging, silently, to his death 300 feet below.

In Boston, George Demeter, who owned the Hotel Minerva, would put an olive crown from Greece on the head of the marathon winner. Before the race, he gave Kyriakides a note written in Greek. It said, *"Ee Tan Ee Epi Tas."*

With the world watching, Kyriakides — in the last stages of the race — broke away from veteran local favorite Johnny Kelley to win by two minutes. Kyriakides ran in a shirt which bore the name of his country and flag. He wore Number 77, and wept joyously afterward.

Kelley walked over to him and said, "It's great that you won, Kyriakides. It's great for your country."

Harry was winning too. He loved baseball the most, and that Spring he dazzled, hitting .575 and having only one error in 148 chances at first base. Classical had a great team and for Harry, baseball was a continuance of those idyllic summer days as a boy when he would stay at Barry Park all day long and hit and run and play, stopping only to eat out of a brown paper bag.

Boston Globe sportswriter Ernie Dalton remembered the first game Harry played that year, at Fraser Field and was so enthralled he told a colleague, Bob Holbrook, to come out to see the kid from Lynn.

"Bob, go watch this kid play. I don't believe what I saw last week," Dalton said.

The next week, Holbrook did. After the leadoff man reached first base against Classical, Harry turned one of the most difficult plays for a first baseman, picking up a ground ball, throwing to second for a force out on the runner, and hustling back to the bag to take the return throw to complete the 3-6-3 double play. He did it so effortlessly Holbrook almost whistled under his breath. "I see what you mean," he told Dalton.

He was such a feared power hitter, even at 17, that outfielders used to back up to the 400-foot mark trying to hold him to singles. Harry won the Fred Ostergren Trophy as the outstanding high school baseball player in the state, his first major award, and was selected to play in the Hearst All-Star game at Fenway Park, where he played for the Massachusetts team against players from other New England states, including another left-handed quarterback and baseball player, Lou Gorman of LaSalle Academy in Rhode Island.

That summer, as he worked for the second year in a row for the city's Parks Department and spent many evenings with his friends at Christy's, a drive-in food stand right on the beach at Lynn, near a road connecting the city to the peninsula of Nahant, Harry was picked to represent New England in the annual Esquire All-American Boy baseball game in Chicago, at Wrigley Field. It wasn't far from where his uncle, Louis Pappas, his mother's brother, lived and his uncle and his family were there to greet him, after a long train ride on which Harry ate peaches and ice cream.

They cared for and fed Harry so well that he kidded he could barely bend over to pick up ground balls. One of the players Harry met there was a tall, lanky southpaw from Virginia named Chuck Stobbs, who was regarded as one of the country's best high school pitchers and quarterbacks. They talked a little and posed for photos. Harry's coach, Honus Wagner, picked him to start ahead of his own son. Harry walked his only time up as the pitchers would not give him anything good to hit.

It was a great summer. Harry was working at the playgrounds, playing All-Star games, hanging around with his friends at Lynn Beach and at the amusement park at nearby Revere Beach, which featured one of the biggest roller coasters in the country. They went to Christy's in Lynn often, and Harry was able to land another part-time job. The Boston Red Sox had established the Lynn Red Sox, a Class A minor league team, in the city.

Their scout, Neil Mahoney, had been keeping an eye on Harry for a couple of years already and they hired Harry's football and baseball coach, Bill Joyce, to be president of the team. A returning veteran, Dick O'Connell, was the business manager and he had Harry doing odd jobs and fixing the team bus, and occasionally he would work out with the team.

And one day when he was sitting around Vrees' diner in Lynn, owned by brothers Andy and Jim Vrees, who had several businesses including a car dealership, Harry and George Bullard, the short, pugnacious athlete Harry had played against on the sandlots, talked about starting a local baseball team

The Vrees All-Stars were born.

With Jimmy as manager, the Vrees' got the best high school players from miles around, including Somerville, a hotbed for high school baseball. They played the Lynn Red Sox, the Boston Hoboes and athletic clubs all around New England, touring on a bus the brothers provided.

They beat college players and semi-pro teams as word spread quickly, and soon they were being covered by the newspapers as if they were a professional team, sometimes attracting as many as 2500 people. Harry and Bullard were the stars, hitting and fielding, and attracting fans.

It was a busy Summer for Harry, but now he was looking forward to the 1946 football season almost as much as Joyce was.

NIKE ◆ VICTORY ◆ NIKH

The first football game of the year would be against a lightly-regarded Class C team, Winthrop, which had played Classical very tough the year before, losing only 7-6. That Winthrop team was led by a great halfback, Bomber Neil, one of the few black players in the league at that time. He was not coming back, but the Winthrop coach, Doc Conner, was worried his team would be wary about the build-up surrounding Classical, and playing in Manning Bowl, which held 20,000 people and could be a raucous, dispiriting place for opponents.

The Friday night game was such a social event that fans came from other towns in the North Shore. They would eagerly pile into cars in Somerville and East Boston and towns from close by and far away, for the drive up to Lynn. When they got there, there was excitement in the air. Vendors were outside yelling, "Peanuts, ten cents," and you could get two candy bars for fifteen cents. Hot dogs and Cokes were a dime each. The stadium was so big that ushers helped fans find their seats, and many men came dressed in coats and ties.

On the field, Classical came roaring out in green-and-gold new uniforms and the school mascot for the Rams, Orphelia, a ram, was dressed in a red-and-white fabric harness and leash held by the school's eleven member all-male cheerleading squad. Harry was now wearing Number 33, after his sports idol, professional quarterback Slingin' Sammy Baugh, to whom he had written a letter.

Also on the sidelines was a young boy, Angelo Karayianis, who was Harry's biggest fan. He was crippled and needed braces to walk. Harry's teammate, the Albanian Orthodox Vic Pujo, saw Harry walk over and hug Karayianis and shake his hand for good luck. The boy smiled broadly. Harry did the same before every game.

It didn't take long for Harry to make the crowd yell. Classical led only 6-0 at halftime, but he led them on a second-half rout that finished with a 39-0 win. It was the start of a season of rolling wins, 12-0 over Arlington, 38-14 over

Revere, 44-0 over Lowell, 27-0 over Gloucester. The Classical backfield of Harry, Dave Warden, Pike and a line that included captain Dick Crombie, Ray McClorey, Bob Anderson, Harold Potter and Fred Smith, and Chipouras at center, was a physical bunch who played rough.

Bullard, who was a star shortstop on the baseball team, was a fierce and fast defensive halfback too, pairing with Harry to make it almost impossible for receivers and runners to get past the secondary.

It wasn't just the scores garnering attention for Classical. It was the way Harry played. He was decades ahead of his time at quarterback. In an era when quarterbacks would drop back and stay in the pocket, he was a scrambling dervish who ignored oncoming linemen and would roll back 20 and 30 yards, picking out receivers at the last moment and firing left-handed line drives. He was a master of deception at faking handoffs and was so strong he could just shove aside some tacklers who got near him.

Fans were intriqued watching a left-handed passer. Harry would have crowds gasping and standing as he whirled around, and the bowl was filled with 20,000 fans and more. Tickets were so hard to come by that scalpers were getting premium prices for a high school game. Harry made sure his family always had seats though so he could see them while he was playing. But his mother would not go.

Heading to the big Thanksgiving Day game against rival Lynn English, which, after losing its first three games by close scores was now also pounding other teams, Classical had only one close game, against nearby Salem, which was led by a fleet running back named Andy Konovalchik. More than 22,000 fans came.

Konovalchik got through the Classical line several times, but he couldn't get past Harry or Bullard in the backfield. "He was the greatest player I've ever seen. He stopped me cold several times," Konovalchik said. With the score tied, 7-7, in the fourth period, Classical scored 19 points to break away to a 26-7 win.

Early in the game, Harry had the ball on Salem's 1-yard line and, instead of going in on a quarterback sneak, handed it to Pike, who was the state's leading scorer. "I don't want fans to think I'm a fathead," Harry said.

Harry had been befriended by Joyce and line coach Harold Zimman, who became especially close to him with the death of his father that January. Zimman ran the concessions at the field and Harry found it easy to talk with the man who would give him advice about playing, and how to handle life.

Joyce had once told his players to have their friends stop calling for them to be put into games. "Stop calling, 'We want Sonungapaw,'" Joyce said, calling up an Indian name for Strongheart. Harry was not afraid of jousting verbally with his coach, who was autocratic but loved his players. He liked the sound of it and called Joyce "Sonungapaw," after that.

Joyce and Zimman were kind to Harry, but Joyce had to stay after him to pass more. Harry preferred to hand the ball to his teammates, or occasionally run himself because he thought it was a more effective technique against teams who were expecting him to pass. Opponents had never seen a passer like Harry, a 6' 2" southpaw who could throw the ball long and hard, or feather it softly to teammates breaking out of the backfield. One of his favorite plays was to drop a flare pass into Bullard's hands and let the speedster break away from linebackers and linemen who couldn't get their hands on him. They were a deadly combination.

Classical came into the English game with an eleven game winning streak and was regarded as the best team in the state, although a rating system which cost them points for playing smaller schools like traditional rival Winthrop had them ranked behind Melrose.

But in the Classical-English game, records meant little. Friends who played with each other on the playgrounds were now battling each other for bragging rights in the city. Which school you attended depended on where you lived. Best friends who were a street apart could find themselves in different schools and playing against each other.

Mike Frangos and his brother Charlie went to English. Charlie, a hard-charging lineman, would find himself trying to block Harry, although they went to St. George's Church together. Players on both teams had best friends on the other team. It was the biggest day of the year for the players and families of both schools, and the bowl was filled beyond its capacity of more than 20,000, and fans were standing everywhere, including on a hillside.

The game didn't start well for Classical when Charlie Ruddock steamed 30 yards around right end for a touchdown. Classical blocked a punt at midfield and five plays later, Harry scored to tie the game.

After a Ruddock run set up another English score, Classical came back on a short touchdown by the state's scoring leader, Pike, but Dooley's placekick was wide and English still led, 14-13.

A Classical fumble in the third led to another English score before Pike added his second touchdown to narrow the lead to 21-20. After one of Harry's passes was intercepted in the fourth period, Nick Ricciardelli scored his third touchdown, but English missed the extra point and led, 27-20.

Then, with only a few minutes to go, Harry had a weaving 15-yard punt return and five plays later, Pike ran 10 yards to make it 27-26. On the extra point attempt, as English players poured through trying to block the kick, Harry showed his imagination. He was holding for the extra point kick, but, when he saw it might be blocked, he stood up and calmly threw to a wide open Pujo in the end

29

zone to preserve the tie, and Classical's unbeaten season.

After the English game, which salvaged the unbeaten season for Classical, Harry and some of his teammates, and some rivals from English, teamed up to help the North Shore All-Stars beat the Greater-Boston All-Stars, 14-7, as he threw two touchdown passes.

On December 3, he was honored by the Greek-American Legion at the Oxford Club. Harry, dressed in a suit, had to stand up and speak to a large group,but not before others spoke about him first.

Joyce said Harry had remained modest. "He never has an unkind word for anyone. He takes the bumps and comes up smiling. All boys who have played against him have high praise for him. He never uses profanity and I know he will carry on the high ideals of sportsmanship," he said. Joyce wasn't done yet.

"I doubt anyone in this hall will have the honors heaped on him during his lifetime that this boy already has won," Joyce said. "But I have no fear this will twist his head. He is a boy of splendid character and I have never once heard him say an unkind word about anybody nor utter an oath or curse. In all my 28 years of coaching boys at Classical, he is the first boy from whom I have actually learned, and from whom I actually sought advice."

Harry was presented with a gold watch, by Post Commander Charles Chronopoulis as family members watched proudly. Standing tall in his shining suit and looking earnest, Harry said "My greatest years of my life I know will be my three years with Bill Joyce and I wouldn't give them up for anything in the world," he said. Harry was called "Mr. Football."

St. George's Church President Charles Demakis was there, along with Harry's family, and Rev. Christopher Argyrides, and other Greek-American athletes who were being honored, including Peter and Charlie Frangos, Bob Ansoulis, Pujo, Chipouras, and Jim Varzakis. War veterans, including Christopher Karaberis, a Congressional Medal of War winner, were there. It was a proud night for Harry and his family, but he didn't let it to go his head.

Lynn Item sports columnist Red Hoffman, who had become close to Harry, saw him one night at the diner owned by Andy and Jimmy Vrees. Harry, who had stepped behind the counter to work for a moment, had a request for him. Harry called him into a corner and asked him, politely, "Please don't write my name in the paper so much. I don't want people to think I'm a hot dog." He meant it, Hoffman knew.

"I'd be happy to, Harry," Hoffman said casually. "If you'll just stop throwing touchdown passes, shooting baskets and ringing basehits all over Fraser Field."

The 11-0-1 season earned Classical an invitation to play Granby High of Norfolk, Virginia. in the Orange Bowl in Miami on Christmas Day, in a game sponsored by the Shriners to benefit crippled children. Classical had scored 326 points, but would be meeting a formidable powerhouse in Granby, which had won 33 consecutive games in three years. The only close game had come a week earlier when they beat Clifton, New Jersey, 6-0 in a bowl game.

Granby was led by a left-handed quarterback and multi-sport star too, and it was someone Harry knew: Chuck Stobbs, with whom he had played in the Esquire All-Star baseball game in Chicago. Stobbs was highly touted, but he thought Granby had a better player and athlete in lineman Hank Foiles, a tough brawling type who was also a great baseball player.

Granby had outscored its opponents by 1186-79 and had 15 shutouts in the 33-game streak. Most of the players on the 1946 team had been together for almost all those games, and several had been All-South selections. Granby's Blue Comets had rolled over opponents with scores like 66-13, and 50-0. But Lynn was ecstatic and the Classical players felt they were unbeatable.

Stobbs said he told his players about Harry and to be wary. "I knew who he was," he said. "We knew we were in for a battle."

Hundreds turned out for a rally in Lynn before the players, coaches, staff, Mayor Albert Cole, forty-fivefans, and reporters boarded a train at South Station for a forty-five-hour ride of 1,618 miles. For the players, most of whom were sixteen or seventeen years old, it would be the time of their lives. They would spend the time down going over some game strategy, but also talking, playing cards, joking and making sleeping arrangements in the overhead sleepers in the old pullman cars.

Team Manager Nathan Goodman said Classical, which had made a lot of money for the school during the Manning Bowl games, brought down $7000 worth of equipment. By the time the team arrived two days later, the temperature was already in the 80s and the players spent some time looking around and taking photographs of each other in front of palm trees. Reports were that professional gamblers were trying to rig odds to make Classical an early favorite, but the team was a 6-point underdog.

There were reports as much as $500,000 to $1 million would be bet on the game. One man from Lynn gave up 6$\frac{1}{2}$ points and bet $600, several months salary. *Lynn Telegram-News* Sports Editor J.F. Williams said there was a brimming confidence amongst the players though.

On December 21 he wrote that "After watching Classical scrimmage, it is going to take a super team to beat them as I talked with all the boys who say 'We want to win this game. Granby will have to be extra special to win.'"

Although he wasn't a starter, Bullard was being touted by reporters in the South as a dangerous runner. When he ran, Bullard looked like an angry bulldog, but with the speed of a greyhound. It would be a good prediction by game time, because Joyce wanted to give him plenty of time to complement his backfield of Dave Warden, Dick Dooley and George Pike.

Harry took time out to go to St. Sophia's Church in Miami with the other Greek players, and many of the other players went to churches too, or to a local Temple. The team also went to the Latin Quarter where they were the guests of E.M. Loew, but they were mostly talking football and not entertainment. Harry went to the dog races but only stayed for one race. Lynn restaurant owner Harold Standel took Agganis, Crombie, Dooley and Pike on a sightseeing tour.

By game time, the odds had swung and Classical was made a 6-point favorite, angering Granby coach Elmer "Snookie" Tarrall. "They can't do that to us. How can they make the champions underdogs? We'll show 'em on the field who is the favorite. They'll never take a team that has not lost a game in three years and has a record of thirty-three straight. Phooey on the bookmakers."

He was very upset, reporters said. *Lynn Item* Sports Editor Ed Cahill said Tarrall pointed a finger at him and said "Classical a favorite! Most of the boys (Granby) have been with the team three years and several of them have never seen a Granby team defeated." Granby looked big, tough, and rugged and its players were on the average a year older than Classical.

Three Granby supporters sneaked into a practice and were belittling the Classical team how they were going to bet $3000 on their team. It didn't bother Harry or his teammates. The starting team would be Agganis, with Dooley, Warden and Pike in the backfield, and Nils Strom, Harold Potter, captain Dick Crombie, Chipper Chipouras, Ray McClorey, Bob Anderson and Vic Pujo in the line. The scrappy Chipouras was at center and his job would be to keep Foiles from getting to Harry.

By game time, it was a warm, starless night and the fans were hatless and coatless. Back in Lynn, thousands of fans had jammed Central Square in the cold on Christmas night to stand and listen to big loudspeakers placed outside the Lynn Item building, huddling together and hanging on every word of the broadcast back home, which in Lynn was being handled by Curt Noyes, a sports columnist from Lynn, who was doing the play-by-play. It was the largest radio audience ever for WESX, covering the North Shore.

Nearly 25,000 fans turned out for a high school game, including players from the University of Tennessee, in Miami to get ready for the Orange Bowl game on New Year's Day, with their legendary coach, General Bob Neyland. The band opened with "Let Me Call You Sweetheart."

On the first play of the game, Pike fumbled and the ball was recovered by Granby, but after an initial 8-yard run, they were stopped. It would quickly become a rough game. There was an early crisis for Classical, when Harry's left hand, his throwing hand, was stepped on and badly injured by a cleat. He went to the sidelines to have it looked at and Joyce wanted to have it wrapped, but Harry declined. He didn't want the Granby players to know he was hurt or to make his hand a target.

But the injury meant he could not rely on his passing game, even though he had won so many games in the past by running and using the threat of the pass to keep opponents guessing. The hand swelled quickly, but Harry didn't want to come out of the game, and he didn't want to let even his own teammates know how badly he was hurt.

Classical drove to the Granby 37-yard line before Stobbs, who, like Harry, was a strong defender too, intercepted one of his passes. And then Foiles intercepted Harry's second pass of the game, setting up a score to put Granby ahead, 7-0. Harry's hand was hurting and he wasn't throwing well. There was doubt he could throw any more.

In the second period though, he drove Classical on an 87-yard march and set up Pike with a deft handoff for a short run for a touchdown. And then Dooley came off the bench but faked the extra-point kick. Harry, who was holding, threw to Pike instead to tie the score, 7-7.

Late in the half, Granby scored on an unusual play. Stobbs threw to a teammmate on the 7-yard line of Classical. With only seconds left, Classical stopped a run, but was penalized for roughness and the ball was placed on the 1-yard line. Granby scored on the last play. Foiles' kick was wide, but another roughness penalty gave them a second chance and the kick was good to give Granby a 14-7 lead. There was groaning in Central Square.

The Classical players were drinking orange juice instead of water during the game, to keep themselves hydrated in the warm night. They went into the locker room tired and dirty, but not defeated.

In the third period, Harry took a punt back from his 28 to the 45-yard line, and started a drive that included a 20-yard run by Pike to the Granby 26. Pike's nose was badly injured when he was hit by Foiles. A few plays later, Pike drove his knee into Foiles in retaliation.

It wasn't the only encounter between Foiles and a Classical player. Stobbs said "Foiles was a super football player," and he was a rough 180-pounder. But Chipouras, who was going against him, was a tough Greek kid who knew how to hit too.

When they lined up, Foiles drawled at Chipouras: "Ahmm Awl-South."

Chipouras didn't blink. "I'm All-America. Let's go boys," he said.

Bullard ran to the 22. Then Bullard took a lateral from Harry and passed to Pike, who ran in for the tying score, but Classical had bad luck again. A referee placed the ball on the 11-yard where, he said, Pike had stepped out of bounds. But Warden ran to the 7-yard line, and, after Pike was stopped for no gain, Warden ran to the 1-yard line. On the next play, Bullard bulled his way in and Classical had tied the game, 14-14.

Although smaller than Granby, Classical had more team speed, especially with Bullard and Harry. In the fourth period, the speed paid off when Stobbs, trying to pass from his own 35-yard line on fourth down as Granby gambled, had the ball knocked down by Bullard, who then ran twice to put the ball on the 23-yard line before Harry ran a quarterback sneak to the 20-yard line.

Then came the game's biggest play. Granby thought Harry wouldn't throw any more. But he faded back and spotted Jimmy Varzakis all alone and hit him between the eyes on the 3-yard line with a hard pass. Varzakis simply stepped into the end zone untouched, and Classical led, 21-14.

There was delirious cheering in Lynn. Although he had thrown two interceptions, Harry had completed the most important pass of the game.

Granby tried to come back behind Stobbs' passing, and almost did. One of his passes was dropped by a receiver in the clear on the Classical 10-yard line as time was running out. Both teams were offsides and Granby was given another play. Harry knocked down a desperation pass as time expired.

Nike.

Lynn Classical was the national high school champion, sportswriters said. Stobbs and Harry met at midfield, took off their helmets and shook hands. It wouldn't be the last time they would meet on a playing field. Harry walked off the field arm-in-arm with Stobbs after both teams huddled to exchange cheers.

The game had been brutally rough. Classical was penalized nine times for 72 yards, upsetting the coaches because Granby had been penalized only once, for five yards. Classical penalties included roughing the kicker, and unnecessary roughness, but the defense held Granby to a total of 66 yards, after the Southerners had outscored 1946 opponents by 335 points. Classical wound up with 248 yards, but Harry's hand limited him to 52 yards passing.

Varzakis said, "My dreams came true. Every night I was dreaming about making a touchdown and I did. It was a great throw by Harry. It certainly gave me a great thrill to see the hands of the officials go up."

Stobbs was downhearted. "We lost and we weren't too happy about it. They beat us physically. They were tough, they were the toughest team we'd ever played and they had a lot of speed," he said. Granby had lost one of its best players to injury before the game too, he said. But Tarrall said Classical had deserved to win. "That's the greatest high school football team I have ever seen," he said.

Foiles said, "I never saw so many fists fly in one game." And Classical's T-formation had confounded Granby. Neyland, the Tennessee coach, was impressed watching Harry. 'That young man could step into any college backfield right now," he said. Stories abounded later that professional gamblers had lost heavily on the game by beating Granby, although Classical was favored by game

34

time.

The locker room was bedlam, as the Classical players posed with Mayor Cole in wild exhultation, and players kissed each other in joy. Even the usually stern Joyce was grinning, and he was dunked in the shower. He was given the game ball and had to fight back tears. Cole stood right next to Harry.

The man who had bet several months salary on Classical, and given up 6½ points, was perhaps the happiest of all. He had won his bet by a half point, and was so delirious he walked into the shower with his suit on.

At the Hotel Robert Clay, many Lynn supporters gathered. The Shriners gave the team a silver bowl that night at Peter Panesis' Boulevard Cafe. He was from Lynn originally and hosted the team. The 41-inch high trophy cost $300, an enormous sum for an award in 1946.

The ride back on the train was joyous and Lynn was ready for a celebration. The players had been gone two weeks and were anxious to share in the fun at home too. More than 500 fans were waiting at South Station on December 31, New Year's Eve day, and another 1000, including most of the student body, was waiting back in Lynn. A police escort picked up the players at South Station and took them back on buses, with sirens blaring when they hit Lynn.

They circled the Lynn Common before going to the Armory for a reception. Harry said the officiating was so bad, "We beat fifteen men out there. They are a good team but we should have won easily. I hurt my hand in the first period and that is why I didn't throw any passes. I tried one long one as I gripped the ball around my hand."

Crombie was overjoyed. "I played the best game of my high school career. That Henry Foiles is certainly tough. I hit him hard and I got hit hard. We were up against a tough foe, but we have a good team and that is why all opposition cannot stand up against us," he said.

For Harry, 1946, which started with the death of his father, had wound up very good indeed. But there was more to come.

THRAMA ◆ DRAMA ◆ ΔΡΑΜΑ

Harry wasn't limited to sports. Character was built on study and intellectual pursuits too, and the arts. He was starring again for the basketball team, excelling as a defensive player and scorer, with more than twenty points in several games, and he made the Essex County League All-Star team. Harry was also the nucleus of his church team, which was in the midst of a long winning streak against other church teams.

On January 14, 1947, Harry was spotted skating on Lynn Common, which had been turned into a winter wonderland. He was using the skates of his older brother, Jimmy, which were twenty years old. He was so adept though that the next day the Lynn Item reported that "Those who saw Agganis on skates declare he would soon learn to become a hockey player, and that the stickwork would come as natural to him as batting, kicking and what not have in other sports."

He wanted to try acting too. Joan Fitzgerald was in the drama club and Harry wanted to be in a play. On January 17, 1947, Harry had the lead part in "Stage Door." Joan had a starring part too and Harry, she said, was as good an actor as an athlete. He enjoyed playing a different part, stepping out of the athlete's role and expanding himself.

Later, Harry had a starring role in "The Willow Pattern." Before the play began he told one of his friends, Jim O'Brien, "I'm going to get bigger laughs than anyone tonight."

"What do you mean, Harry? I've got funny the funny lines," O'Brien said. Harry just smiled at him.

A short while later, after the play had begun, O'Brien turned to Harry and delivered a set up line that was supposed to end with Harry driving a sword between O'Brien's arm and chest, to make it appear as if he had stabbed him.

O'Brien said his line. Harry just stood there. O'Brien said it again. Harry just stood there. O'Brien said it again, while the faculty advisors were fretting openly, wondering if Harry had forgotten his lines. He hadn't.

O'Brien turned away, putting his back to Harry, unsure what to do since the play called for him to fall as if he'd been stabbed with a sword.

Harry came to life and jabbed the sword playfully into O'Brien's buttocks. The crowd roared and couldn't stop. "Harry gave me the best looking goose that Classical ever saw," said O'Brien.

In April, Notre Dame Athletic Director "Moose" Krause wrote to a local booster in Lynn, Ralph Wheeler, for help in recruiting Harry when he would graduate the following year. "We are anxious to get Harry interested in Notre Dame and would appreciate anything you can do to help us. Could you get the boy to write us a letter asking for information on the school, after which we can correspond with him personally?" Krause asked.

The 1947 baseball season would be Harry's best. Classical also boasted Bullard and Saul Sherman and Lou Pollack, all All-Scholastic players. Harry was thumping the ball and fielding brilliantly, although he had broken his thumb, and he took his team into the Eastern Massachussets tournament where they made it to the final against a tough Newton team.

And there, before 3,000 fans at Fenway Park, it looked like Classical's luck had run out. They were down 6-2 in the seventh inning, and were still behind, 6-5, with two out in the ninth inning and a man on first base. Gus Moran hit a long fly ball that the left fielder had in his glove for the final out—but he crashed into the "Green Monster," the 32-foot high wall of Fenway, bobbled the ball and dropped it, letting the tying run score, as Moran raced to third base. Then a hot ground ball was bobbled too and Moran raced home with the game winning run to beat Newton, 7-6, and send Classical to the state final against Ludlow.

Classical came into the game at 17-1, and this would be on their home grounds of Fraser Field in Lynn. More than 5,000 fans showed up and Classical romped, 14-2. Harry went 2-for-5 and saved several wild throws from being errors. He made an unassisted double play in the eighth inning. That season he had hit several towering home runs that would have been out in most major league fields.

Against Ludlow, Bullard, drawing a lot of attention from scouts with his slick fielding at shortstop, went 4-for-5 hitting. Harry, who hit .352, was chosen captain of the 1948 baseball team. He wasn't through with baseball for the year yet, though.

He led the North Shore All-Stars to a 6-1 win over the Catholic All-Stars with a booming home run, in a game witnessed by 2,000 fans. And, once again, Harry was selected to play in the Hearst All-Star game at Fenway Park, where selections would be made to the national All-Star team to play against the New York stars at the Polo Grounds.

Before that Harry came over to Fraser Field to watch a friend play for the Lynn Red Sox. It was Chuck Stobbs, the quarterback for Granby High, the team Classical had beaten six months before in the Orange Bowl. After graduating, Stobbs had signed a contract, for a $30,000 bonus, with the Boston Red Sox, who assigned him to Lynn.

On July 5 that Summer, Stobbs hurled the Lynn Red Sox to an 8-2 win over Pawtucket. Harry went to the dugout to visit him and the two were photographed again. "What a small world it is," Harry laughed.

At the New England Sandlot game at Fenway, the teams were managed by Red Sox Manager Joe Cronin, and Lou Boudreau, who was a minor league coach for the Red Sox. There were 30 players to be split into two squads for the game, which was free and played after the Red Sox played the Cleveland Indians. Harry and Walter Keany, a third baseman from Dedham, were selected to go to New York. Harry had three hits, including a triple.

More than 2,100 high school players across the country had tried out for the U.S. All-Star team. It didn't take Harry long to show his ability. In a practice at the Polo Grounds, he was the only player to hit a home run. Manager Oscar Vitt, who had managed the Indians, walked by and said "The ball Agganis hit into the right field stands was a high inside one with plenty of smoke on it." Harry hit two other long drives, off Ken Fingeroid of Oakland, who had three no-hitters in games leading up to the contest. Harry's homer came on the first pitch.

Keany did not start the game, but Harry did. And when he came up to bat on August 13, it would prove to be his most embarrassing moment in uniform. With 29,000 people watching the game, Harry walked up to the plate for his first at-bat. A big wave of applause broke out behind him, but he kept his head down. He stepped into the batter's box.

His name had just been announced, but he was wondering why there was so much applause. He was used to being recognized in Lynn and Boston, but didn't think his name meant anything in New York, so he just kind of ducked his head and pawed at the ground with his spikes. But, instead of stopping, the applause got louder and louder. He started blushing, he didn't know what to do or what was going on.

"I didn't want to be a jerk altogether," he said later. So he finally turned toward the stands and tipped his cap. What he didn't see was a man walking down the aisle to a front row box and waving to everybody. It was Babe Ruth, being cheered to the skies. "I felt like a crumb," Harry said. "It's a good thing everyone was watching the Babe." It was one of the few times in his life he would ever be upstaged. Ruth and golfing great Babe Didrikson had been chosen honorary chairmen of the game.

Harry was wearing Number 1 and batting fifth. Coach Ray Schalk said "I am putting plenty of faith in Agganis." It wasn't misplaced. The U.S. All-Stars routed the New York team, 13-2. After the Ruth incident, Harry walked, moved to third on a wild pitch and was forced at home on a hot ground ball to the pitcher.

In the third, he walked again as the pitchers were being careful with him, then executed a perfect steal of second, hooking his spikes around a throw that seemed to have caught him. Then, moving to third, he was spiked in the shin and had to leave the game. Keany got in in the eighth inning and hit a double. Harry had gotten to play with Bill "Moose" Skowron, Billy Hoeft, and Dick Groat, future major league stars.

Harry played again that summer for the Frasers and for the Vrees All-Stars, including one game against the Boston Colored Giants, who had a tough 50 year-old pitcher named Cannonball Will Jackman. The Vrees' All-Stars won.

PNEUMA ◆ SPIRIT ◆ ΠΝΕΥΜΑ

In Harry's senior year, the expectations were high for Classical's 1947 football team, although they had lost many players from the 1946 club that had won the national championship. A spirit of optimism prevailed throughout the city. The population had soared past 100,000 and there was almost total employment.

Harry and Bullard were back, as were ends Nils Strom and Vic Pujo, and Chipouras was back at center. But the 1946 backfield of Dave Warden, Dick Dooley and state scoring champ George Pike had graduated, as had virtually the entire line.

Joining the team was a black player, Paul Pitman, who was the state's 100-yard dash champion. He was going to play in the backfield with Bullard, who was almost as fast, and who had beaten him in a shorter dash one time. Bullard was the state's 60-yard indoor sprint champion. There was also another black player, Tom Smith, who would be a tackle and defensive back.

Their reputations were astonishing for high school students, and led to a request for Classical to play an exhibition game at the Veteran's Administration hospital in Bedford. They were scheduled to play in the preseason game against a Catholic school from Lowell, Keith Academy. But their opponent was replaced by Waltham, a strong team which had beaten powerful Brockton, and which featured a shifty halfback named Joe Terrasi.

A crowd of 1,800 was expected, including 700 disabled veterans who asked Joyce to play Harry as much as possible so they could see the high school sensation. "The veterans would like to see Harry Agganis in action. I hope you can see your way clear to use him," Joyce was asked by a commander.

In an abbreviated exhibition, Classical beat Waltham, 13-0. Harry had a 75-yard punt return for a touchdown nullified by a penalty, a run on which he used a stiff arm to bury a tackler into the ground.

Classical came back to score when Harry handed off to Bullard at the Waltham 42-yard line. Bullard faded back and passed it back to Harry, who caught in on the 35-yard line and raced in to score. Terrasi was astounded at their ability.

After the game, Bullard and Harry toured some of the wards to talk to bed-ridden patients who weren't able to come out and watch. It had a profound effect on Harry, one which would stay with him. He and Bullard felt uncomfortable when they saw some rooms with padded cells, and the veterans, some of whom didn't even know where they were.

When he and Bullard were coming out, Bullard said he saw a man who used to work at a bowling alley in Lynn. He was outside the hospital pushing a cart of peanuts as a concessionaire for the game. Harry and Bullard were still unnerved by what they saw, but the peanuts salesman wasn't disturbed by the surroundings, and he broke the tension with his sense of salesmanship. That broke Harry and Bullard into a relieved laugh.

"Nuts for the nuts!" he yelled. "Nuts for the nuts!"

But Harry was very affected by human suffering. Few knew that he would often go to visit an elderly woman from Ireland named Mary Maloney, who was living in Lynn. She was dying.

Harry had heard about her through Bullard, whose family was related to the Maloney family. It was a touching sight, the young Greek-American boy sitting by the edge of her bed, trying to comfort an Irish-American woman in her last days.

When Classical opened with a 20-6 pasting of Winthrop, there were predictions of another unbeaten season. Before the game, Winthrop coach Doc Conner was so worried, remembering the 39-0 beating the year before, that he took his team into the stands at Manning Bowl for a pep talk.

It worked for a little while. Winthrop was losing only 6-0 at halftime to the national champions. Paul Millerick, a halfback and defensive back, said his team was elated. It could have been a lot worse, but he said he thought Harry was taking it easy. "He was trying to make us look good," he said.

The game had opened with Pitman taking the kickoff and blasting past Winthrop defenders like they were tied to trees, going 98-yards for a touchdown. But it was called back on a penalty and, after Millerick intercepted one of Harry's passes, Classical settled into a routine rout.

"They had to work out a lot of kinks because they had lost a lot of players from the year before," said Millerick, who scored his team's touchdown. There was no stopping Harry.

Then came Peabody. The Tanners had Jimmy Smyrnios back at halfback, and a defensive line shored by a pair of 250-pounders. There were ominous omens for Classical when fullback Harry Rosenblatt fumbled several times and Harry was staying with a running game instead of passing. And then Bullard fumbled as he was switching the ball between hands—just as he was about to walk in for an easy touchdown.

Smyrnios scored two touchdowns, including one in the last moments of the game, on fourth down from Classical's goal line, to give Peabody a 12-7 lead and it was too late for Classical to come back. Joyce had told Harry to pass more but he hadn't, and the fumbles were costly.

Harry completed eight passes, but threw only ten, and Classical was upset. But Smyrnios was more relieved than anything that Peabody had somehow managed to escape Classical, and Harry.

"He was the best player I ever played against. It wasn't the fact he was so fast, but that he was so evasive," said Symrnios. Another Peabody player, halfback Joe Regis, said he was worried all week before the game. "When you knew you were playing Number 33, you had butterflies," he said.

Peabody's quarterback, Charley St. Paul, said players from other schools would go to Manning Bowl just to watch Harry when their teams weren't playing. "I've never seen anything that comes close to what he produced. He had a mental attitude and ability to think on his feet that was uncanny. He was a coach on the field," St. Paul said.

Symrnios' brother, George, said Classical was intimidating even before the game. Peabody players had old leather helmets and uniforms, but Classical had new Green-and-Gold uniforms with shining gold helmets. "You'd say, 'Oh, my gosh, how are we going to play against this god?'"

In the crowd of Classical players, all the Peabody players were only looking for one: Number 33. Regis said, "Thank God we escaped and didn't have to play him again."

It was a dramatic ending. With Peabody losing, 7-6, Regis was stopped on a third down right on the Classical goal line with only seconds remaining. On the next play, Smyrnios spun off right tackle and slipped into the end zone, for the winning score and Classical had only the next kickoff to try to salvage the game. Shortly before that, with time running down, Harry told one of his linemen to check with the referee how much time was left in the game.

"Get the time! Get the time!" Harry told him.

The player went over to the referee and ran back breathlessly. "Harr, Harr, Harry," he spit out in between labored breaths, "It's 20 minutes to four." Harry, and Bullard, just looked at him, astonished.

The Peabody fans got a huge ovation as they left the field, and were taken to dinner by the city's mayor that night. George Symrnios, who had been a star for Peabody, was delirious.

"You guys became immortal by beating Harry," he told his brother and his teammates.

Joyce was furious at Harry, who had been calling most of the plays. He ordered Harry to pass more in the next game, setting a quota of at least twenty-five passes. When Gloucester came to Manning Bowl, they were brimming with confidence they could play Classical after the Peabody upset.

Joyce told Harry if he didn't pass, he was coming out of the game. Harry said he preferred to hand the ball off to this teammates, so they could share the glory, and thought running when the other team thought he would pass was better strategy.

"Go in there and pass all afternoon. When you stop passing, you stop playing," Joyce said adamantly.

"How about letting some of the other guys run?" Harry asked.

"Never mind the other guys. You pass. Remember, Harry, you come out of there if you don't."

He did what Joyce said. Harry was 10-for-14 passing in the first period, for 125 yards and three touchdowns, including eight consecutive completions as Gloucester couldn't contend with him. He finished 23-for-32 with four touchdown passes in leading Classical to a 28-0 pasting of a good Gloucester team before a full stadium.

After his first period start, Harry came off the field and over to Joyce.

"Now can we run with the ball?" Harry laughed.

For his performance, he won a pair of shoes donated by a local company, Spencer Shoes. Gloucester's star player Joe Palazolla said "Agganis was ahead of his time. He could roll out, scramble, and pass."

He proved it in a series of triumphant games, beating Arlington 25-6, a game in which he was 13-for-17 passing, with four more touchdown passes. Then Haverhill fell, 41-0, and schoolboy football fans had the game for which they were waiting the most eagerly.

The next game would be against big and powerful Everett, a school whose football team had been the subject of national magazine articles.

Everett coach Denny Gildea had his team come out and march around the field and right through the Classical players who were warming up. Harry and Bullard, punting to each other, paid no attention to 200-pound linemen charging like elephants.

There were more than 23,000 fans in the stands and standing everywhere. Tickets for the game had been so difficult to obtain that even the governor had to scramble to be there. Harry was ready though.

During the week, Joyce told reporters he estimated Harry had thrown more than 25,000 passes in the offseason and in practices, and that neither he nor his team would be intimidated by the aggressive Everett players. Even Gildea was concerned the game might be rough, and he came over to Harry to warn him.

"It's not my doing what's going to happen here today. These guys are fired up," Gildea said.

Harry was not concerned. "It's okay. Everything will be fine," he said.

Both teams punished each other physically and Classical led only 6-2 at the half, although Harry had runs of 35 and 48 yards off fake passes and was bewildering in the open field. Early in the game, Classical's Tom Smith, one of two black players on the team, intercepted a pass on his team's 6-yard line and ran it back 92 yards to the Everett 2-yard line. Harry quickly threw a touchdown pass to Pujo. In the second period, a snap sailed over Bullard's head on a quick kick, giving Everett a safety.

It was still 6-2 going into the final period. But Harry, mixing running with deft passing and faking, led Classical on drives of 94 and 66 yards, with Bullard running for touchdowns on runs of two and 12 yards.

After the second touchdown, Harry's pass for a conversion failed, and Everett defender Dick Lionetti, who was 6-4, straddled a prostrate Harry and refused to let him up, and took a swing at his head.

Both teams started to scrap. Harry, displaying anger for the only time in his high school career, leaped to his feet, fighting mad as Lionetti tried to put him in a headlock. Police came running to the sidelines and the field to quell the disturbance. Joyce briefly took Harry out of the game.

Lynn Telegram-News sportswriter Fred Bowler reported "Speed in deception triumphed over weight and power as Classical, digging in to turn the tide at critical moments, absored terrific punishment from a gargantuan Everett eleven and then staged a fourth-quarter runwaway to win its most crucial game of the season, 19-2, before a record crowd of more than 22,000 goggle-eyed fans at Manning Bowl last night."

Drama continued to follow Harry. Salem High coach Glenn O'Brien had said before the Everett game he thought the Everett players would make Harry "eat the ball."

After Classical had beaten Everett, some Classical fans showed up the next day at the Salem-Lowell game with signs that said "You Eat It, O'Brien. Agganis Isn't Hungry," and "Classical 19, Everett 2. Your Turn Next, O'Brien." It was a harbinger for the next showdown between the teams.

O'Brien said he was misquoted, but Classical was ready. Still, Salem was up 6-0 at the half before Classical's other black player, Paul Pitman, a speedster, ran for a touchdown, and Classical took a 7-6 lead.

Harry, passing sparingly, completed only two of six passes, but was dazzling with his running, evading many would-be tacklers in the open field. On defense, he was stopping runners and knocking down passes.

In the fourth quarter, still holding to the one-point lead, Harry took a dangerous gamble. Classical had a fourth down on its own 10-yard line and Harry, practically defying Salem to stop him, handed the ball to Bullard instead, who ran for a first down.

Harry led Classical on a long touchdown drive and later, after he had a 58-yard touchdown called back, Pitman ran 66 yards for the final score to seal a 20-6 win. Harry was embraced by Joyce as the game ended, and his coach was beaming with joy.

After the game, a Lynn newspaper put together a composite photograph showing Harry handing a ball on a plate to an unsmiling O'Brien. The Salem coach though was gracious in defeat. He wrote a letter which stated "Harry Agganis is not only a gentleman, but the finest football player ever to grace a high school gridiron."

In October, Harry was named captain of the high school All-American football team, after a poll taken by more than 100 sportswriters. There was going to be a game between the best high school players in the country, but it was never played. Still, Harry became the most famous high school athlete in the country with the designation, and his awards were mounting.

Also that month, University of Georgia Athletic Director Wally Butts wrote Harry directly. "The University of Georgia is very interested in boys of your type and would like to talk with you at a later date," he wrote.

Classical would not be stopped now. The next week, they beat Saugus, 20-7 and Harry was matched against his cousin, Ernie Anganis, whose family name had been Agganis. Most of the games were being played at Manning Bowl because of the capacity, and because the gate receipts of sold-out games were benefitting both teams.

The next week, Classical faced Lowell. But this was not the Lowell team the Green Wave had demolished in a shutout a year earlier. The Red Raiders had hired former pro football player Ray Riddick, a tough coach who preached hard defense and a smashing running game.

In a few years, he would become one of the best known high school coaches in the country and take Lowell High on a two-decade run as a powerhouse that included wins over the North Carolina All-Stars and in bowl games in Florida.

Harry had a passing duel with Walter Kulis and would finish with 10-for-19 for 263 yards. Lowell, behind Kulis and running back Tarsy Kouchalakos, a shifty open field scatback, kept the game close throughout before losing, 32-20.

Classical's reputation meant every opponent was determined to play well, trying to knock off the national champions, and some games were being carried on an experimental basis by a budding new media called television.

The next week, Lynn was up only 13-12 in brutally cold weather against Revere when coach George Kenneally took the Revere players off the field to protest what he felt was poor officiating. It was a dramatic moment as the Revere players headed under the stands at Manning Bowl, and Joyce had to come over to plead for their return.

Kenneally was angry that a referee's decision over a botched lateral had given Classical the ball on his team's 2-yard line, but he brought the players back. Classical scored and went on to a 27-12 win.

That set up the annual Thanksgiving clash with Lynn English, the team which had kept Classical from having a perfect record in 1946. They couldn't wait to get at each other again.

PAREEFANIA ◆ PRIDE ◆ ΠΑΡΙΦΑΝΙΑ

This time English had Harry's friend and basketball teammate at St. George's, Lou Tsioropoulos, whose family had moved to a section of Lynn which required him to switch schools the year before. He was outside the Classical section by only one street.

Tsioropoulos had missed playing on the Classical team which went to Florida for the Granby game. He was a fearsome player, a tall and strong runner and punishing defender. Playing with him was a strong lineman, Charlie Stephanos, and Mike Frangos' brother, Charley, who liked to lead blocks for Lou.

Elias "Lou" Tsioropoulos was an impressive athlete. In Lynn though, the big story was still Harry, especially among the Greek-American fans and families. Tsioropoulos was 6'2" then and 165 pounds, but would grow into a willowy, strong 6'5", with the look of a predator bird.

And besides Harry, Classical had Bullard, who was the leading scorer in the state and who had more points himself than either English or Medford, ranked ahead of Classical because of a system which gave Classical fewer points for playing some smaller schools.

As before though, English played especially hard in the traditional rivalry which pitted good friends against each other. English took a 19-7 lead with only three minutes remaining in the half. Billy Whelan had run 50 yards for an English touchdown a moment earlier, after a Tsioropoulos interception of one of Harry's passes had set up English's second touchdown.

But on the kick off from English, Harry took the ball and put it in Bullard's hands on an disguised reverse play they had often practiced. It was so cleverly done, virtually everyone on both teams and in the stands was fooled.

Bullard took off on an 83-yard touchdown run. Days after the game, *Boston Globe* sportswriter Ernie Dalton asked Harry and Bullard, in civilian clothes, to do the play again and said he still couldn't see how they had done it.

In the third period, Bullard had a 30-yard touchdown run and Classical went up 20-19, and Classical wore down their rivals for a 32-19 win. Bullard finished the season as the state scoring champion, like George Pike had for Classical the year before. Bullard's four touchdowns against English gave him 127 points.

Tsioropoulos thought English was finally going to beat Harry in that 1947 game, especially after going on top, 19-7. Then came the reverse play with Bullard. "Harry was *poneeros* (clever) He pulled that thing on us," said Tsioropoulos, who was an angular man with a narrow, tight and handsome face.

When Harry gave the ball to Bullard on the reverse, Tsioropoulos tried to backtrack and catch Bullard, but the Classical runner was the state's 60-yard dash champion and impossible to catch from behind when he got a step.

"I started to chase, but Bullard went down the middle and every five yards he was getting five yards ahead of me. He put on his afterburners. That Harry was clever, he knew how to screen the officials when he slipped it to Bullard," Tsioropoulos said.

Even though Harry and Lou were good friends, and the two predominant

Greek-American athletes in a city which produced many well-known stars in baseball and football, they were fierce competitors with each other and didn't let up in competition. Once when Tsioropoulos was getting ready to hit Harry with a hard tackle, Harry gave him a stiff arm that braced his good friend to the ground.

Tsioropoulos grew up on Charles Street, right around the corner from Harry's home on Waterhill Street, and near Loumis' grocery store. They used to hang together at the store, and the older kids from Barry Park would come down to recruit Harry to play baseball and football because he was so good.

Like Harry's family, Tsioropoulos' family was from the Laconia region of Greece. Tsioropoulos' mother, Stavroula, was from Kotrona, just outside of Kalamata and north of where the Agganis family lived in Logganiko. Tsioropoulos' father's family was from Oikala in the same region. And, like many other Greek-American immigrant families in the early 1900s in the United States, the mother was a lot younger than the father.

Stavroula was born in 1905, and was fourteen years younger than her husband, Costas, who quickly became prominent in Lynn, where he was a foreman in a leather factory and became secretary and president of St. George's Church.

"He knew all the Greek people," said Tsioropoulos. Costas, like Harry's father George, was a strong, proud man. He had been a sergeant in the U.S. Army in World War I and married early in the 1920s. Tsiropoulos' older brother, George, died in 1932 when he was only five years old, when his mother was carrying his sister, Georgia.

Tsioropoulos was born in 1930 and lived in West Lynn most of his school life, until his family moved to another neighborhood when he was in high school, just one street from the boundary line which would have let him keep going to Classical and play with Harry. They had gone to Breed Junior High together.

Tsioropoulos grew up speaking mostly Greek, used exclusively by his mother, although his father could speak English. His sister, a brilliant student, was mistakenly thought by teachers to be retarded because she was speaking only Greek and having a tough time in elementary school. His father made them start speaking more English.

At Classical, while Harry was starring as a sophomore, Tsioropoulos, who had not started sprouting as fast as had Harry, played on the sophomore team.

Harry was one of the stars of the St. George's church basketball team that included Mike and George Frangos, Pujo, Hippocrates Kyros, Jimmy Kirios, Pete Cuomo, George Manos, Charley and Pete Laganas, George and Socrates Maravelias, Chippy Chipouras, Tom Sfikas, and Jimmy Orphanos. It was a team that would win seventy-one straight games in church leagues and tournaments, including against those from Catholic churches and even Jewish synagogues.

Harry played center and guard and was a redoubtable defender, usually being called upon to hold down the opponent's leading scorers. "He had a good way of pumping everybody up around him and he did that well," said Tsioropoulos. "He liked the camaraderie and he said nice things about everybody else and liked it when they did well," he said.

Harry called Sfikas, who would become the scoring leader of the Essex County League, "King" for that achievement, a nickname that would stick for a lifetime.

Before his family moved, Tsioropoulos played basketball at Classical with Harry, in the winter of 1946-47. Kirios and Pujo were on that team Tsioropoulos said Harry "was very talented and very steady and he had a good shot around the pivot. He could rebound and play defense."

"The thing with him was that he had such a court awareness of where he was, he could easily focus on what he had to do. He seemed to bring it to all the other players and make them better from playing with him. As opponents, we became better for playing against him. He had fantastic balance and I've never seen a better football player. He could throw long, short and he could run and he could kick. He embraced people around him. He had a good sense of humor and humility. He had a sense of confidence too that he weas ready and he could do well, and he loved his home town," Tsioropoulos said.

When people met Harry and said they had heard a lot about his mother, said Tsioropoulos, "He would say 'You want to meet her?' and put them in the car and drive them there to see her."

It was typical of the times too. "We had great role models in our families who worked so hard in industry and business. We saw them come to church dressed up and we saw the family and we saw them work, and there's no way anybody would be egotistical, and we looked up to them because they had such great work ethics," said Tsioropoulos.

The Greek boys had their own Boy Scout troop that was an extended family. "It was known any young Greek boy did not misbehave. It was bad for the community. All the Greek mothers and fathers told their children that. They had a sense of pride up and down the street," he said.

The younger Greeks also looked up to men like Jimmy Andrews, veterans who came to their games and encouraged them, and who demonstrated not only a sense of ethnic pride, but of patriotism as Americans. "We were fortunate to be Depression babies and be around during World War II, when patriotism was at its highest and we became patriotic," said Tsioropoulos.

The win over English was Harry's last regular-season game for Classical, and, for the first time, he cried after. "I'll never wear the Classical uniform again," he said to Joyce, not knowing that he would.

That night, films of the game were shown in the Paramount Theater in downtown Lynn, drawing more crowds. Streamlined fountain pens worth fifteen dollars were given to players on both teams who had scored the first touchdowns.

Classical finished at 10-1, with nine straight wins and only the improbable upset to Peabody keeping them from a perfect season. It was good enough to earn them another bowl invitation in the South. But there was a difference from the year before. Classical had two black players, Paul Pitman and Tom Smith, and they weren't going to be invited.

The Classical players declined the invitation unless they could bring all their teammates. There would be no bowl trip for the defending national champions of high school football.

But there would be more football for Harry and Bullard, who teamed with some English players and other Massachusetts schoolboys to go to Dover, New Hampshire and play the New Hampshire All-Stars. It was a one-sided contest as Harry, playing for the first time with a big end from Watertown named Tom Oates, led a 40-0 win. Harry was perfect, going 8-for-8 passing for 124 yards and two touchdown passes.

Oates had come up to Lynn several times to watch Harry. "I wanted to see if he was that good," he said. "He was the one high school player the players talked about. Until he became my teammate, I had no idea of the talent and skill he had. He was a gifted, great athlete in many ways. He could throw a football and he could punt it. He was a magnificent defensive player and he was a fierce competitor. I loved being a teammate of his."

Oates realized just how good Harry was in another way. While Harry's mother couldn't bear to watch football and didn't go to any of his games, Oates' mother went to all of his, and watched only him.

After the All-Star game, Oates was proud of his performance, catching passes from Harry and asked his mother what she thought of his play.

"I didn't even see you play today," she said sheepishly. "I was watching Harry."

Oates shrugged. "That's the kind of magnetism he brought. He was such a fine kid and a good guy," he said.

Oates caught a touchdown pass from Harry. "I became very conscious he threw from the left side and I had never seen that before and it took me a few minutes to adjust. The ball came at you differently and he threw with such a nice, tight spiral. If you needed the ball in a tight situation, he gunned it at you, absolutely gunned it. It was you or nobody. If you had a step on the defense, he just floated it in. He just had such a great touch. There was no doubt about his ability to sense that instinctively. He was a pleasure to play with," he said.

On December 6, Classical was host to the New Hampshire state champions, Nashua, coached by Buzz Harvey. Classical had been denied the state championship under the rating systems again because they had played smaller schools Winthrop and Gloucester, traditional rivals school officials did not want to drop.

The state title went to Medford, which refused to accept a showdown game, giving Classical the opportunity to play Nashua for the so-called New England championship instead.

It was almost as one-sided as the All-Star game against the New Hampshire stars. Classical pounded Nashua, 38-6 as Bullard scored four touchdowns and Harry scored the other two. "We don't face that kind of competition up in Nashua and when my team goes up against an outfit like the Classical club with Agganis and Bullard, the boys have a chance to learn a lot," Harvey said.

The next day, Harry led the North Shore All-Stars to a 19-6 win at Manning Bowl against the Greater Boston All-Stars. This time, Oates was on the opposing side and was even more impressed at what he saw. Harry went 13-for-19 passing for 160 yards, into a stiff wind.

Oates, a 195-pounder who played defensive end too, came at Harry like a hurricane on one play. "I was going to nail him. I thought I had him flushed out, but I never put a hand on him. He was very strong. One of the times when I got to flush him out, I thought I had him. He just put his hand on my helmet and pushed me aside. He changed my charge to going right by him and I wound up with a handful of nothing. That was the first time anybody had been able to do that to me," he said.

One of the Greater-Boston coaches said it was easy to see why his team lost. "Agganis plays and thinks like a twenty-five-year-old college player. He is terrific and he makes all the difference between the two teams," he said.

On December 12, Bill Graf, athletic director at Manlius Prep, a strong academic school which was a noted football powerhouse and military school, wrote Harry that he had been in contact with Notre Dame football coach Frank Leahy about him. "You should hear from him soon," Graf wrote.

Harry had brought more than headlines to Classical. The team played to more than 160,000 home fans in 1947 and grossed more than $110,000 for the school, bringing in a $40,000 profit off football, an enormous sum for a high school program. He was called a "one-man Chamber of Commerce."

Harry was again named to the All-Scholastic team. His number 33 was retired and was never worn again by a Classical player. In his three years at Classical, he had led his teams to a record of 30-4-1. In the two years he was the quarterback, the record was 21-1-1, and he garnered more awards than any other high school athlete in the country, as shown in one memorable news photo where he was sitting with his mother in front of an array of awards. It was designed by Kirios.

In his schoolboy career, he completed 326 of 502 passes for 4149 yards and forty-eight touchdown passes, scored twenty-four himself and kicked thirty-nine extra points and was a booming punter and ferocious defender against passing or running.

NEOTEES ◆ YOUTH ◆ ΝΕΟΤΗΣ

It was almost unbelievable how much Harry meant to people, even those who didn't know him. John and Frances King of Salem were honeymooning in New York City in the Fall of 1947 when Frances called her uncle, Patrick O'Connor, at Pat's Brass Rail in Lynn and put her new husband on the phone. He heard some good news: he had two tickets for the sold-out English-Classical game on Thanksgiving. The Kings cancelled their plans to go to New Hampshire the following week, and came back to Lynn just to watch the game.

It wasn't just football for Harry that Fall, as great as he and Classical were. He loved to sing and act and appeared in October in a presentation of the "Classical High Varieties," led by Gertrude Norris. It was a typical song-and-dance and variety act for high schools of the time.

The students sang "Don't You Love Me Anymore," and "Remember." There was a ballet dance and violin solos like "Scheherezade," by Elizabeth Dryer, and tap dances and piano solos, and the Gay 90 quartet, featuring Harry, Chipouras, Pujo and Ted Roderigue. The show wound up with a barn dance.

Kirios, who had a face like an amazed pixie seeing only joy all around, loved it when Harry broke out in immproptu songs and their banter over singers Frank Sinatra and Bing Crosby were as much fun for Harry as throwing a touchdown pass.

Harry loved to kid Kirios too over what he called his friend's little laugh. When Kirios smiled, only the top half of his lips would move and, when he laughed, all that came out were two barely audible words, in slow-motion— "ha, ha." Harry's laugh was boisterous and rolling like a Scottish burr that wouldn't stop, and he couldn't stop poking fun at his friend for being so reticent and not laughing out loud.

In public though, it was Harry's performances on the field that were best known. He was so good during the 1947 season that he got an astounding endorsement from an unlikely source. Clipper Smith, coach of the professional Boston Yanks, who were desperate for a quarterback, had been told by his owner to find the best one in the country.

He came back and said "There's a kid who can play regularly on my team right now and I wouldn't be surprised if he could make every team in the league."

The owner was delighted, until Smith continued, "We're going nuts for a forward passer and the best one in the United States is a schoolboy we can't touch."

Aldo "Buff" Donelli, the new head coach at Boston University, who had coached in the pros, was watching. He said, "Agganis is the best high school prospect I have ever seen. He is a superb caller of plays and knows how to develop an offense. I'd give anything to have him." He was already looking ahead—as were a lot of other coaches—to trying to persuade Harry to go to his school after graduation.

Harry went to Cambridge the day before the Harvard-Yale game and was enthralled by the gaiety and festivities around the campus along the Charles River. It was a preview of college life. He was watching touch football games being played at fields everywhere and moved from one to the other just to look.

"This is something," he said joyously. "All these fields, all these games. There are games for guys who wouldn't be allowed to wear uniforms at other places. And those guys are having a wonderful time. This is college sports at its best."

Boston Traveler Sports Editor Arthur Siegel asked Harry what he would advise high school seniors on how to choose a college. Harry hesitated briefly and said, "I'd go where I belong. I'd figure out what my future might be. If I wanted to come home after college and live the rest of my life around here, then I'd go to a school near home. That's where I belong. If I wasn't planning on returning home after college, then I'd consider where I would like to spend my future days. Then I'd go to college in that area. Because that's where I would belong and that's where I'd make people accept me."

At Christmas, the team had a party at which principal Frederick Buckley talked about the academics expected at Classical and how many students went on to college. Charlie Connelly, a well known candy king, gave gold footballs to the lettermen, along with a half pound of chocolates. A large cake was presented by Phil "The Baker" Freedman, and was placed at the head table with a photo of the 1947 team.

But the highlight of the night was a show by the variety players featuring a barber shop quartet, including Dick Cushing, Chipouras, Roderigue and Harry, who were dressed in straw hats and striped coats.

Dickie Harris, son of a local photographer named "One Shot" who took many of the pictures of the Classical games, gave a rendition of the classics in boogie-woogie and it was reported, "He can certainly tickle the ivories."

Bullard and Bert Freedman dressed like girls for a comedy song in which they were featured as "The Classical Girls." Joyce announced the captain for the 1948 team, the first without Harry since 1945, would be Don Cheever. But

Joyce would not coach for Classical again.

As 1948 began, Harry spent the winter starring again in basketball. One of the biggest games came against arch-rival Salem. Harry was called upon to defend 6'5" Al Kendall, who was the second leading scorer in the league and had gotten fifty-six points in his first three games. Tsioropoulos, now playing for Lynn English, said he had seen first hand playing against Harry how tough he was as a defender, and now Kendall found out too.

Kendall did not score.

Salem Football coach Glenn O'Brien said later that "I know that Harry is a great football player and equally great in baseball, but I hadn't expected he would come up with such a stellar performance in basketball." Harry could score too, often getting more than 20 points in some games, and finished the basketball season as a league all-star, and selected captain. He was also named All-Scholastic.

Classical coach Jim Twohig, who had taken over the team from Art Rogers, said Harry picked up the intricacies and nuances of basketball quickly and naturally. Twohig said Harry learned to dribble with either hand in five minutes.

And in one game against Haverhill, the league leader, Harry demonstrated his uncanny instincts. In the last few moments, a play had been set up in which he was supposed to pass to a player, but Harry saw a man cutting and fed him instead.

"Anybody else would have waited for the man to come across, but he saw the open man and said the heck with the play," said Twohig. Harry had a good surrounding cast too, including Pujo and 6'7" Ernie Bulpett, who had developed into one of the best big men in the league that year.

Sometimes, they forgot who they were playing. In one game the year before, when Tsioropoulos was playing for Classical, he said they were talking to each other in Greek, telling teammates to tip the ball forward or back, "*Embros*," or "*Peeso*."

Tsioropoulos said one of the Salem players, whom they didn't know was Greek, laughed and said, "Don't worry, I'll be there too."

The church coach was Mike Kosky, the only Greek-American teacher at Classical. The players admired him. The manager was Harry Brown. The boys played so well together because the church was the nucleus of life for their families. They attended church, went to Greek dances and picnics and festivals.

By now, college scouts and coaches were calling and camping outside his door at Waterhill Street and Harry sometimes had to jump over the fence at the rear of the house to avoid them. The list was growing and would soon surpass seventy-five to eighty-five schools who were beseeching him to play for their school. There were some famous names who came knocking.

Bullet Bill Osmanski of Holy Cross, one of the greatest runners of the era, came to Lynn and met with Harry for two hours, and brought some local alumni. Boston College thought they had an edge because two players from Lynn who knew Harry well, Angie Nicketakis and Walter Boverini, were talking to him. Cornell was making the best pitch, and Dartmouth was interested.

University of Massachusetts Athletic Director Warren McGuirk said Harry was too good for college play. "This boy is ready for the National Football League right now," he said. The biggest push came from Notre Dame coach Frank Leahy, who came to the Hotel Edison in Lynn to meet with Harry, while Harry's family was in the next room waiting.

Joyce had met Leahy earlier at a football clinic in Atlantic City where the Notre Dame coach was the guest speaker. Leahy walked over to him and said, "I hear you have a pretty good boy up there, Agganis, isn't that his name?" That led to Joyce sending Leahy some game films that had the Notre Dame coach in wonderment. Leahy had called Harry "The finest prospect I've ever seen."

Columbia sent Gene Rossides, their great All-American quarterback from a few years earlier who had led his team to an upset of Army, hoping the Greek-American connection would work for them.

Harry had a proclivity for not telling anyone what he was thinking, and he didn't want to let on what he felt about where he would go to college. He had been a role model during his high school years, although sports had taken so much time he had to work hard to achieve moderate grades.

He continued his acting too. His starring role that Spring came as Captain Hook in Peter Pan, during a sold-out series in early April. Harry looked the part of a swaggering villain and played it to the hilt. He had to. Joan Fitzgerald, his girl friend, was playing one of the lost boys. Playing with Harry were many of his teammates, Strom and Cheever and halfback Jim Brown and Pujo. They were a raggedy band of pirates.

It was acting that helped Harry become more comfortable talking in public. Despite his fame, Harry's humility, a Gary Cooper-like shyness, made it hard for him to talk before groups when he was a younger teenager.

Joyce talked to him about the growing demands on his time to speak. Harry told his coach, "I'm not an orator. I can't talk and I just don't want to stand somewhere and be looked over like a freak."

Joyce knew Harry would blossom, although Harry's nature was more introspective. "Harry could develop into a spellbinder in no time. You know he had fine talents as a dramatist, inherited from his Greek forebears, I imagine." Joyce said Harry had no problem learning lines, especially in the demanding role of Captain Hook. "He learned them fast, a real Barrymore. He filled our bowl every Saturday and he filled the school theater two nights running," Joyce said.

Harry and Joan found time to take trips to New Hampshire's White Mountains, where they walked along The Flume, a river carved by glaciers aeons before, and to visit Dartmouth with some friends. His high school years were winding down now, although he stepped into the baseball season again, relishing the 1947 state championship and trying for another.

Classical had another great team, but baseball is a fluid, dynamic game and in a single-elimination tournament where anything can happen, Classical lost in the state tournament, but Harry was named All-Scholastic for the third straight time, and was named New England's best high school athlete.

Harry was more admired in Lynn than even pro athletes. When a sporting goods store hired Red Sox star Johnny Pesky, who had married a woman from Lynn, the Army and Navy Store countered by giving Harry a part-time job. "All the youths from miles around jammed his tiny store just to have the privilege of buying something from Harry," the *Lynn Item* reported.

SOPHIA ◆ WISDOM ◆ ΣΟΦΙΑ

While Harry was trying to keep his thoughts to himself, he told assistant coach Mel Palumbo what he was thinking one afternoon that Spring while Palumbo, who had gone to Boston University, was driving him home.

Harry had turned sour on Boston College, and getting into an Ivy League school might be tough because Harry's grades were just average, but Cornell was interested in a package that would bring him and Pujo and Chipouras there. His teammates received scholarships there in anticipation Harry would follow. Another Lynn great, Billy Whalen, was going there and the school knew there were great athletes in the city.

Palumbo looked over and told him, "If you go to Cornell, you'll meet a lot of nice people and they'll help you later in life." Harry was thinking.

Then he said, almost casually, "What's wrong with B.U.? You went there and my mother's alone and I don't want to be too far away from her."

Palumbo was stunned and didn't say anything for a moment.

"There's nothing wrong," he said, surprised but satisfied.

Palumbo called Zimman, who knew Donelli and B.U. administrators, and they drove over to talk and he said they agreed B.U. would be a good choice for Harry. Donelli said he was delighted to get Harry.

"He wanted to be local," said Palumbo. "He wanted to stay home because of his mother and he lost his father two years before, and he didn't want to lose his mother. B.U. was just coming up and we were beginning to show some life and I think he picked B.U. because he thought he'd be a lot more happy here."

His sister, Mary Raimo, said those reasons were true. "He chose B.U. to be near my mother," she said simply.

Harry though had seen what had happened to Boley Dancewicz, the Classical great who had chosen to leave the area and go to Notre Dame. He had been a great player there too, but was mostly out of sight of his family and the people who meant the most to him. Harry basked in the affection of his friends and family and wanted them to see him play.

On May 18, the *B.U. News*, the school paper, was the first to report that he would be going there, although there had been no public announcement and Harry had promised to tell reporters what his decision would be, when he made it finally.

He denied it at the time, because he said he hadn't made up his mind, although it was clear by then that Donelli, Palumbo and Zimman were talking to him extensively. And May 18 was the date Harry's application was received at the school. He was going to study at the School of Education and listed as his references Rev. Argyrides, Bill Joyce, a local police inspector, John Hines, and Palumbo.

His principal, Frederick Buckley, gave him only a lukewarm recommendation though, giving him highest grades for sense of honor, self-control, responsibility, perserverance, loyalty and leadership. He stated "There is no doubt of his willingness to do college work."

Three days after he applied, Harry was accepted. He would receive a full scholarship. And there was another reason why B.U. seemed so attractive.

It was John and Tom Pappas, who were one of the most successful and rich Greek-American business families in the country. Judge John Pappas had attended Boston College and received his law degree from B.U. in 1925, when he was only 20 years old.

In 1946, he had purchased Suffolk Downs, a horse racing track in Revere, one community south of Lynn. Pappas plunked down $350,000 as a down payment for their $3.6 million deal. One of their investors was a wealthy Louisiana oil man named William Helis, known in that state as "The Golden Greek," and who supposedly had an income of $10,000 a day, a fortune in 1946.

Pappas was a big fan of the Red Sox and B.U. and wanted Harry go to to his school, which had many Greek-Americans and opened doors to many working-class students. He could offer him part-time work at the race track, which Harry, who was living alone with his mother would need, even if he had a scholarship to pay for his school costs.

Pappas and his brother were role models too. They had worked long hours as boys in their father's small grocery store, called Gloria, in Boston.

When he was attending B.U. Law School, John Pappas used to get up at 5 a.m. to open the family market and work there for a few hours before going to school, and hustle back to work at the store later before studying. He and Tom and their brother, Arthur, used to get fifty cents a week for their work.

While John was becoming politically-connected as a prominent leader of the Democratic party in Massachusetts, the little grocery store business had evolved into C. Pappas Company, a large export-import firm which he and Tom took over, and diversified into real estate development and liquor wholesaling and related businesses.

They, with only a few other Greek-Americans, like Hollywood movie studio president Spyros Skouras of 20th Century Fox, were among the most influential in the country. When John married Katherine Plakias in 1939, the ceremony was presided over by Bishop Athenagoras, leader of the Boston Archdiocese, and attended by 400 guests.

Tom was daring and shrewd and once went to Italy and bought that country's entire crop of tomatoes. Unlike his brother, he was a prominent Republican. He had been a director of the Greek War Relief Association and was involved in many charities. He and his brother were primary benefactors of the church.

Harry was attracted by the work ethic and success of the Pappas family, and was impressed they were interested in his attending B.U. John Pappas knew Red Sox owner Tom Yawkey too, who wanted B.U. to play at Fenway Park and thought Harry would be a big draw.

Lou Perini, owner of the rival Boston Braves of the National League, had Boston College to play at Braves Field and Yawkey thought Harry could make B.U. a draw at Fenway Park. John Pappas used to go to Red Sox games and sit in a box held by a well known liquor distributor, and knew Yawkey well.

John Pappas told Harry that B.U. had been good to him and many Greek-Americans and told him "You going there will help the school." Pappas was a trustee of B.U. Harry, who had already decided on B.U., was more convinced than ever.

Donelli said "Pappas told him if he did well in the classroom there would be a good job waiting for him when he got out. This made it easier for him to live in Boston without relying on his mother," or his family, he said.

On June 9, with Cornell coach Eddie Pierce in Lynn still hoping, Harry announced he was going to B.U. He asked Joyce for some nickels. He was going to keep his promise to call sportswriters to tell them the news.

When the President of B.U., Daniel Marsh, heard the good news, he said to Harry, "I hear one of the reasons you're coming here is because of your mother."

"That's right," Harry said.

"She must be a terrific woman. I'd like to meet her," Marsh said.

Harry drove him to Lynn and marched the president up to the second floor apartment to meet his mom. They sat in the kitchen and had coffee.

But first he had to graduate, on June 11, 1948. Harry was pictured, smiling broadly, his arm around Joan Fitzgerald and his friends. High school glory days were over.

He had joined the Marine Reserves and was about to embark on his biggest odyssey, college, where he knew he would be under more scrutiny than ever as sportswriters tried to see if he could elevate B.U. into the upper reaches of college football.

But first, he would spend the summer playing semi-pro baseball. Harry decided to play for the Augusta Millionaires in Maine. Billy Porter from Lynn had gone up to play in that league too, and it was in Augusta that Harry met Ted Lepcio, a rugged high school football player who had gotten noticed by major league baseball scouts at a tryout camp in Oneonta, New York.

Lepcio had played for Augusta in 1947. It was a casual league, unlike the more organized Northern League, which played in bigger places like Montpelier and Burlington, Vermont.

The Augusta team, made up of a lot of top high school and college players, toured through places like Portland and Auburn, Maine, and small towns like Brewer, and Farmingham and Kennebunkport, which was stocked with Ivy Leaguers and owned by a man who later owned the New York Mets.

When he saw how good Harry and Lepcio were, he laughed and said "What are you guys doing playing against these kids?"

Lepcio was a slick infielder, and he took an immediate liking to the big, fast, powerful kid from Lynn with the big swing, and a bigger appetite for life and fun.

They were looking for a place to live and wound up staying with the McCarthy family, twelve miles from Augusta. The boys had to hitchhike back in the dark after night games. A month later, they moved into Augusta.

Ben Howser was the coach. He was an old-time fatherly type who watched over his young players. Harry took Ted to a Greek diner, owned by a man named Chris. Harry introduced Lepcio to Greek salads and feta cheese and souvlaki, lamb and vegetables on a stick. They ate there every day and Harry liked speaking Greek to the owner.

Lepcio and Harry were the stars of the team, and Harry would frequently hit deep into the outfield gaps and make the outfielders start backing up. They played four times a week at least, almost 60 games that summer. Both were being looked over carefully by scouts for the Boston Red Sox.

All the games were at night, except for Sundays, when it was an afternoon game and the first one to hit a home run would win a pig. Because it was a semi-pro league and they weren't supposed to be paid by the team, the players had jobs at a local shoe factory, but all they had to do was show up to get paid. They played at lobster festivals and against prison teams too.

Games would draw as many as 2,000 to 3,000 people and occasionally the Millionaires would play teams like Harry's old club from Lynn, the Vrees All-Stars, who would bring up George Bullard and a young catcher from Fall River, Massachusetts, named Tom Gastall. On one road trip, Harry almost got the team tossed out of a hotel after he and Lepcio had a watermelon fight.

It was an idyllic Summer of innocence, playing baseball almost every day in small New England towns, basking in the sun and touring with friends, with high school over and college on the horizon. These were boys of promise.

The Millionaires would be practicing by 10 a.m. and the day often would not end until 11 p.m. After night games, Harry and Ted would go to the diner for something to eat, or to a dance at the Island Park Recreation Center.

"The local guys didn't like to see us show up," Lepcio smiled. "Because the girls all came to Harry."

PATHOS ◆ **PASSION** ◆ ΠΑΘΟΣ
1948 – 1950

T he excitement and news about Harry arrived at Boston University before he did in September of 1948. Alumni and friends were still amazed he had chosen the school over Notre Dame, Cornell, Georgia, and even Boston College, despite what Harry had felt was the anti-Hellenic attitude displayed by officials at the Jesuit school when he heard they were displeased that Lynn's Angie Nicketakis had been selected captain of the football team.

Harry's brother, Phil, remembered when Nicketakis had come to the family home on Waterhill Street as Harry was trying to decide on a college. Phil and Angie had played some semi-pro football together. Angie had starred at Lynn English before going into the service during World War II, and, like so many veterans, returning to college after the war. Phil was surprised to see him nonetheless.

Phil invited him in and they went into the kitchen to talk. Angie looked anxious. "I was sent here to try to talk Harry into going to Boston College, but I'm not going to do that," he said. Phil asked why.

He said Angie told him about being elected captain in 1947 by his teammates, and that some alumni and school officials weren't happy about a Greek Orthodox student leading the team at a Jesuit college. Nicketakis, immensely popular with his teammates and on campus, was hurt.

Phil was unhappy with the news too, because Greek-Americans were still subject to some discrimination, although their work ethic had elevated their acceptance.

If Nicketakis felt there was prejudice, he hadn't told his teammates, said Jack Farrell, a star of the B.C. team. "It didn't happen," he said. Farrell said he thought B.C. had a good chance of getting Harry because the Eagles had Nicketakis and another Lynn friend of Harry's, Walter Boverini, and there was some surprise at the school when they didn't land Harry.

But Harry was set on Boston University. He came to the school as a mature nineteen-year-old who looked as if he were thirty years old, and had the poise to show it. He was undaunted by upperclassmen, or even the coaches, although he was respectful to each.

He was enrolled in the School of Education but one of the professors with whom he had his closest relationship was a fellow Greek-American, marketing professor John Alevizos. The two would often have impromptu debates in the school's lounge and cafeteria, raging passionately over politics and life and philosophy over coffee and soft drinks.

Harry liked B.U. The main campus was on Commonwealth Avenue, along the Charles River, midpoint between where Massachusetts Institute of Technology and Harvard, its more prestigious neighbors, on the other side in Cambridge.

B.U. was a growing school that attracted many students from blue-collar families, and had a large following in the Greek-American community, some of whom were already influential there, one of the reasons Harry felt more comfortable at the school.

There was no arrogance around Harry, only an imperial confidence that was contagious and made his teammates want to reach the same level. He came as a touted quadruple-threat quarterback and safety who could lift B.U. into national prominence, and the players knew it too. They wanted the left-handed number 33 to pass, run, kick and defend them into the headlines. They would get a role model, a young man who didn't smoke, drink, or use profanity, who went to church, loved his friends and family, and was loyal to them.

John Toner from Nantucket, also a left-handed quarterback, was a junior and the starter on a good team, but he said he could see the potential already in Harry, and especially the way everybody took to him.

"Everybody loved him and there were a bunch of seniors on that team and a lot of us were GI's," he said, men who had seen service and combat. The football players lived together in small quonset-like dormitories near the practice field in Weston, about fifteen miles west of the campus, and had a chance to develop a camaraderie, living two to a room and talking football when they weren't playing it.

Charlie Kent of Arlington, a sophomore, was a star running back on on B.U.'s undefeated freshman team of 1947, but he said there was no jealousy or envy when Harry arrived, even by the upperclassmen, many of whom were combat veterans of World War II. They were taken aback by his poise.

"We were thrilled. It gave us an opportunity to get a little attention. We knew he was wanted by everyone. We were kind of a sleepy little football team over there at B.U. and when he came on the scene all of a sudden national sportswriters showed up. We never saw that before and he was a great guy," said Kent.

Because freshmen couldn't play varsity in 1948, Harry would have to wait a year until playing for the man who had recruited him, Aldo "Buff" Donelli. But even Harry's mere arrival on the practice field caused a sensation, and he tried to downplay it.

"I'm on the spot this year. Everyone has written about me, forgetting other players for some reason. As far as I'm concerned, I'm just another guy in uniform with a job to do, so I don't pay much attention to publicity," he said, even while surrounded by photographers and reporters.

Trying to answer questions and deflect the hub-bub his first day at practice, he scuffed his cleats in the dust and looked down, a little embarrassed to be showing up his teammates, and the varsity at the other end of the practice field in Weston.

"I don't know whether I like football or baseball best," he said. The questions about his future persisted. He answered politely. "Yes, I may turn pro after graduation but it all depends on which sport seems to suit me," he said, after posing for more than an hour for photographers.

Cliff Sundberg, sports publicity director, said Harry handled the attention like a veteran. "He was a pro, just the way he posed for pictures. I never had to tell him anything. He knew just what to do. He had been through much of it in high school and he was well versed in it. There was no problem for him. He never had a big head," he said.

Later, Harry said, "I'm only a freshman, but you'd think I'd made the varsity already. And from some of the stories you might get the idea I'm the head man. That isn't fair to the other fellows on the team, and I'm the first to realize it. Thank goodness they're so level headed and a lot of them are older. They understand the situation."

In another interview inside one of the administration buildings, he praised teammate Pete Sarno, who stuck his head in to watch. "Hey Pete, another writeup," Harry yelled, laughing.

Trainer Mayo Donelli, Buff's brother, said, "Never mind that stuff 'Flash Bulb.' Let's get into the uniform and out on the field."

Harry laughed, but came back quick seriously and said "I found out long ago that football is a team game. You have ten other fellows out there with you all the time, and no team ever can get any place unless all eleven are trying on every play. That's why it's silly, when you analyze it, to publicize one player and overlook the rest."

Harry praised his brothers, Paul, Phil, Demo and Jimmy for giving him the chance to play sports. "They would have been great athletes only they had to go out to work and support the family. I was the baby so they made it possible for me to finish high school," he said.

The upperclassmen included a few friends who knew Harry well, like Bobby Whalen, who had played at Lynn English, and Dick Fecteau, who grew up in Harry's neighborhood. "Everyone was always waiting for him to make a mistake, but he never did," said Fecteau. He was prouder than ever about his West Lynn colleague.

Whalen would be especially important to Harry because he was a fast and strong running back who came from a family of great athletes. His father had briefly played professional baseball, and professional football with the Canton Bulldogs. His brother, Billy, played at Lynn English the same years Harry was at Lynn Classical, including the 27-27 tie of 1946, and had gone on to Cornell with Harry's Classical classmates Vic Pujo and Chippy Chipouras. Billy also had played baseball with Harry for the Vrees All-Stars.

Bobby Whalen had graduated high school in 1945, several months before Harry started his career at Classical. Whalen briefly went to Notre Dame, but left and went into the Navy for a year. He came back to Lynn and went to B.U. and was on the undefeated freshman team of 1947.

He told some of the upperclassmen how much Harry would mean to B.U., and was surprised Harry had not gone to Cornell or another college. He had seen the Classical-English game of 1946 and was wowed by Harry's performance. The two schools produced many athletes who would go on to star in college.

At B.U., Harry for the first time would meet even freshmen who were older than he. Whalen said the varsity couldn't wait for Harry to play with them. "We realized how much he was going to help us. There was no jealousy or anything like that," Whalen said.

Harry met a senior he liked right away, a passionate man who laughed and talked loud and loved to talk about his Italian heritage the same way Harry was proud to be Greek. His name was Silvio Cella.

Cella met Harry in the trainer's room and right away liked the freshman who wanted to talk to everyone, and who wasn't daunted by seniors or coaches.

Harry took a liking to Mayo too and was engaging him in conversation when Cella came in.

Cella, who played for Revere High School, not far from Lynn, looked at him and said, "Harry, if you played against me in high school you wouldn't be here. You know why? Because you've got Greek eyes and those eyes deceive you and I know exactly where you're going to throw the ball, how you're going to throw the pass," he laughed.

Cella was a demonstrative, outgoing man who was a resourceful pass defender, and he couldn't resist ribbing Harry. Harry knew how to come back, and the conversation cemented a friendship.

"You're kidding me, what, are you kidding?" Harry laughed.

"I'm telling you, I've know that for a long time about you, those eyes give you away," he insisted, waiting to see how Harry would take it, his own eyes twinkling with mischief.

They came from the same kind of working-class backgrounds, where food and family meant everything. Cella's parents, Michael and Louise, emigrated to the United States from Avellino, Italy.

Cella, who spoke fluent Italian, called Harry an "*Aveva Politica*," a man who was wise, astute and had the rare ability to make everyone like him right away. Despite the age and difference in their years at B.U., they went out often and taught each other their native languages.

"Harry, say '*Com-e stai*,' it means 'How are you'," he said. And "*Bene grazie*," which meant, "Well, thank you." Harry learned "*Tu sei bella*," to tell a woman "You are beautiful." And "*Buona notte*," which meant "Good night."

Harry gave Cella "*Tee kanees*," how are you, and "*Kala*," which means good and "*O Anthropos eenai kalos*," which means, "The man is good." There would be nightly lessons in Greek and Italian in the dorm. They didn't talk football, because there was too much Mediterranean passion in the air, as their debates raged into the night over culture and philosophy and life.

The upperclassmen took such a liking to Harry, he would come to Cella's room, where they would be joined by veterans like Billy Tighe and play the ukelele and bass fiddle with Everett Dorr, who had been wounded fighting in Iwo Jima.

Cella would sing. Harry would get a chair, sit in the middle of the floor and laugh and listen and banter with the seniors. Next to sports, music and singing were his passions.

It all came to a head one night when Cella told Harry "Italian food is much better and richer than Greek food." Cella had had enough of Harry spouting that the Greeks were responsible for just about everything great in he world. "It's time to go to Felicia's and get some Italian food," a popular spot in Boston's Italian North End, Cella said.

As they were walking up to the second-floor restaurant in the crowded neighborhood, Cella introduced Harry to Felicia, who was standing on the landing. "*Com-e stai*," Harry tried out his Italian. He turned around to Cella, and in the same breath, but in English, said, "Can she make the Greek peppers?"

"They don't make Greek peppers here. We make everything Italian. This is the North End, Felicia's!" Cella roared back, his arms flying in exclamation. "We're in the North End, we're eating Italian food!" he said.

They had a wonderful Italian meal, after which Harry said, "I've never had the Italian coffee, espresso, can you order one for me?"

A week later, Harry turned to Cella and said, "I'll show you where you can get everything to eat." He took Cella to a Greek restaurant, the Olympia. They had stuffed grape leaves, cabbage, a lasagna-like dish called pastitsio, a Greek salad and a traditional dessert of crushed nuts and honey called baklava that is irresistible and dripping sweet.

Cella wound up his meal having some Greek coffee, a muddy thick concoction in a demi-tasse that is stirred with a tiny spoon and savored slowly. It is an acquired taste that is too bitter for some tastes. "How is the coffee," Harry asked.

"The Greek coffee is good," Cella said.

Harry smiled. "I told you Cella, even the Italian coffee doesn't compare with the Greek."

The friendships were part of the camaraderie on campus, but those times were too few because of the demands of football, and the expectations that came with Harry. B.U. had a good team in 1948, but there was already some looking ahead to when Harry could join the varsity the next year.

Even Donelli, who had a good team in 1948, got caught up in some enthusiasm. "Next season? We can't miss. Look at the material. Look at the depth." And when it's mentioned to Harry that B.U. and company are on the march, he sad "Okay, but be sure to put the COMPANY in capital letters."

Harry had become close to Donelli, who had wisely used connections in the Greek-American community to help convince him to come to B.U. Donelli had been brought to B.U. the year before to upgrade the program at a school that was one of the ten largest in the country, but had been mediocre in football.

He was one of the best coaches in the country and once had coached Duquesne University and the Pittsburgh Steelers at the same time in 1941.

He was an old-school coach, tough and disciplined, the result of having been a star athlete himself. In 1934's World Cup of soccer, Donelli scored all the U.S. goals in a 4-2 victory on June 27 over Mexico that led to one headline that read: "Donelli 4, Mexico 2." He also scored a goal in a losing effort against Italy, the last time an American had scored against that country in World Cup competition.

Cella said "Buff's soccer background was evident at B.U. because he had us practicing onside kicks years before other teams thought about it. He did things then that pro teams were doing decades later."

His players gave him the ultimate respect of rarely deigning to approach him, content more to listen and heed his admonitions. Veteran players, especially those in the late 1940s who had been in the service and seen combat, were less apprehensive, but respected Donelli's intense preparation.

"He never belittled anyone, and he had a good sense of humor," said John Simpson, a senior. "He was very demanding, but he wasn't abrasive."

Donelli was short, but strong, and rough looking, with a broken nose and gray hair. He could have played a strongman in the popular 1940s film noir detective movies because, for all his kindness, there was a hint of menace about him, a sense he was not a man with whom you could trifle.

He liked to wear a dress hat with his suits that made him look commanding. He had played for the Steelers in an era of two-way football and little money. When he coached in 1941, the players were getting fifty dollars a game.

He didn't have to scream to get his player's attention. After an off-tackle B.U. play called "B-36, right" failed to work against New York University one year because Donelli thought his players hadn't executed, he ordered them to run only that play most of the third quarter until they got it right.

"There was great respect of his knowledge and ability to organize," said Simpson.

Donelli quickly developed a close and avuncular relationship with Harry, who, after his father's death in January of 1946 had attached himself to strong male role models like his brothers and high school coaches Bill Joyce and Harold Zimman. Donelli loved Harry and the Greek-American family whose upbringings were so similar to Italian-American homes, of closeness and sharing and moral values.

Donelli didn't let up on Harry though when he thought it was needed, although that was rare indeed. One day before practice in Weston, Harry showed up in a Cadillac he had borrowed from some friends, the Vrees' brothers.

"Where the hell did you get that car?" Donelli snapped.

"A guy gave it to me," Harry said.

"I don't care who gave it to you. You get it out of here, and you with it," Donelli snorted.

Harry came back with another car from the Vrees', a yellow convertible with no roof. When it rained, Harry would just drive it and get wet. He was singing in the rain.

He was having a good time after practices too, entertaining teammates in the room he shared with Tommy Oates, a tough pass receiver and defensive end

Harry had recruited himself to come to B.U. after they had played with and against each other in high school all-star games.

All the freshmen, and most of the veterans, were a little frightened of Donelli and few got his ear. "You didn't get too close to him and he made you work," said Whalen, who said he once lost 20 pounds after a series of double sessions and went down to 155 pounds.

Donelli wanted Harry to run the Wing-T formation which would give his team more flexibility and options to pass, which could happen only because Harry was such an outstanding passer and a danger to run any time he dropped back to throw.

Harry had to play for the Freshmen "pups" team of the Terriers. He was no ordinary freshman though. That first day he came on to the practice field, there were hordes of reporters and photographers following his every move.

There were a few good-natured jibes from upperclassmen at the other end of the practice field in Weston, but awe from many who had heard of his high school reputation. It didn't take long before they saw what he could do.

Irv Heller, a veteran and tough varsity lineman from Revere, said Harry had such a big reputation he was anxious to knock him down. "I'd had some success and I wanted to work him over to see what makes him tick. It ended up the other way around and that's when I gained a lot of respect for him," he said. "He was the greatest all around football player I'd ever seen,' he said. "He was a great passer but a great defensive player too."

And, said Heller, there was another element to Harry that players soon discovered—usually too late—about him.

"He was tough," said Heller.

ΕΡΙΤΗΥΜΙΑ ♦ DESIRE ♦ ΕΠΙΘΥΜΙΑ

Harry got a chance to lead the freshmen against the varsity in a scrimmage. The varsity had a good team that year, including the freshmen from the undefeated 1947 team. Harry led his underclassmen on an impressive 80-yard touchdown drive.

With Harry playing for the freshmen though, there was a problem for the varsity: getting fans to go to Fenway. Many preferred to see Harry play. In his first college game, as a freshman, Harry methodically led B.U. to an easy 20-7 win over Wentworth, a technical institute in Boston better known for its academics than its football.

"Ever see a robot in action?' wrote Al Harmon, a reporter for the school paper, the *B.U. News*. "This robot, who goes by the name of Harry Agganis, mechanically swept 55 yards down field for one touchdown, mechanically kicked two extra points, mechanically displayed a radar set for a left arm; and mechanically handled a wet ball like a magician as he deftly directed Russ Peterson's T machine ... in short, Agganis did everything but call penalties." He had arrived.

With his team down 7-0, Harry faked a handoff and ran 55 yards for a score. He ran the second half kick back 45 yards and on the next play, with a magical sleight of hand, gave the ball to running back Charlie Hanson, who ran 45 yards for a touchdown while the Wentworth players were mesmerized watching Harry. He was his own best decoy.

"So expertly did Agganis fake possession of the ball that one Wentworth player claimed sorcery on the play," Harmon wrote. Harry wanted more than sports from school though. In the late 1940s, campuses were serene ivory towers, places for study and sports and socializing.

It was a different, quieter time, the post-war years when Americans wanted to regroup from the depression years and the war years and wanted stability. Ex-GI's were back to buy homes and go to school and start families, and college campuses were havens. There were signs of imminent change, however, as the new medium of television was catching on and 200,000 sets a month were being sold, far more than the peak of 165,000 radios monthly. America, and the world, were changing.

The school paper had ads for his and hers Jantzen sweaters for $7.95 and $8.95. The students in the ad wore matching white buck saddleshoes and were touted as having the "Big Game Strategy ... Perfect Together."

And, in an age when kissing and petting were big topics, when AIDS and the horrors of sexual plagues were far away, there was a different type of admonition about sexual behavior. A story in the school paper warned that "The modern college graduate is a man without morals," according to certain religious educators. But Dr. Walter G. Muelder, Dean of Theology, said "This is a blatant half-truth."

Singer Frank Sinatra, who made his bobby-soxer fans swoon with want, suffered a throat hemorrhage, and Perry Como and Frankie Laine gained some popularity with Sinatra on the sidelines. Stan Kenton nosed out Woody Herman to lead the country's favorite jazz band, but some critics thought they could detect a change in music too.

Students thought of careers and families, even if for women that meant those who didn't go to college—and many who did—would still wind up with aprons and children and not careers.

An ad offered a career opportunity in insurance. "Want to earn $9,000 a year?" Radio comedians Bob and Ray were scheduled to appear on campus, with their deadpan, low-keyed dry sense of humor that had no sense of scatology.

But an editorial on October 26 lamented that despite good weather the previous Friday night, there were only 8,000 in attendance for the football game, prompting a Boston newspaper to write that "Boston University yesterday proudly boasted a new high enrollment of 30,694. But the students either aren't allowed to go out nights or they have a grudge against their football team."

The editorial stated that Boston College had an enrollment of 6,300 but drew 26,000 to its first home game, causing ire at B.U. "The present situation is a disgrace to the university and a good part of the blame rests on the shoulders of the student body," and asked them to fill Fenway Park. Harry wasn't yet playing at Fenway to fill the seats.

Some students later complained of high ticket prices. Phil Bateman wrote that B.U. games were costly. "Too much dough. It sets a fellow back at least $3.60 when he goes on a date," He said. And that didn't include the popcorn.

Harry got a measure of revenge in his next game against Dartmouth, a school which had recruited him. B.U. blanked Dartmouth, 39-0, as Harry went 6-for-6 with two touchdown passes, following that with a 34-0 thrashing of another Ivy League club, Harvard's freshmen, which drew 6,000 out to Weston.

Harry was 8-for-16 for 134 yards, threw a 20-yard touchdown pass to Hanson, punted to the Harvard 2-yard line and scored a touchdown himself. After three games, he was 17-for-29 passing and a sensation on campus.

"He has punted superbly, displayed crafty running abilities and exhibited an uncanny accurate left toe. His quarterbacking has been technically flawless. One observer who has seen all the great T formation quarterbacks compared Agganis and Frankie Albert, the former Stanford All-American," the school paper raved of his performances.

But the big talk was of the upcoming game with Holy Cross' undefeated, untied and unscored upon freshmen team. The Purple Crusaders were touting their own sensational freshman quarterback, Paul Gallo from Westfield, a small town in western Massachusetts.

The matchup was made and the game proved irresistible, and was getting more attention than varsity games. Donelli was trying to convince reporters to come watch his varsity, which, after an opening game 27-0 loss to Muhlenberg of Pennsylvania, then a football power coached by Ben Schwartzwalder, was in the midst of a winning streak.

When he grew weary of complaining, Donelli said, "Ok, go and look at the freshmen. You'll see the greatest eighteen-year-old football player I've ever laid eyes on."

Even as a freshman, Harry was averaging more than fifty minutes a game, and was savaging receivers and runners from his safety position, where he could leap effortlessly from one side of the field to the other to knock down passes, and was a punishing hitter whom runners couldn't get around.

So when B.U. went to Fitton Field in Worcester for the year's most celebrated freshman game, there were 18,000 fans ready to watch the battle royale. For one of the few games in Harry's life, it was a letdown.

Gallo was unstoppable, with touchdown runs of 92, 19, 44 and 12 yards, leading Holy Cross to a 38-12 pasting of B.U., with Gallo and Arlington's Mel Massucco dominating the game. Harry was 8-for-23 for 125 yards, although injuries to B.U. had limited their ability.

A headline later proclaimed "Gallo Outshines Agganis" and the story in the school paper said "Harry Agganis, the Pup's prize possession, was lost in Gallo's blinding performance, but he passed, kicked and directed the team in precision in a losing cause, going 8-23 for 125 yards."

Whalen though said there was a reason why B.U. didn't play well that day. During the week, Agganis had led the freshmen in scrimmages against the varsity, which was getting ready for Fordham, and several of the best players on the freshmen team had been hurt and didn't play against Holy Cross.

During the Fordham game at the Polo Grounds in New York, an announcement was made that Holy Cross, a Catholic school like Fordham, was beating B.U. "The place went wild," said Whalen. The varsity beat Fordham though, 33-7.

Massucco, a highly-recruited running back had been denied admission to B.U. because, like many young men in the 1940s, he had left school early to join the military and had received a "war diploma.," He said the loss was not Harry's fault, and that Holy Cross had a great team.

"Harry was no stranger to me," said Massucco, who had read of Harry's high school exploits. He said beating Harry's team "was pretty thrilling. And from what he did afterward, it meant even more because he was quite an athlete." The Holy Cross defense was geared simply to stop Harry.

Harry did not dwell on his failure. In his last game as a freshman, he led B.U. to a 15-8 win over Marianopolis Prep, a military school that at the time was known for its football teams as well. He went 8-for-15 passing and had a 70-yard punt, and ran for a touchdown. The punt went from his team's 20-yard line to the Marianopolis 10. He finished his freshman year throwing 29-for-52 for 429 yards and five touchdowns. And he was quickly becoming one of the most popular figures on campus.

CHARA ◆ JOY ◆ XAPA

The attention given Harry for his athletic prowess already was drawing reporters from around the country, too, and coincided with the arrival of Donelli a few years earlier to improve the football program at B.U.

The campus was spread out though, from Commonwealth Avenue along the Charles River, down past Kenmore Square and Fenway Park, to Copley Square two miles away.

It was a good, innocent time to be in college, even if there were inequities in America's social fabric, with discrimination against minorities and limited opportunities for women. But there was relatively little violence and divorce was still something that would get people's attention.

Colleges still seemed reserved for white, relatively well-to-do students and those with means or jobs to put themselves through school.

At the movies, film noir was popular, and the toughest language actor Alan Ladd would ever use was "You big lug." Clothes were stylish and elegant, and there was a sense of grace. Television had just come out, a harbinger of what would soon become a more fast-paced world.

The end of World War II a couple of years earlier had brought some tough and hardened and older students back into colleges, those who had seen the world and death and were not awed by a university. It would mean that Harry would have to deal in his sophomore year with teammates who would not be daunted by his high school reputation, either.

Around the B.U. campus on Commonwealth Avenue, where there wasn't even a good street light yet, most students were going about the business of trying to get a degree, and have a good time. Harry would soon join the fraternity Sigma Alpha Epsilon, in Brookline, and become one of the most popular pledges.

And, after his freshman year, he had moved from the football campus in Weston to the Myles Standish dormitory in the middle of Kenmore Square, a large building that put students in the midst of a teeming business area. And he would, of course, continue to commute frequently back to Lynn to be with his mother and family, and often bring his teammates there.

On the campus, the school inaugurated a date bureau to aid students in their social life. Before big games for the varsity, there were pep rallies, like the "Beat Iowa" parade that included floats. It didn't help the varsity, which, after a six-game winning streak, lost its last game, at Fenway Park, to Iowa, 34-14.

In December, the *B.U. News* carried a feature on Harry, in which he said he looked forward to his sophomore year and playing on the varsity.

"We ought to roll through our schedule. We've got the best coach in the country and most of the top players are coming back," he said. Harry rated Slingin' Sammy Baugh of the Washington Redskins as his favorite football player and Ted Williams of the Boston Red Sox as his favorite baseball player. Harry had chosen Number 33 back in high school because that was Baugh's number.

While the 1940s were a time when many women seemingly were in college looking for husbands, there was some sentiment poo-poohing that idea.

Dr. Herbert Lamson wrote that colleges are "not marriage mills." He said "Less than half the co-eds at college in recent years trekked to the altar with men from the same college."

He said, "Today's co-ed, after graduating college, wants to work and acquire a skill which she may use in case the marriage fails." That was in contrast to the advertisements and tone of the times.

A Phillip Morris cigarette ad in the school paper tried to give vocabulary lessons while pitching the product. A cartoon character was shown entering a movie with a woman on his arm. "Lucky me! About to behold the kaleidoscopic undulations of Greta Gayheart—and escorting the most glamorous gal on campus," he said.

And she, with covetous gaze, said back "Romance certainly seems to be on the horizon, my gay Lothario."

In the winter, Harry had time to study because his coaches didn't want him playing basketball, a sport at which he was an all-state performer in high school, even often outshining his one-time Lynn Classical teammate, Lou Tsioropoulos, who was headed to Kentucky. Harry's coaches were worried too that he would be using different muscles for basketball.

He would spend a lot of time with Jimmy Kirios, who had gone to Suffolk University, and with his schoolboy friends. They especially liked to sing. Kirios had a rich, toneful voice that had a sweet melancholic tone, and Harry admired his ability.

They would go to the Willy House near Lynn, and Farmer's in Nahant, the peninsula attached to Lynn by a narrow road running along Lynn Beach.

Harry loved music almost as much as sports, and he and his friends would dance the jitterbug and fox trot and waltz with women they would meet. Harry liked to go to Greek dances too, at the Pan-Samian Hall in Peabody, where he would often lead a line in folk songs, leaping up and slapping the front of his foot and yelling "OPA!"

In May, Harry went to Fenway Park for a workout. He was a familiar face at the field, and Mary Trank especially liked seeing him. He got a chance to bat against his old adversary, Chuck Stobbs, and hit several long drives off him. They were good friends now.

In the Spring of 1949, Harry went to football drills—and the attention returned. Photographers kept him busy with their demands, asking him to pose in different positions and drawing some more ribbing from his teammates, including the varsity, against whom he would have to play again, this time with a freshman season behind him for experience.

George Winkler, a great pass-catching end, was with the varsity at one end of the field in Weston when Harry came on, followed by a gaggle of photographers.

"What gives here?" he said. Some of the varsity players snickered too. "We're going to knock this guy down a peg or two," they said.

"We thought this guy has to be a cocky son of a gun, but wasn't. He had a lot of confidence. He was a regular guy and he had a great smile for everyone and you learned to love him because he was a regular guy ... for all the God-given talent he had he didn't lord it over everyone," Winkler said later.

"He gave all his teammates the credit and he always showed great respect to coach Donelli and all the coaches. What endeared us to him was that this young man, as great as he was, could have gone to any college in the country and he wanted to stay in Boston because of his mother. He loved his family and he wanted to be near his family."

But Donelli told reporters he wouldn't commit to giving Harry the starting job in the Fall, because he had John Toner, another left-handed quarterback with experience.

In an intrasquad game, Harry picked up a fumble and ran 60 yards to score and threw a touchdown pass to lead his team to an 18-6 win. A few weeks later, in the annual Alumni-Varsity game, Harry overwhelmed a talent-laden alumni team, directing the varsity to a 39-12 win, including a 28-yard touchdown pass.

But his friend Silvio Cella intercepted one of Harry's passes. Harry laughed, "Good old Silvio. Can you imagine that, my old pal Cella intercepted me. Isn't that something," glad his friend had a moment to shine too. Even the usually terse Donelli had to laugh.

"I guess Cella knows you, you and your eyes," Donelli roared. Whenever Harry saw Cella after that, he would laugh too. "See those eyes, don't they sparkle?" he said.

It wasn't long before the track coach came by to inquire if Harry would be interested in throwing the discus and hammer for his squad, but Harry had to decline, because the baseball team needed him more. The football season and studies had taken their toll though, and the expectations for Harry in baseball were just as high.

He started off miserably. For someone who had been hitting major league and semi-pro pitching, and had played the previous summer for the Augusta Millionaires in Maine with Ted Lepcio and some major league prospects, there was concern. Harry went 0-for-19. He was hitting the ball hard, but right at defenders.

With the short Spring season for New England colleges, there was little time for recovering from slumps, but Harry came on strong and finished at .268.

There was Augusta to look forward to again, the idyllic summer of barn-storming through small New England towns, playing baseball every day and hanging out with his friends. Harry went back up to Maine for the season.

He had become especially close to Lepcio, and had lived in the same house with him and another player, who were put up by local residents interested in the league.

And there was a lot of interest. A crowd of more than 2,500 attended one game during a warm Summer afternoon, although many of the games were played at night in small New England towns.

The Millionaires played the Boston Bearded Hoboes in one exhibition game, although Harry missed some games because of tonsilitis. In one game against the Portland Pilots, he hit two long home runs that went behind a snow fence more than 400 feet in the outfield.

It was a joyous life.

PROVLEPSIS ◆ ANTICIPATION ◆ ΠΡΟΒΛΕΨΙΣ

Donelli was nervous. His team was going to open an arduous schedule at Syracuse for the first game of the 1949 season, in September. Ben Schwartzwalder, who had coached Muhlenberg to an embarrassing shutout route of B.U. the year before, had moved to Syracuse, and Donelli didn't want to lose to him a second time. He told the players, "If you don't win, you're going to walk back from Syracuse."

This was a strong B.U. squad. Winkler and George Sulima were exceptional pass-catching ends, and Bobby Whelan, the flashy running back from Lynn English, was the fastest man on the team, and the only one who could beat Harry in a dash. The line was strong too, anchored by Artie Boyle and Irv Heller. But Syracuse had the reputation and was a favorite in the game.

B.U. had not played particularly well in a recent scrimmage against powerful Army, especially Harry, who had trouble directing the attack. Toner was scheduled to start. Worse, it was a rough ride in bad weather and Donelli didn't look good as the plane was bucking.

Harry, smiling, came up the aisle in the plane and tapped his coach on the shoulder. Harry was barely twenty-years-old and hadn't started a game in college yet and he was talking to a man who was one of the best, and toughest, college coaches in the country and who had handled pro teams too.

Donelli was loosening his tie and fretting, and getting out some play sheets and then discarding them a dozen times. He suddenly felt a tap on his shoulder and looked up. It was the smiling face of Harry, in an open shirt and windbreaker.

"How's it, coach?" he said, casually and confident, grinning. "You worried?"

The plane suddenly bucked hard, but Harry, loose-jointed and stolid, rode with it. "Don't worry coach, we'll take 'em," he said. He slapped Donelli on the back, walked back to his seat and picked up a magazine. Donelli didn't know what to think, although he was a little resentful of the cockiness.

"What business had a boy just out of high school to notice the worrying of an old stager like me?" he said. But he started laughing at himself a moment later.

"You try to teach your boys poise, but here you are getting a lesson from a fellow you've hardly begun to teach," he thought to himself. From that point on, Harry was something special to Donelli. The boy had taught the coach.

On Friday night, the team went to dinner and Donelli became irate when he saw steak coming out. "We have Catholic boys here and they are not eating meat on Friday!" he bellowed. "You people are inadequate," he told the staff. "We are getting out of here." The team left.

In the locker room before the game, Harry got taped early and sat with his eyes closed, not a sign of worry anywhere. It was moments before his first varsity game in a stadium filled with raucous fans, and it was raining hard.

By game time, the weather had worsened and it was a driving rain. Toner was on the kickoff team too and, when B.U. fumbled, he suggested to Donelli to let Harry start instead. Donelli left it up to Toner to decide what to do.

"He was a helluva player. It was an opportunity for Harry to come in and get the job done," said Toner. It was the start of a college career in which Harry would almost never come out of a game, playing both ways.

Harry responded by mixing up his running and passing, making a wary Syracuse overlook Whelan, who was running well. That set up an early Agganis touchdown pass to Winkler, but it was called back on a penalty. With fog settling in, Harry coolly responded by throwing a 17-yard score to Sulima.

Whelan had a 48-yard touchdown run called back on a penalty, so he went on a 78-yard scoring run to take B.U. up by 20-0, shocking Syracuse. And Harry had kept Syracuse backpedaling with his throwing, dazzling running, and field generalship, commanding the veterans and calling his own plays and sometimes making up new ones.

In the rain-soaked huddle, Harry thought for a moment and, on one knee, looked up at Whelan. "Bobby, can you get behind that back?" in the defensive backfield, he asked.

"No question. He's not even looking at me because you can't throw the ball that far in this weather," Whelan said.

"Don't worry about it," Harry said. "You get out there behind him and I'll get you."

And he did.

Winkler said he was awed. "We had the feeling no matter how far behind you were or the problem he'd take care of it. He was a big, strong man," he said.

Before the game, B.U. players had been as anxious as Donelli. "We had a lot of respect for them and the name," said Winkler. "Slowly but surely we grew in confidence the way Harry conducted himself, called the plays. I could remember other years when there would be some grumbling … with Harry, no one spoke. He did all the speaking and he was the general and he called it. We soon found out we keep our mouth shut. He was in charge."

Winkler said it was easy to catch Harry's passes because they were so precise and timed so well. "He made me a great receiver. If I went 12 yards down and out and turned, the ball would be there."

"When he said you run a 15-yard sideline, I just had to run without worrying about looking back, and make my break, and when I had to look for the ball, there it was. I didn't have to worry about looking over my shoulder," he said.

Whalen was impressed at the way Harry had taken command. "Because of him, it made it awful easy to run. It's because Harry was such a great quarterback and passer that they had to think of him first," he said. Harry didn't yell in the huddle.

"You're going to take the ball this time and you'd better move," he told Whalen on one running play. Harry was kneeling in the rain and mud and looked up at his friend and smiled. "You couldn't help but like the guy. He always had a smile on his face and he always made you feel good," he said.

Syracuse got two quick scores and Heller, one of B.U.'s best linemen, got thrown out for fighting. And then Syracuse took a 21-20 lead in the third period, rocking B.U. and worrying everyone, it seemed, except Harry.

Whelan ran 74 yards for another touchdown and then Harry threw a clinching 12-yard touchdown pass to Winkler. He had thrown the ball only six times in the driving rain, two for touchdowns, but Syracuse was so worried about his versatility, the field was opened. Whelan had 240 yards rushing in 18 carries, his greatest game.

B.U. had the stunning upset in Harry's first game, 33-21. And Toner said he knew he wouldn't be playing quarterback any more, and would go onto defense. He didn't mind. The sacrifice would later earn him the school's award for sportsmanship.

"We never, ever talked about it, but down deep I knew once he got settled in he was going to be the quarterback. There were plenty of other places for me to play," he said.

Winkler was impressed with Harry's confidence. "He'd say we're going to get a first down on this play and he was always positive in his thinking. We'd look to Harry for the play that was going to bail us out because you got accustomed to it. Harry never wavered, even after falling behind 21-20. He always felt we're coming back."

The next week, also away, B.U. crushed Colgate 40-21, as his friend from Lynn, Tommy McGee, and Harry Zingus, who were roommates, hitchhiked to upstate New York and arrived at 3 a.m., sleeping in a hotel lobby. They were standing by the side of the road in New York, holding a megaphone, when a car came by and stopped. It was Harry's brother, Phil. He gave them a ride.

Colgate was favored too, but Harry scored a touchdown, passed to Whalen for three and set up a fifth. Whelan scored three touchdowns, and the Lynn Connection was connecting. Harry was 8-for-15 for 137 yards and intercepted two passes at safety.

Whalen had an easy day. "Harry had the knack, if it had to be hard it was hard, if it had to be feathery and plop in your hands it was just that way ... he would just put it in there so easy you couldn't believe it," he said.

Harry had discovered early on that Colgate was double-teaming his great receiver, George Sulima, who was a tough and resilient player. Harry looked to Whalen in the huddle.

"Okay, Bobby, we'll throw it to you instead," he said.

The Colgate win and Harry's performances, which were drawing attention from papers across the country, set up a wild anticipation for B.U.'s first home game, at Fenway Park where the Red Sox played. More than 19,000 fans turned out for the game against West Virginia, the third highly-rated favorite in a row for the Terriers, who had scored 73 points in their first two games under Harry's direction.

After the Colgate team, Harry went over to Donelli and said, "Hey coach, I'm ready. When do we play Army?" It was the day after Army had beaten Michigan in a clash of national powers in the year's most important game to date.

"Gol' dang it," Donelli grinned. He knew Harry meant it. But he was more interested in trying to get Harry to pass more. As in high school, Harry still often preferred the running game and to let his teammates have some glory too.

West Virginia had been the Sun Bowl champion in January. But they hadn't played against Harry. B.U. crushed the Mountaineers, 52-20 as Harry, passing sparingly, was 8-for-13 with three touchdown passes, to Winkler, Sulima, and Tom Oates of Watertown, against whom he had played in high school all-star games. In three games, Harry had eight touchdown passes.

B.U. fans talked of renewing a rivalry against Boston College, still the main rival for newspaper attention. B.C. officials though said they didn't want to play B.U. in 1950.

B.U. pummeled NYU 38-0 as Harry had two more touchdown passes. Before the game, Donelli gave Harry an ultimatum: throw at least 25 times. During the game, Donelli was still harping on Harry to throw more, even as

Harry was a handsome boy even when he was a youngster at Burrall Elementary School in Lynn.

Harry (No. 12) at Lynn Classical with (front, l to r) Lou Tsioropoulos, Hippocrates Kyros, Dave Warden and Vic Pujo. (back, l to r) Jug Greenbaum, Boe Martin, Jimmy Kirios, Seymour Fishman, Peter Pujo, and coach Art Rogers.

With coach Bill Joyce and William Dragon Jr., Spring, 1948.

Harry before the 1946 National high school championship game against Granby High of Virginia in the Orange Bowl in Miami.

Harry starred in several plays at Lynn Classical. He's in the middle here as Captain Hook in Peter Pan, surrounded by pirates, including some of his teammates.

The Classical football team went to Washington, D.C., in 1948 after refusing to play in a bowl game in Florida because two African-American teammates were not allowed to play.

Harry was the most celebrated schoolboy athlete in the country and he showed those awards for photographers, but first making sure his mother was with him.

Harry loved his high school coach, Bill Joyce, who was close to him. This letter sweater Harry's wearing has a patch designating the 1946 national championship team.

Harry represented New England in All Star games throughout the U.S. as a first base man.

Harry with two of his mentors, high school coach Bill Joyce (left) and Aldo "Buff" Donelli (right), who was to be his coach at Boston University.

The 1949 B.U. team, Harry's first, was one of its greatest. (Front l to r) George Winkler, Hugo Primiani, Dave Barrett, Art Boyle, Lou Salvati, Irv Heller, George Sulima. In the backfield is George Luker, Charlie Kent, Harry, and Bobby Whelan.

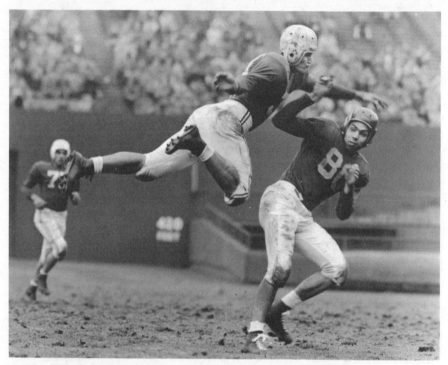

At B.U., Harry's defensive play terrorized opposing players with his hard hitting and acrobatic plays. He set a still unbroken record of 27 interceptions in three years.

In an article for The Saturday Evening Post, *Harry took some time behind his home in Lynn to play with his nephews.*

Harry made a dramatic appearance at B.U.'s Night at the Pops in 1954. He came with B.U. President Harold Case (l.) and Mrs. Case and participated in a sing-along.

In 1952, Harry received an awarded from the American Hellenic Educational Progressive Association (AHEPA) and Athens Chapter No. 24 President Harry Demeter, Jr., as the outstanding Greek-American athlete.

Harry wasn't just a great passer, he was a powerful and elusive runner, as many B.U. opponents discovered trying to tackle him in the open field.

B.U. was routing NYU.

"Pass it, ding it, pass!" Donelli was yelling.

"What's the matter coach," Harry yelled back. "Aren't we scoring enough points?"

In four games, the Terriers had scored 163 points and there was talk about a bowl game.

B.U. went to 5-0 and continued its scoring pace with a 46-6 rout of Scranton, and Harry had four more touchdown passes. After intercepting one pass, he threw a 64-yard score to Sulima. He finished 14-25 for 218 yards.

"He was sensational at shaking off tacklers, shedding them like a duck sheds water," one report stated. B.U. was now leading the nation in offense with an average of 443 yards per game, with 517 versus Scranton.

Winkler described Harry's knack. "Before we broke the huddle, he looked to me to say you get there and the ball would be there. He could do so many things well. If he couldn't find a receiver, he'd dance around and run for daylight or until someone got open. He had a great knack and great mobility, quick release and strong arm. He made passing a precision for the B.U. receivers. We never had to look back for the ball until the time was right. When we did look back and he was scrambling around we broke off our patterns, and, if you got open he'd get the ball to you."

Suddenly, the nation was discovering what fans in Massachusetts and New England had known about Harry in high school. He was decades ahead of his time, a prototype, a big passing quarterback who could scramble and defy defenses, coolly standing back in a pocket or running dizzily around gasping defenders to pick out a receiver at the last moment. And his kicking was booming, as he was leading the nation in punting.

The nicknames started. Although he was known as "The Golden Greek," he was called "Lighthorse Harry" and "Hairbreadth Harry" and he was named on four straight UPI polls as an All-American candidate, going 37-for-67 in passing with 14 touchdowns, beginning to challenge the NCAA record of 22 set by Nevada's Stan Heath the year before.

"You can break the record," Donelli told Harry.

"Who wants to break records?" Harry said. "Let's win the ball games."

Donelli was brought up short. "Sometimes, I wonder who's the coach and who's the player. He calms my nerves."

Harry had been late coming onto the field against West Virginia because equipment manager Jim Bradley had forgotten to leave a stick of gum in Harry's locker, a superstition he had picked up, along with sometimes wearing pajamas to practices before changing out in Weston.

He had his gum for the next game against Temple, B.U.'s fourth consecu-

77

tive home game. He was being called everything from "The Golden Greek" to the "Avenue Apollo," now because B.U. was located on Commonwealth Avenue.

But, for Harry, it was not a good game, although he threw his fifteenth touchdown pass of the season and lead his team to a 28-7 win. He completed only four passes and continued to throw only reluctantly, as he had so often in high school.

Despite his prowess, Harry still favored the running game and Donelli had to stay on him to get him to throw the ball more. At Toner's suggestion, Harry cut the sleeves up high on his arm to allow more movement for throwing the ball, and the stylish decision showed off his powerful biceps and arms too.

The win against Temple propelled B.U. to 6-0 and was the prelude to the big game against vaunted powerhouse Maryland, who would come into Fenway Park a big favorite despite B.U.'s perfect record.

APOGOETEUSIS ♦ DISAPPOINTMENT ♦ ΑΠΟΓΟΗΤΕΥΣΙΣ

On campus, Harry was leading a poll as the most popular football player for the upcoming varsity dance, where tickets would be $1.20. And the college's first radio station, WBUR, was set to start broadcasting, with 250 watts of power.

The Maryland game would be the biggest for B.U., and brought national attention to the school, and Harry. *Washington Post* sports columnist Maury Povich had noticed him too. Povich wrote "By birth, he is Greek-American. By performance, he is All-American."

Maryland fans blocked Route 1 and paraded around the B.U. dorms the night before the game until 7 a.m. More than 1,000 of them had come up for the game at Fenway Park, and they were being bolstered by students from M.I.T., anxious to tweak their cross-river counterparts at B.U.

The Maryland fans sang rebel songs and waved Confederate flags, while the B.U. fans countered with their own cheers and songs in the stands. On top of one of the baseball dugouts behind the B.U. bench, McGee was dancing and exhorting the B.U. fans to raise their voices. More than 35,000 fans turned out.

Harry quieted the Maryland fans quickly, when he opened the game by bringing his team down to the Maryland 23-yard line, evading the constant rush of heavy defenders trying to pursue him like hounds going after a fox.

But a harried Harry had a fourth down pass intercepted and Maryland's All-American fullback, Ed "Big Mo" Modzelewski came back with a touchdown to put Maryland up, 7-0.

Toner intercepted a pass on Maryland's 38-yard line. Harry brought B.U. down to the 27, dropped back to pass and, when he couldn't find a receiver, ran nine yards to the 18.

A penalty against the aggressive Terrapins put the ball on the 3-yard line and Kent ran in for a touchdown. Andy Dell Ollio's extra point attempt was blocked after a high snap and Maryland still led, 7-6. It was a crucial difference.

In the third period, Whelan was crossing the Maryland goal line for a 17-yard touchdown, but fumbled and Maryland recovered. B.U. blocked a punt and Whelan ran in for a 32-yard touchdown to give B.U. a 13-7 lead, after an extra point. Then came the drive that ended in controversy.

Harry brought B.U. back down to the Maryland 3-yard line and the chance to go up by two touchdowns. With third and less than a yard to go, Kent drove into the line for what looked like a first down. But he was pushed back and the officials did not mark his forward progress, leaving B.U. inches short.

"I'm going to throw to George (Sulima) in the corner for a touchdown," Harry said. His teammates, for the first time, weren't sure if it was the right call and urged him to give the ball again to Kent for a first down.

"No, no, it's only six inches. Let's go for the first down," several teammates urged.

Harry paused, then relented for the first and only time, and Maryland packed the line looking for a handoff. Kent plunged again, driving hard into the line, pushing and scrambling and going what looked at least a yard before he was pushed back after the play had ended. He seemed to surely have the first down this time.

But two Southern officials thought different. Referee H.V. Hooper stepped into the pile after Kent was pushed back, and picked up the ball and placed it short of the first down.

"Gentlemen," he drawled. "I'm going to place the ball heah," he said. Donelli after the game would scream, "The officials stole the game!" and *Boston Herald* columnist Dave Egan suggested the referees be given a varsity letter from Maryland because of the calls.

Kent said he made the first down—twice. "It was just a straight buck. Our line was such that they were moving their line pretty well so I knew we could get through. I felt no question I had made beyond the line of scrimmage, probably one or two steps. We were all pretty upset."

Winkler was blocking. "They never gave us the full yardage. On the third down we felt sure we had it but we were short. But (on the fourth down) we all felt we could make this so we crashed into the line and once again it was forward progress, and then thrown back and the spot killed us each time. We made a first down on those two downs. They had a great line. They had a great football team and several All-Americans."

Whalen, who had run out of bounds to set up the first down plays, was a decoy on Kent's runs, and was able to look directly down the line of scrimmage to check on Kent's progress. "He was at least a yard over for the first down," he said.

After it was ruled otherwise, Whalen said he and his teammates second-guessed themselves for not listening to Harry, who wanted to throw to Sulima for a score that would have put B.U. up by two touchdowns. "It was something they weren't looking for," he said.

Maryland came back to score a touchdown and take the lead, 14-13, holding on as B.U. drove again late in the game. Winkler said, "I never wavered that somewhere down the line Harry would do something to pull this out. I don't fault him one bit. He played a heck of a game against a great team. Everyone played their hearts out."

Maryland fans, hooting and hollering at the end, stormed onto the field and tore down a set of goal posts. At the other end of the field, the B.U. band was under the other posts when they were attacked by the Maryland horde. The band played The Star-Spangled Banner trying to stop them, and several members were tousled by Maryland fans.

New York Times sports columnist Red Smith, the most well known in the country, said he saw the director of the B.U. band stave off at least half a dozen swarming Maryland fans in a wild finish that looked like a riot in a Civil War movie scene.

Although Maryland was favored, Modzelewski said they were glad to win and had been briefed about Harry extensively by the coaching staff.

"I remember reading about him. I was just a young guy coming up too and I said 'Oh my God, look at what he can do.' We played B.U. and everything was Harry Agganis, and even after that it left an indelible mark on me that we were from the coal mines of Pennsylvania and able to play against him," he said.

There were scouts from the Orange and Sugar and Gator Bowls watching. Toner sighed later. "If we had won that game B.U. football might have been forever changed upward."

Instead, there was a tremendous letdown. A strong St. Bonaventure team, quarterbacked by Ted Marchibroda, came to Fenway and shut out Harry for the first time, 19-0.

Harry did throw one pass for 65 yards, but another was intercepted on the goal line. B.U. finished 6-2 and set a season scoring record of 250 points, but the two consecutive season-ending losses meant there would be no bowl bid, and, for the first time in his career too, Harry had to deal with losing. Sulima edged him out in the balloting for the most popular player and lineman Lou Salvati was chosen captain for 1950.

Still, Harry was named to the All-New England team and was named an honorable mention All-American. The expectations were very high indeed. Enrollment at B.U., passed 30,000 and the school was now one of the ten largest in the country. Harry had brought school officials what they wanted.

He finished with 55 completions in 108 attempts for 15 touchdowns and 762 yards, had run for a 5.4 yard average and scored two touchdowns and the nation's best punting average of 46.5 yards. He had 15 interceptions and averaged almost 60 minutes a game.

After the B.U. season ended, a disappointed Harry and Whalen decided to hitchhike to Philadelphia to watch their friends at Cornell play Pennsylvania on Thanksgiving weekend. They were on a lonely road in Sturbridge, Massachusetts when a car jolted to a stop and a man jumped out, pointed and screamed.

"You're Harry Agganis!" he yelled.

The man was an alumnus of B.U. who had watched Harry play and was an admirer. He was on his way to Long Island in New York and dropped them in New York for the night. With limited money, they checked into a cheap hotel and went to the Latin Quarter.

The next day, the man who had dropped them off called the hotel and said he wanted to see the game and would drive them to Philadelphia. Harry, who knew the Cornell staff, got them passes to sit on the bench at Franklin Field, and that night they went to a party held by the players.

The man was unable to drive them back so they took a bus. At Haymarket Square in Boston, waiting for the last transfer to Lynn, they saw a familiar sight carrying a bag over his back.

It was Lou Tsioropoulos, Harry's former football and basketball teammate at Classical who had transferred to Lynn English in his junior year.

Tsioropoulos was 6'5" now and had been recruited by Kentucky basketball coach Adolph Rupp, and was quickly becoming a star there. But he had wanted to play football too, forbidden by Rupp, and had left school to come home to Lynn. They took the bus home together. A week later, Rupp called Tsioropoulos and convinced him to come back.

It had been a good year for Harry. He had joined the fraternity Sigma Alpha Epsilon and became a pledgemaster. After his games, his fraternity brothers would break into a chorus of "Harry makes the world go 'round, world go 'round," when he came to the fraternity house.

Harry was popular with co-eds too, and found an active dating life, often with very beautiful women. And he resurrected school spirit.

Alumni who hadn't sung the school song in years found themselves singing the words "O glorious thy name and fame, resplendent from thy youth, O radiant the holy flame that lights the lamp of truth, O Boston University, alma mater dear." And they were going to the games too, helping to fill Fenway Park, cheering: "B-O-S-T-O-N!"

"B-U!"

"B-U!"

"Fight, team, fight!"

On April 14, 1950, the George K. Menichios Greek-American Veterans Post, honored Greek-American athletes, including Harry, Angie Toyias of Boston Tech, James Toyias and Harris Jameson of Boston Latin, George Spaneas and Menil Mavraides of Lowell, and James Lakis of Northeastern. Former New York Yankee Bump Hadley, also from Lynn, was the guest speaker, and George Condakes and George Rodes were the post officials who had invited them.

What Jameson remembered most though, besides the thrill of the schoolboys meeting their idol, was what Harry said to them. They were talking in a small room before going into the hall and Harry brought them together, huddled around him. Harry was smiling as usual and said to them, with emphasis, "Always be proud of your Greek heritage. Be proud to say you're Greek."

A couple of weeks later, Harry was invited to speak at the Charlestown Boys and Girls Club in a Boston neighborhood that was predominantly Irish-American, and which had produced some well known boxers and athletes.

Harry was at ease before them too. "It doesn't matter what you are, Irish, Polish, Greek, as long as you've got the heart and give your all, nationality doesn't matter when it comes to competition," he said.

He was making a lot of appearances now, for youth groups and charities, including the Lynn Boys Club in his hometown. The club was still trying to raise $50,000. He was out a lot, trying to balance his studies with his athletics, and constant demands for his time. He was looking forward to some time to himself.

With the excitement of his first varsity year in football behind him, and with another summer looming with the Augusta Millionaires in Maine, Harry had a scintillating sophomore baseball season, hitting .332, teaming with many of his football teamates like Winkler, who was a three sport star at the school. Harry was named B.U.'s Athlete of the Year, for the first time.

Despite his fame and celebrity, even Harry was not immune to criticism and discrimination or slurs. One night that Summer, Harry and his friend Jimmy Kirios went into the diner in Lynn owned by the Vrees brothers who had put together the All-Star baseball team on which he had played.

Harry was a few steps ahead of Kirios and, as he entered, heard a big man inside bellow as they entered, "Here come the goddamn Greeks." The man was sitting on a stool and looked to be more than three hundred pounds.

Harry didn't change complexion, but walked over to the man, put his arms around him, lifted him up off the stool and dropped him. The man blanched, but didn't move and didn't say another word. Harry and Kirios went to a booth in the back, sat down and ordered a cheeseburger. "It was over," Kirios said.

Harry thought he would have another carefree summer and was looking forward to the 1950 football season. Because of him, Donelli had done well recruiting and was expecting the next year's team to be one of his best.

He had put together an ambitious schedule too, including powerhouses like Miami, Syracuse, William and Mary, and a season-ending finale with one of the country's top teams, College of the Pacific, to be played in California.

Then, Harry's fame would be spread coast-to-coast.

KATHEKON ◆ **DUTY** ◆ ΚΑΘΗΚΟΝ
1950 – 1951

The Summer of 1950 was a chance for Harry to get away from the head-lines and back to the languorous days of small town baseball in northern New England. He had gained national attention for himself and B.U. in the 1949 football season and into Spring baseball in 1950. But he was looking forward to going back up to Maine to play for the Augusta Millionaires and see his friends again, including Ted Lepcio, another promising infielder whom the Red Sox were watching carefully.

The league was where major league teams would place prospects, and was a mix of potential major leaguers with college players and some of the best amateurs in the region. It fit the times, games played in bucolic settings without the pressure of professional leagues or scores of sportswriters.

The decade of the 1950s would, for the most part, be an innocent era of families. World War II was behind Americans and, although there was the bur-geoning civil rights struggle in the South and a fight for racial equality, most people were looking forward to a time when there was no war or strife, although there was grumbling about the American involvement in Korea, where the country had been divided after World War II, with the Soviet Union and Communism taking hold of the northern part of the country.

President Harry Truman had ushered the country through the post-War period after his stunning upset of New York Governor Thomas Dewey in the 1948 Presidential election. By 1950, there were no thoughts of the upcoming election, although there was talk that General Dwight D. Eisenhower would be a formidable candidate.

Truman was trying to convince Americans why the United States was involved in Korea and was battling with World War II hero Douglas MacArthur, who was his commmander there. Harry had joined the Marine 2nd Infantry Organized Reserve Batallion in 1948 after his high school graduation, along with other friends. He had been sent to basic training at Little Creek, Virginia.

Harry Botsford, an assistant freshman coach at B.U., had gotten Harry and George Bullard into the reserves at the behest of B.U. coach Buff Donelli, who was worried that Harry might get drafted into the military before he could get to school.

At that time though, some reservists were dropped from their companies if they had not attended regular meetings. After his enrollment at B.U., Harry had missed a series of meetings and was not sure of his reserve status. And, he was working part-time at Suffolk Downs and for the Judge John Pappas at the C. Pappas Company trying to make money to support his mother while he was going through school.

Botsford said he had told Harry to get his discharge from the Reserves. "Harry, get your damn stuff turned in so you can get a discharge. As long as you have your seabag and you haven't turned in your clothes, they can come and get you," he said.

Many families had been displaced by the post-war period and were working more than one job in many cases to keep themselves intact. With growing fighting in Korea, which involved the United Nations, and many soldiers from Greece—where the country was trying to get over a divisive Civil War—Truman was feeling pressure to either get out of the fighting or step it up.

Greece had always been allied with the United States and, despite the ravages of World War II which caused starvation and destitution in the countryside, Greek soldiers would go to South Korea and re-established the reputation for courage they had earned with ceaseless resistance against occupying German armies. Greek-Americans, including those in Lynn, followed the exploits of their countrymen because they had many relatives there who were involved in the fighting in Korea.

The United States had sent troops into South Korea after World War II, but removed them in 1949 and Truman indicated early in 1950 that Korea was outside the main U.S. defense line of Asia, giving the Communists of North Korea an opening to invade.

On June 27, Truman tried to stop the Communist advance and ordered U.S. Naval and Air forces into South Korea and the United Nations asked its members to assist. Congress supported Truman, but no war was ever declared. But Americans troops went to Korea to fight what would be called the forgotten war. Reservists who were called up faced the possibility of being sent there too.

While Harry was playing in Maine, American troops started fighting against the North Koreans on July 5 at Osan, and a build-up was beginning, with expectations some reservists might be called into action. Donelli was worried that Harry might be caught up in a call-up.

On June 22, Donelli had football on his mind though, and sent Harry another letter giving him plays and a questionnaire and told him he would be quizzed later. He also sent a code and told Harry to keep it confidential. "The code is to be read by you and nobody else," he said. "We can have a good season if you know all the answers," to his questions, Donelli wrote. He was a taskmaster who prepared assiduously, even though Harry was wont to make up plays in the huddle or go to with his Barry Park instincts too.

On July 7, Donelli wrote Harry up in Maine, telling him to study plays that would be used in the 1950 season. "Before you begin to study the cutback series, I want you to write up in detail what you know about the use of the slant series," Donelli wrote. Donelli insisted all his players be ready for a season long before practice began at the late summer drills held at a camp in Peterboro, New Hampshire.

By August 3, Donelli was showing signs of worry about what was happening in Korea. He wrote Harry, who was staying at the YMCA in Augusta, urging him to get back to B.U. in a hurry. "I would suggest that you get in right away (and don't waste any time) so that you can sit down and have a talk with the Colonel at the head of R.O.T.C. (Reserve Officer Training Corps) and find out what chances you have of getting into R.O.T.C. for your last two years in college," Donelli wrote.

Donelli had been in contact with Botsford, who was now a lieutenant, to find out what the chances were of reservists being called into active duty. "You are in the inactive Marine Corps, but according to Botsford, you will be gone if your group is reactivated. If we can switch you into R.O.T.C., you can be saved. So get down here immediately!" Donelli wrote to Harry.

But it was too late. Just before the start of the football season, Donelli lost Harry and, with it, a chance to build on the success of the year before when Harry had captured the attention of the nation's sportswriters and B.U. had almost gone to a bowl game.

On September 18, at practice, as Donelli was putting together what he thought would be his finest team ever, a veteran-laden club that would have Harry with a season's experience, came some bad news. Harry had just finished beating all the running backs in a 50-yard dash and was eating peaches out of a can when the word came he was being called into active duty, and would be sent to Camp LeJeune in North Carolina.

The services had called into duty many well-known athletes who were reservists. Quantico, a rival of Camp LeJeune, had stacked its baseball and football teams with All-Americans, including another left-handed quarterback, little Eddie LeBaron of College of the Pacific.

Donelli called Botsford again. "Can you do anything? They called up Harry," he said. Donelli said the Marines were going to send Harry to Quantico too, where the officer candidates were trained.

Botsford, who was stationed with another football star, Jim Landrigan of Wakefield, Mass. went to the Camp LeJeune football coach, Bruno Andruska and told him. "Hey, they don't need two quarterbacks. How about getting Harry down here?" He did.

Donelli and B.U. fans were upset. "Donelli Reshuffles Personnel As Marines Claim Agganis," the B.U. News headlined. Donelli called Harry "One in a million, a Sid Luckman who comes along only once in a coach's life," comparing him to a famous professional quarterback.

And, the school paper said "His passing, for moment means a rewriting of the script that had 'Harry Agganis And Co.' as the up-and-coming team in the East. However, no one is writing any obituaries or funeral dirges, as Donelli continues to drill his finest team in four years."

Students were in a period of campus contentment for the most part. Harry was photographed getting on a train and heading away from Boston. But the games were going on, and students of St. Bonaventure came into town and hung their school flag off the B.U. bridge before the game.

At Holy Cross, Paul Gallo, the wonder boy who had outdueled Harry in the 1948 freshman game, had left school for a time to get married, but returned, although he would never match Harry's status again.

Donelli had to open the 1950 season with a capable quarterback, Billy Pavlikowski, but he broke his arm only several games into the season and Donelli had to turn to an outstanding fullback, John Kastan of Glassport, Pennsylvania, who was on the 1948 freshman team with Harry, to play quarterback.

Kastan was not a good passer, however, and the team didn't respond to the uncertainty at quarterback. Harry followed the news from Camp LeJeune unhappily, worried too that Donelli was having such a rough year without him.

But Harry's loss would be keenly felt. After opening with a 21-7 win over Duquesne at Pittsburgh, B.U. lost 25-21 to St. Bonaventure, and was belted in succession by Miami and Syracuse. It would be an up-and-down season, although Donelli had many veterans back. But he didn't have Harry.

Harry would play football that fall for Camp LeJeune, but would also have a regular tour of guard duty. Although his mother was dependent on him, he didn't try to seek a hardship to prevent being called into the service or to duck his duty.

He came in as a private, number 1032484, but also as a celebrated player pressed into service immediately. When he arrived, a tough Tech Sergeant, Florio Sampieri, a sixteen-year veteran who was working with the camp's football team, was surprised to see a tall, strong, good-looking kid with an easy air of confidence walk up to him. Sampieri was standing, wearing a T-shirt.

"Go tell the coach that Agganis is here," Harry said casually.

Sampieri was flabbergasted. Recruits were supposed to be timid and nervous as squirrels. Harry was just smiling.

"Agganis? I never heard of you," Sampieri said.

But he took him in to see the coach, Andruska, who was in the storeroom, checking uniforms. Sampieri sauntered over to the counter to issue gear and said, "Coach, Harry Agganis is here."

Andruksa leaped to his feet, ran past some of the lockers and practically fell into Harry's arms. He stopped to pump his hand in a shake that didn't stop. Sampieri was even more stunned. "This Agganis must be SOMEBODY," Sampieri thought.

A few minutes later, Harry came up to him for some football shoes. Sampieri handed him a pair of 9-D's. Harry just stood there waiting and smiling.

"Where's the other pair?" he asked.

"What d'ya mean, the other pair," a startled Sampieri asked.

"Agganis always checks out two pairs of shoes," Harry said.

"Tell you what," Sampieri said. "You show me two right feet and two left feet and I promise you, you'll get two pairs of shoes," he said. From then on, they got along just fine.

Just before the start of the football season, Harry came up to Sampieri in a bashful way, leaning in very close to his ear and almost whispered. "Sam, I gotta favor to ask."

"Sure kid, what d'ya want?"

"When you give out the uniforms to the team, would you do me a favor and save Number 33 for me. It was my number in high school and college and I'd feel a lot better with it on my back during the coming season." Sampieri agreed.

Halfway through his first game, Harry already had a section of rooters starting to follow him, electrified by his dazzling presence and a style unseen in the 1950s when quarterbacks dropped back and stayed in the pocket. Harry could scramble like a rabid dog looking for a drink or somebody to bite.

He was in the Special Services, there primarily to play sports, although he went through the rigors of basic training and was photographed on the rifle range and with a bayonet.

And he had presence. He was always smiling and usually was chewing gum. And the Camp LeJeune crowds roared. Word quickly spread about the big Greek kid who could throw and run, and civilian fans were coming to the games, like Takey Crist, who lived nearby and wanted to be a doctor.

Before you knew it, there were more people in the stands, and each game attracted more. "The stands were filled watching that Number 33 working and calling the plays. You couldn't help watching that big Number 33 driving toward the goal line," Sampieri said. Harry was getting most of the attention, but he had some great players with him too, like Big Jim Landrigan, Wally Williams and little Minnie Minihan. And Botsford, who had suited up.

The crowds were entranced, watching Harry dance away from trouble, shifting his feet and legs to dart away from tacklers. He wasn't sacked once that season. "Watching the Golden Greek play was a great thrill to me. The kid was great," Sampieri said.

When he was tackled, Harry would bounce up and help up the man who tackled him. It amused Sampieri and fans. "Even the men on the other side of the line respected Harry Agganis," Sampieri said. He said Harry reminded him of Cleveland Browns quarterback Otto Graham, who was leading his professional team to a string of championships. "They never could catch Harry from behind. He had that go-go-go," Sampieri said.

PISTIS ◆ FAITH ◆ ΠΙΣΤΙΣ

The service teams were strong and played a schedule that included many colleges. Harry led Camp LeJeune on a 48-0 destruction of the Amphibs of Little Creek, throwing four touchdown passes, scoring two others and running an interception back for a third.

LeJeune coach Bruno Andruska had plenty of New England help on his coaching staff, including Botsford and Landrigan, who played at Holy Cross and Dartmouth, Major Dick Opp, who played for Northeastern, and Captain Wally Williams, who had won eleven letters at B.U.

Harry was a special favorite at Camp LeJeune too because it was where the enlisted men trained, and there was a special rivalry against Quantico, where the officers were trained. The schedule favored LeJeune to go undefeated until meeting Quantico on November 10 at Butler Field, the officers home field.

Quantico had the great little All-American quarterback, LeBaron, and sportswriters were wondering publicly why so many great football players were being called into the Marines as reservists when others weren't. LeJeune had many college students, and graduates, like Harry's B.U. teammate, John Simpson. Some of the LeJeune platoons were as educated as the officers.

But, in their second game, LeJeune was upset by a strong University of Tampa team, although Harry had his team on the opponent's one-foot line as time ran out. After the upset by Tampa, Harry led LeJeune to an 87-0 rout of Turner Air Force Base, a 55-7 win over Bolling Air Force Base, and a 27-13 win over Ft. Jackson.

In one of the games, on October 3, Harry wrote Donelli that Camp LeJeune had to settle for a 0-0 tie with Cherry Point because the game was played in such a driving rain that "The ball was so wet, if you squeezed it, water would come out of it." But he said also he thought he would not be called into action in Korea.

The big game at Quantico drew a large crowd and featured a lengthy game program billing the matchup as Agganis vs. LeBaron. While LeJeune had a strong team, Quantico was packed with the best college players in the country and gave LeBaron a big edge.

Quantico beat LeJeune, 42-7, despite heroics from Harry. They got all the good players because they were officers. Quantico was stocked with All-Americans. As usual, Harry was left to imagination and improvisation, although he had many solid college players on his team too.

Still, Harry led Camp LeJeune to the Sixth District Naval Championship with an 8-2-1 record against some powerful teams, including a 32-7 rout of Keesler Air Force Base in the Electronics Bowl, a game in which he ran for three touchdowns, passed for another and kicked two extra points.

Harry was glad to see Simpson, his B.U. teammate from the year before, who had graduated and was called back into duty too. Although he was a college graduate, Simpson didn't want to be an officer. When Harry got to Camp LeJeune, he had been helped by Donelli's friend, Botsford, and Harry persuaded the football coach to add Simpson to the team late in the season.

When LeJeune was invited to the Electronics Bowl in Biloxi, Mississippi they couldn't take their whole roster. Harry went to his coach and said he wanted Simpson to come, but Simpson declined. "Harry, I've only been here for a game and some of these guys have been here since September," he said.

LeJeune finished third among all the service teams nationally, behind only Quantico, and MCRD San Diego. Harry was named to the second team All-Marine selection by Leatherneck magazine, behind LeBaron.

There was more than sports at LeJeune, although Harry had quickly established himself as an approachable star. Among the friends he made was a young man from New York named Gerald Solomon.

He told Solomon one day during a discussion about a philosophical point that would be raised many years later, using a football analogy. "It's like Notre Dame beating Slippery Rock 69-2, but saying Slippery Rock won the game because they scored the last two points," Harry said.

Harry had walked over to Solomon's barracks to visit another Marine, and everyone in there was agog at seeing him. "He was so famous as a football player," said Solomon, who was a nineteen-year-old from a small town in upstate New York, who had found himself living with a lot of city kids from Brooklyn.

Solomon said the two biggest names in sports among the Marines were Ted Williams and Harry. "We all worshipped Ted Williams and along comes Harry Agganis, who is another athletic hero to us. It was exciting and he was such an inspiration and you really looked up to him, and you were proud to be a Marine because he was one" Solomon said.

As he stood in the barracks telling his story, Harry was surrounded by recruits. "He was like a magnet, people were drawn to him because of his whole disposition," Solomon said. "Agganis would just excite everybody, everybody he touched, even those of us who weren't on the team," he said.

Solomon never forgot that day, or that story Harry told.

Harry met a fellow Greek-American from Florida, Leo Thallasites, son of a Greek Orthodox priest. Thallasites, who was born in Dover, New Hampshire, had joined the Marines briefly in 1943 to fight in World War II, until the authorities found out he was only fourteen-years-old, and kicked him out.

He went into the Navy and back into the Marines when he was old enough. He was a skilled martial artist and formidable fighter with a strong physique and deep, abiding respect for religion, family, and dedication to his country, as well as his body and spirituality. Like Harry, he was a humble man and they quickly became friends.

The two would often pray in their bunks and go to church together, faithful to their Greek Orthodox upbringing. Harry had done the same when he was traveling with his football teams, seeking out Greek Orthodox churches. Harry and Leo trained hard as Marines too.

Harry confided in Leo that he wasn't sure yet which professional athletic career to seek when he got out of the Marines and college. "Leave it in God's hands, Harry," he said. Thallasites, who earned three Purple Hearts in combat in World War II, including fighting at Iwo Jima and Okinawa, admired Harry. "He was a good Marine," he said.

Although he was a great athlete, Harry didn't try to get out of his other Marine duties, and Thallasites recognized he was a skilled hand-to-hand fighter who would have performed well in combat. He taught Harry how to fight with a baton as a weapon.

Harry soon saw some familiar faces too, including his old high school friend and teammate, George Bullard, who had signed to play with the Detroit Tigers right out of high school. Bullard was a phenomenal athlete too, fast and quick and strong. But, he told friends, he had problems with authority and saluted an officer with his left hand when he arrived, making Harry laugh.

Donelli and B.U. were suffering through a disastrous season without Harry, after having so much promise following Harry's sensational year in 1949. The Terriers went 3-5 without him, including a season-ending 55-7 crushing defeat to College of the Pacific in California, in a game played in fog, an eerie end to an awful year without Harry.

"A spark was lacking this year," the school paper reported. "We were not a hard-hitting team." Attendance at Fenway Park, which Harry had helped fill, had fallen to 3,000, one-tenth its capacity.

Not knowing when Harry would be getting out, Donelli had recruited several prospective replacements, including little 5-5 Johnny Nunziato of Somerville, Massachusetts, who played on an outstanding high school team, and two All-Scholastics, Phil O'Connell of Brockton and Tom Gastall, who was also a standout baseball player and all-around athlete. But O'Connell and Gastall were freshmen and wouldn't be allowed to compete.

In November, Harry was featured alone on the cover of *Sport Magazine*, the best-known sports magazine in the days before *Sports Illustrated* began. Although Harry's exploits had already been featured on sports pages across the country, mirroring the publicity he received as a schoolboy, the four-page article detailing his athletic prowess and dedicated family life helped boost him into even more national prominence.

Writer Al Hirshberg, who knew Harry well, said when Harry was called into duty after thinking he wasn't eligible, "Harry accepted their decision with characteristic amiability."

The article helped spawn new fans for Harry too, who had so much attention at B.U. that Themis Stoumbelis, Donelli's secretary, had to seek help from two assistant football managers to handle all the mail that poured in. Harry had six official fan clubs at B.U., but that was not new to Harry, who had been receiving fan mail since his high school days at Lynn Classical.

"None of this amazing adulation has gone to Harry's head," Hirshberg wrote. But while Donelli could only hope that the Marine schedule would keep Harry honed in tough competition, he was worried too that he might be kept in the service through another season.

KAKOUCHIA ◆ HARDSHIP ◆ KAKOYXIA

In February of 1951, Dr. Harold Case became the President of B.U. and Jim Argeros, a leader of the school's prominent Hellenic community, was elected as the Man of the Year. B.U. was upgrading its academic commitment too, including the work of a young thirty-one-year-old researcher at the medical school, Dr.Isaac Asimov, who was getting as much attention for his science fiction novels as his work in cancer research.

While Asimov said his heart was in his work in cancer research, the school newspaper carried ads for cigarettes, urging students to light up. Greyhound bus fares to Hartford were only $2.60 and you could get to Los Angeles for $52.60. Although the Korean War was causing consternation in Congress and fret among Americans who wanted war behind them, there was a growing sense of optimism in the country. Mass production of housing was creating an economic upsurge. Even Truman's bickering with General MacArthur over the direction of the war in Korea couldn't deter Americans from thinking about better times that seemed to be coming quickly.

Women were still second-class workers in pay and opportunity, but the American family was still a two-parent association, with the father the primary wage-earner. There was still a significant respect for authority, although looming on the horizon was the burgeoning beat generation of writer Jack Kerouac from Lowell, Massachusetts, a team Harry had played against from 1945 to 1947 in football.

Kerouac had been a football star at Lowell, and briefly at Columbia. He was an agitated young man who played to the simmering undercurrent of unrest from those who felt disaffected by the surface tranquility of the times.

For Harry though, the product of an immigrant family to whom America had given opportunity and hope, there was a duty to be upheld. Although he was playing sports for the Marines, he was still subject to being called to Korea.

Harry didn't dislike his duty or time in the Marines. He used to borrow Botsford's car and when he was driving through the gate, the guards recognized it and thought that Botsford, an officer, was driving and they would salute. Harry loved that. "Hey coach, I just got saluted by three more sentries," he would say.

Botsford said the Marines admired Harry. "I always felt if I had a son that turned out as good as he was, I would have been a successful parent. There was just something about him that was sort of magical. He was a real clean-cut, nice young man," he said.

Back home in Boston, Donelli was getting anxious too. The 1950 season left him reeling. Unless Harry could get out, 1951 would be even worse, he feared. On April 18, he wrote Harry that Harry's high school coach, Bill Joyce, had told him "You have a good chance of getting out."

Donelli said he needed Harry back. "Nunziato doesn't have the experience, but I think he'll be a pretty good quarterback by the time next Fall rolls around." He wrote he had heard about Harry's performances playing baseball for the Marines. "I hear you are hitting the devil out of the ball," he said. And, he said, that might go against Harry.

"The thing I'm worried about is if they do let reservists go, they might want to hold onto you," Donelli wrote.

Harry was having one of his best years ever as a baseball player, against outstanding competition and service teams that included pitchers who had played major league baseball. He was the best player on the Camp LeJeune baseball team, hitting .362 while leading his team to a 72-17 record. Simpson was in the stands often, watching and helping lead cheers for his friend.

So was Sampieri, who said he would always remember Harry's smile and that he was a gentleman. "He never smoked, never drank, and I never heard him use a word of profanity during the year he worked for me," Sampieri said.

After playing or performing his duties, Harry would usually go to an early movie and come back to the barracks and go straight to bed, or talk with his friends. But he was getting anxious too about what was in store for him with the Marines.

Donelli was getting worried about 1951 as the Summer wore on, although Harry got home once on a break and, in a home run hitting contest at Braves Field, beat major leaguers when he hit five home runs deep into the stands.

Harry had already missed one year and was in danger of missing a second, which would have meant many of the teammates with whom he'd come into school would be moving ahead, and Harry would have players with whom he was unfamiliar when he returned. Donelli tried to accelerate his release.

Harry was worried about his mother. When he was at B.U., he still spent much of his time at the Waterhill Street home caring for her, bringing down friends for dinners which gave him a chance to keep an eye on her. She was now sixty-six-years-old, and had been suffering from an arthritic condition in her back and left knee. Worse, while Harry had four brothers and two sisters, they all had families to care for, besides helping out with their mother, a financial hardship for all. Harry, the youngest, had been the only one living at home.

Harry had been sending so much of his Marine paycheck to his mother in an allotment that the Marines eventually stopped it. This was her primary income, apart from what her other children could provide, and Harry was getting worried. He wrote Donelli asking for help.

"I'm in a very depressive mood," he wrote, uncharacteristically, complaining that he was also broke. "The thing I'd like to do is get out on a hardship case.

Since my mother is no longer receiving any income, that would be the best way," he stated. He asked Donelli to visit his mother and take his old high school coach Bill Joyce. "See what she has to say. Find out just where she stands financially and the bills she owes," he asked.

A hardship dependency was not easy to obtain though, and Harry would have to prove not only that his mother needed him, but that he had income to give her. He couldn't just return to school to study and play football. He was worried too what people would think otherwise. "That will eliminate a lot of questioning. They'll probably say 'Where is he getting money? He is only going to school.' So if I have a job, that will solve the problem," he wrote.

Harry was one of a relative few number of reservists who had been called into the Marines at all the previous year, and he could have undoubtedly avoided his obligation by filing a hardship dependency at that time. But he said he had to fulfill his duty, especially since some of his friends were already serving, like Simpson.

Donelli had been thinking of ways for Harry to get out as far back as April, when he sent Harry a letter describing the prospective line-up for the 1951 season. "Bill Joyce tells me that he had a letter from you and you thought you might have a good chance of getting out," he wrote. "If you can manage to handle that situation so that you can be free and be out of there next fall we will have a greater football team," he added.

Harry responded that he had been playing a lot of baseball and performing guard duty at night, and said Simpson was also visiting him, and they would talk about B.U. He pointed out that the 1951 schedule for the Marines posed a problem for him: on October 12, they were to play B.U., and Harry wasn't sure how Donelli or his B.U. teammates would take it.

"About playing this football game, I feel good and bad. The good point is being able to play in Fenway Park (home) again. The bad part is playing against the boys and you. It just feels, well, I can't win either way," he shrugged.

On May 17, Donelli was a little more optimistic, and maneuvering to help. "It would be wise if you could go directly to your General or get to some officer who is very friendly to you who could get to a General and discuss this thing on a personal basis first. Explain to the General that since you came into the inactive Marine Corps and they are now about to be discharged and that you will have completed one year of service by September and if you were to be discharged by September you could get to school this year to complete your education. However, if you were discharged in the middle of the year you would lose a whole year," he suggested.

The hardship dependency was the best way, he knew, especially because of the condition of his mother. But Donelli had another option. "If this plan wouldn't work then you could turn to the political angle," he wrote.

He told Harry he was also talking to Red Sox owner Tom Yawkey for possible help if needed. A month later, Donelli wrote that he had Case, who had been talking to Missouri Congressman Dewey Short, House Chairman of the Armed Services Committee, trying to find a legitimate way for Harry's discharge. "In the meantime, however, we will investigate this problem of your mother and see if this is not a better approach," Donelli added.

On July 10, Case got a letter from Short congratulating the B.U. president on his recent ascension to that job. But he told Case that Harry would have to file for a hardship dependency, given his mother's needs. "When this is done ... I shall be glad to contact the Marine headquarters here and do what I can to be helpful," Short wrote.

A week later, Donelli wrote Harry, who by now was a corporal, to tell him to file the application with his commanding officer. He had some good news too. The Pappas family, Judge John Pappas and his brother Tom, who had steered Harry toward B.U. and were among the most influential and richest in the country, had a part-time job waiting for him at one of their Gloria food stores in Boston.

This would enable Harry to provide income for his mother and still be able to go back to school. So optimistic was Donelli that a few days later, on July 23, he sent another letter giving Harry codes for football plays to study. It was the same day he had received confirmation from Tom Pappas that Harry's job was waiting.

But more had to be done. Affidavits had to be sent to Harry's commanding officer to prove his mother's case. She prepared a statement that showed she had not worked for thirty-five years and was dependent on her family, primarily Harry, for support. The interest on the mortgage for the family home was in arrears and the roof and chimney were deteriorating and needed repairs. Her only income now, she wrote, was six dollars per week from rent of a first floor apartment.

"I have no income to pay my other living expenses and that since my allotment from the United States government was stopped in January, 1951, I have exhausted whatever small resources I had for food and clothing ... the presence of my son, Corporal Harry Agganis, is absolutely necessary for the maintenance of my household and for my own support and if his presence is delayed for any long period of time, that I shall have to give up my home and I shall have to break up my household," she wrote.

On August 9, with the B.U. football season a month away, Harry filed the application and sent Donelli a telegram through Western Union which stated: "Have papers in. Four to five weeks it takes. Write me." Donelli wrote Case at

96

his summer residence in Francistown, New Hampshire. about the efforts to get Harry out and back into school.

Harry told Donelli he had another worry though. "I have to tell the commanding officer to keep it quiet. If it gets to the football coach down here, he might freeze it," he wrote back. This came when Harry was leading Camp LeJeune to the Eastern Services baseball championship, and, a few days later, to the national title over Camp Pendleton in California, beating them three straight games.

This sent Camp LeJeune to the National Baseball Congress in Wichita, a tournament that pitted the best amateur teams in the country against each other. Harry was voted the Most Valuable Player and on to the All-Star team and the Marines finished fourth against the best amateur teams in the country. He played first base and centerfield too.

When he was playing first, Harry chattered away, encouraging his pitcher. And he hit, it was almost always his trademark line drives that seemed to come off the bat like a beam of light. The home runs were prodigious swats. "Not one was a blooper, most of them carried over the scoreboad on a line," Sampieri said. "I saw all the athletes that came through here and that Agganis was the greatest. His mother and father did a great job bringing up that kid."

Harry led his team in virtually every category, with 100 hits, 78 runs, 83 RBI's, 20 doubles, 19 triples, 14 home runs and 35 stolen bases. He had been All-Marine and All-Navy in football and received a certificate from Leatherneck Magazine.

Donelli had his sights set on football though, and was still hoping the hardship application would be approved, and in time to get Harry back into uniform. But it would be close, and Donelli would go into pre-season practice without really knowing who his quarterback would be.

He sent Harry information about plays, but, even if Harry could be released to get back to B.U. before football season, there wouldn't be any time to practice or to learn the new terminology or plays, or get to know many new teammates.

At Camp LeJeune, Harry could only wait.

AGON ◆ **STRUGGLE** ◆ ΑΓΩΝ
1951 – 1952

Just a year after B.U.'s hopes for a successful 1950 season were ruined when Harry was called into the Marines came the news he would be getting out on September 19, 1951, two days before B.U.'s football team was scheduled to open in Virginia against William and Mary. His application for a hardship dependency had been approved so he could return home and go back to school and take care of his mother. It was his junior year.

The decision caused a lot of elation on the campus. "The possibility of Agganis' return has lifted Terrier football prospects to a new high as this week's rumor greatly stimulated the sale of season tickets," the school newspaper reported before he got out.

But there was some criticism that Harry was getting out after only a year in the service, most of which had been spent playing sports. But he had enlisted in the Marines in 1948, while still a student, and subjected himself to a callup which he could have ignored to care for his mother.

There was some isolated criticism over his release. Boston sports columnist Austen Lake wrote that mothers of some sons who were in combat in Korea were irked. "They wish to know how a 'Dependency Discharge' can resume his college studies, timed opportunely to start the varsity football season and fill B.U.'s quarterback cavity, when their own sons are still slogging over Korea's rocky cliffs or rice paddies where things sharp as scythes whizz and sometimes chew ugly holes in people," he wrote.

The criticism didn't take hold, partially because Harry was such a revered figure in Boston and because he hadn't tried to get out of the Marines when he was first called. Lake had a reputation for looking to stir controversy at a time when Boston had intense competition between its many newspapers, including *The Globe, Record, Herald, American* and *Post.*

Red Sox star Ted Williams had become so upset with criticism by some sportswriters, whom he dubbed "The Knights of the Keyboard," he had spit in anger one time. Columnist Dave Egan, called "The Colonel," was constantly harassing him in his writings. Harry's demeanor and dedication to his family, friends and church, gave Lake little more to write about, and fans were more interested in seeing Harry play again.

Even while Buff Donelli was overjoyed at the news Harry would be released, the suddenness meant he had to get him back from Camp LeJeune and into a lineup that included a lot of new faces and teammates with whom he hadn't played. And it meant Harry would supplant little Johnny Nunziato, or the two All-Scholastics, Phil O'Connell and Tommy Gastall of Fall River.

Donelli decided to send his assistant coach John Toner, who in 1949 was the quarterback Harry had replaced just before the Syracuse game, to escort Harry and go over the plays to get him ready. Donelli didn't have to worry about Harry being in shape, because his quarterbacking had led Camp LeJeune to championships in football and baseball. But the sudden transition would be jarring, even to a veteran, and Harry would have virtually no time to prepare himself for William and Mary.

He also had to get back to Boston and register for school and sign in at his part-time job at Gloria Foods, and then back to Virginia to join the team. He was met at the airport in Boston by his mother, his sister, Mary Raimo, and her husband, Tony, and their three children.

After that it was off to Virginia. Toner helped him go over the plays on their way to the Williamsburg Inn, where the team was staying. In his room there, Nunziato, a gritty player who, despite his size had also starred in baseball and basketball at Somerville, including scoring the winning points at the buzzer to beat New Britain, Connecticut for the New England basketball championship, wasn't sure what to think because he was alone. Donelli had paired all the other players, mostly by position.

At about 11:15 p.m. Thursday, two nights before the game, the door opened and in walked Toner and Harry. Two years earlier, Nunziato had come to watch B.U. practice in Weston because his coach was a good friend of Donelli's. Harry had brought Nunziato behind a Quonset hut where the players lived and helped him run some plays and showed him the B.U. system.

Now it was Nunziato who knew the system.

The three men looked at each other and Toner reintroduced Harry and Nunziato, who spoke briefly before going to sleep. The next morning, Harry looked at Nunziato and said "You don't like me, do you?"

Nunziato was astonished. He couldn't believe that Harry Agganis, the idol of high school and college players, was worried what he would think about coming back to the team.

"What are you talking about Harry?" Nunziato said.

"You don't like me because if I wasn't here, you'd be playing," Harry said, worried he had upset the team balance and hurt the feelings of a player about to start his first college game.

Nunziato stammered, "You don't know how glad I am you're here. Now that you're here, we should go undefeated," he said, secretly happy the awesome pressure of starting the game would be relieved. All week long the newspapers in Virginia had said the "Agganis-less" B.U. team would be underdogs and that the unknown Nunziato would be taking the place of Agganis.

Then Harry, towering over Nunziato, asked him a question for which Nunziato wasn't fully prepared.

"Why are you here?" Harry said, wanting to know why Nunziato had chosen B.U.

"Well Harry," Nunziato said. "I got a full ride," a full four-year scholarship which provided a free education.

"You see," Harry said, "That's the difference. I'm here because I want to be." Nunziato gulped quietly and didn't answer, but was thinking that Harry was right. "When the tough times come, you've got to want to be here," Harry was trying to teach him, he told himself.

Harry would have some support from the sidelines. His old B.U. friends Tommy McGee, and Harry Zingus, with whom he would room the last two years of college, had hitchhiked everywhere to watch him play in 1949. Zingus, whose family came from Epiros in Northern Greece, was paired with Harry at Myles Standish Hall in Kenmore Square because Donelli thought his quarterback would like to be with a fellow countryman, and because Zingus had become the team's manager. He and Harry became friends, and would often walk through Kenmore Square to a movie theater on Massachusetts Avenue.

One snowy night, as they were walking, Harry saw a man who was stuck in his car in a snowbank. He insisted they try to help him out. "He didn't even think about whether he'd get hurt," said Zingus. They pushed to get the car out. When they did, the man drove away without thanking them. Harry didn't care. "He always went out of his way to help others," Zingus said.

The two used to go to ethnic dances of Epiros at the Hotel Astor in New York too. Harry met Zingus' parents, Chris and Evanthia, and Zingus' friends. Although his family was from Sparta, Harry quickly picked up the Epirotic dances. In this group, Harry was not famous, and he fit in well with the hardworking immigrants. They came from an area which had never been conquered during the Turkish occupation of Greece.

It was unlike other occasions, when Zingus was frequently amazed at how well-known Harry was. A wealthy Greek-American who had met Harry in the Marines invited him to New York one day, but Harry said he'd come only if Zingus could too.

They were flown into New York, saw Judy Garland in concert, and ate at Toots' Shor's, a restaurant frequented by celebrities and sports figures. "Harry never took advantage of anyone and he always thought of his friends first," Zingus said.

One time, they went to see Holy Cross play out in Worcester, but Harry didn't call ahead. Still, when Zingus and Harry's teammates Chubby Keane and John Hall got there, a Holy Cross official recognized him.

"They just opened the gate and let us in," he said.

Harry was down about ten pounds to 190, and said he'd like to play in the opening game. "It depends on the coach, whether I can work in with the team though," he said.

He briefly went through a drill the day before the game, and Donelli was impressed enough to say he planned to play Harry at safety, and briefly on offense. "Boy, if I'm ready for Saturday's game, I'll sure be ready for the rest of the season," Harry laughed.

But even the terminology had changed, so the plays had different names. It was a tough task to try to start, especially since Harry called his own plays in the huddle. "He's still shaky in calling plays, but if it's necessary, John Kastan can call signals while Harry throws that ball," Donelli said.

William and Mary had a strong team and Nunziato started the game. But it wasn't long before Harry came on to play. And, with little time to prepare or practice, Harry had one of his best days, playing both ways.

He had a favorite target in end Tom Oates, who came up as a freshman with Harry in 1948, and a new one too, tough and tall Bob Capuano from Rhode Island, a leaping basketball player with a wrestler's build and huge hands.

Harry asked Oates what the plays were sometimes and Harry would equate them with the 1949 offense he knew. Oates would interpret it and Harry would call it in the huddle. Harry threaded the ball all day, and was amazed at how Capuano could get to it, especially in a group of defenders.

"Cappy, do you know how lucky we are to be on a team with a guy who can throw it that way?" Oates told him.

Toner, who helped Harry prepare, was happy with his performance, but not the loss. "He had a field day," said Toner. "It was one of the outstanding demonstrations of a true athlete. It was a magnificent afternoon he had down there," Toner said.

William and Mary won, 34-25, but Harry was 8-for-17 with two touch-down passes and should have had another. His TD passes went to Capuano, who, later in the game, was knocked over by two defenders as he leaped for another apparent score. That came a play on which Oates was similarly roughed up on what looked like a scoring pass. Despite Harry's impressive debut, Donelli second guessed himself after the game, thinking the team should have run more.

Harry's performance worried Rip Engle, coach of B.U.'s next foe, a pow-erhouse Penn State team. The game would be in Pennsylvania. "I'll have to admit, we got a little panicky trying to get ready for him, he later told Ridge Riley, editor of school's alumni football letter.

"Our scouts who saw him against William and Mary were scared to death," he said. In that game, Harry also played safety on defense, averaged 47 yards on three punts, including one from behind the goal line for 62 yards. When he was briefly on the sidelines, he often manned the field telephone.

Engle briefed his team, which included a young Joe Yukica, one of his stars. "That boy is really terrific. He could play in the pro league next week," Engle said.

"When you are against that kind of passing, you just have to open up and you're bound to be overbalanced somewhere," he said. He was worried too about the hard-nosed end, Capuano, a leaping athlete who was a star on B.U.'s basket-ball team too.

B.U.'s assistant coach Steve Sinko, who left Donelli two years earlier for a brief stint at Indiana, had come back in 1951 to rejoin him. He said Harry and Capuano had worked together on plays where Capuano would run down and fake in toward the goal post, and then break for the corner of the end zone and Harry would throw what was called a "dew-drop."

"I wouldn't care who was covering him. Bob could outjump anyone else. The maneuver they worked out was absolutely uncanny and unstoppable," said Sinko, because of Harry's pinpoint passing. "He could throw the sideline pass where the end would run down field and break for the sidelines. You've got to be one hell of a good passer to do this and Harry could do it," he said.

The Penn State game was even wilder than the William and Mary game.

B.U., behind Harry, took a 14-7 lead into the halftime. But Penn State came out storming. Yukica made a great catch over Harry to get Penn State rolling, and eight touchdowns were scored in 17 minutes of the third and fourth periods.

After B.U. went up, 21-7, Penn State rallied for a 27-21 lead, until Harry hit John Kastan with a 64-yard scoring pass to put B.U. back on top, 28-27. Penn State scored again to take a 33-28 lead, but Agganis threw a 34-yard pass and Kastan ran it in from the 28-yard line to put B.U. up, 34-33.

Penn State rallied to take a 40-34 lead. But with 1:10 to go, Harry took over for B.U. on his team's 16-yard line. Harry completed two passes to Kastan and then faked a pass and handed to halfback Joe Terrasi, who ran to the side-lines and threw a pass to Capuano, that turned into a dew-drop.

A Penn State defender leaped and tried to knock the ball away, but it was caught by Capuano. He fell flat on his back at the Penn State 9-yard line as time ran out, and the Nittany Lions had escaped. Yukica was exhausted.

Yukica said Engle had warned his team about "The left-handed quarter-back just out of the Marines," but they were skeptical. "We couldn't believe him. Well, by the end of that great performance, none of us would not have bet that if Agganis had time for one more play from our 9-yard-line, he would have beaten us," he said.

Harry finished with 10-for-14 passing for 211 yards and two touchdowns, and kicked for a 48-yard average. It was a performance that had a young assistant coach for Penn State, Joe Paterno, impressed too. He came into the locker room after the game to talk to Donelli, for whom he almost became an assistant coach while thinking of going to B.U. Law School.

Paterno looked over and saw Harry sitting and smiled. "You played a great game, kid," Paterno said, happy his team had gotten out with a win after trying to keep Harry from running all over the field. Penn State defenders on one play had chased Harry 40 yards behind the line of scrimmage, but Harry still managed to throw a completion for a gain.

Paterno had known about Harry since the Lynn Classical days. "He was smart and had great athletic instincts. He was a great athlete," he said. "He almost beat us by himself. He was phenomenal. Trying to sack him was almost impossible, it was like he had eyes in the back of his head. He saw things and had tremendous confidence in his athletic ability," Paterno said in amazement of the game.

Philadelphia Eagles scout Wayne Milner came in to see Donelli too. "I've never seen a college player with such talent," Milner said.

Sinko wasn't surprised. "Harry was an exceptional passer. He had a hell of a good arm and he could throw the ball where it should go. It wasn't that he got rid of it real quick, or he could throw off the backfoot ... Harry was a good sized kid who was quick and he could throw," said Sinko.

Harry didn't like losing though. In two weeks, B.U. had scored 59 points but hadn't won yet, and that made him forget how he had done personally. Donelli and Sinko stayed close to him, anxious how he would take the losses.

"He was like our boy. Buff and I thought the same way. Harry was Harry. He was our kid. He was my son and Buff's son and that's the way it was. We respected him and he respected us and we got along beautifully. It's kind of rare today about how close you could get to a kid. Harry had no father and that made a difference. If he had faith in you he would trust you regardless. What you said, that was gospel," said Sinko.

Next week, B.U. would take on Louisville, a team which had a young quarterback named Johnny Unitas. It was another sterling exhibition by Harry, who was 15-of-21 passing for 227 yards, including a touchdown pass and three extra points, leaving Louisville coach Frank Camp astonished. After B.U. dismantled Louisville, 39-7, the Cardinals most one-sided loss in 10 years, Camp had some advice for Unitas.

"When those game films come back, I want you to study the way Harry Agganis plays quarterback," he said. "He took us apart like nobody ever did."

The game had Boston fans thinking about a possible matchup in 1952 with Holy Cross, which had a great young quarterback, Charlie Maloy, who was being compared with Harry. In 1949, the year after Holy Cross' powerful freshman team had beaten Harry's B.U. freshman team, B.U. had pummeled Holy Cross in a scrimmage. Holy Cross had an open date in 1952, but B.U. was already scheduled to play Wichita. But Harry and Charlie would meet later.

Then came Harry's old mates from Camp LeJeune. He had left there only weeks earlier, when he was worried he might have to play for them against B.U. But the team was still loaded with a lot of college stars. Harry overwhelmed them too, leading B.U. to a tough 16-0 win, their second straight. But few expected what would happen the next week.

SEVASMOS ◆ RESPECT ◆ ΣΕΒΑΣΜΟΣ

College of the Pacific, one of the top teams in the country, was coming to Boston. Less than a year earlier, they had destroyed B.U., 55-7, while Harry was in the Marines. Pacific was still a powerhouse, and had the best offense in the country, and came into Boston a three-touchdown favorite.

Boston Globe sportswriter Clif Keane wrote B.U. "is expected to take a man-sized whipping from the West Coast team, despite the presence of Harry Agganis." Broadcaster Red Barber said "One man can not possibly make that much of a difference."

Even Donelli was worried. He had seen Pacific destroy his team the year before. "Greatest team to play here in 10 years," he said, including the Maryland team that had squeaked by B.U. and Harry, 14-13, in 1949. "I truthfully don't see how we can beat them," he said.

And one B.U. player was so impressed when Pacific players came out, he said, "They looked so big I swear the field tilted." Globe sportswriter Jerry Nason said "It looked like maybe the Los Angeles Rams got their Eastern booking loused up." It didn't seem like B.U. had a chance.

They did. Before 16,030 fans at Fenway Park on a Friday night, Harry took B.U. to a 27-0 lead over a stupefied Pacific team and a delirious crowd. Keane recounted that "They insist that no one man means the difference in a football game, but the Golden Greek was the sole difference last night against a team that looked like a lot of Sherman tanks barging through the line." Pacific had eight players who went into the professional ranks, but even they were awed after the game.

On one play, Harry ran 41 yards before being tripped up at his ankles, and then picked out Kastan from a crowd of defenders for a touchdown pass. Then Harry stopped another Pacific drive by knocking down a pass in the B.U. end zone.

After Pacific threatened again, Harry intercepted a pass at the B.U. goal line and ran it back 36 yards and then threw a 26-yard pass to Oates to set up a 6-yard touchdown run by Lindy Hanson. It was 14-0 at the half and in the third period, Harry dazzled Pacific defenders with a fake hand off and dashed three yards for a score. Then he hit Capuano for an easy touchdown pass after again faking out Pacific defenders. B.U. won 27-12.

A West Coast reporter shrugged at the end of the game that "Well, I'll file the story, but nobody out there will believe it." Pacific had been 26-point favorites and came in first in the country in offense and seventh in defense, and with little respect for their opponents.

Donelli said after the game that "So much is written about Harry's passing and kicking that nobody realizes he is one of the finest defensive backs who ever played." Besides the two interceptions, he also made seven open-field tackles, and one special play Donelli said showed his greatness.

Pacific was near the B.U. goal line and faked a sweep that had defender Lindy Hanson following the wrong man, leaving Harry with two men to cover. Harry leaped about 10 yards and deflected the pass away with his fingertips.

Oates went out for a few beers with some of the Pacific players. "Christ, this guy is a pro," they said about Harry. Oates was used to the accolades given Harry. They had roomed together as freshmen and, even off the field, everybody looked at Harry.

"We would walk into a room and everything would stop. People would turn and look and you could see they were all saying 'There's Agganis.'" Harry would flush with embarrassment at first and leave, but came to handle the adulation, even though he preferred sharing it with his friends.

ZETOKRAUGAI ◆ ACCLAIM ◆ ΖΗΤΩΚΡΑΥΓΑΙ

Sportswriters were getting used to seeing Harry dazzle opponents with sleight-of-hand and his scurrying in the backfield to pick out pass receivers, or mad dashes like an out-of-control dodgem car as opponents careened around trying to grasp him.

Newspapers, especially those in Boston, had Harry headlines in morning and afternoon editions, and he was gaining national fame too. It wasn't just his ability, but his unabashed humility, and the way he changed the game at quarterback as a big, fast passer who was also a powerful runner, and whose instincts made the position one of imagination instead of rote.

Where most quarterbacks were single-dimensional players, Harry brought the strength of his Spartan warrior-like presence into a game. He presided over games like Achilles stalking Troy, tossing aside defenders like toys, pushing underdog teams beyond their limits with his daring.

After the win over Pacific, it seemed B.U. might be able to run out the season with eight straight wins, if only they could get by always-tough Syracuse in the season's finale.

But there came a letdown against Temple, which always troubled B.U. The Terriers were beaten, 20-13 on a 77-yard pass play, the same night that another local hero, Rocky Marciano of Brockton, knocked Joe Louis through the ropes to win the heavyweight boxing championship of the world. Harry was 14-for-23 against the nation's second best defensive team, which had won four straight coming in.

A few days later, three ex-Kentucky basketball stars admitted fixing games in 1949, when Harry's old Lynn Classical teammate Lou Tsioropoulos was a freshman there. Tsioropoulos was on Kentucky's NCAA 1951 champions, but had wanted to play football at Kentucky. He was not involved in the scandal.

In their next game, B.U. matched its scoring record, beating New York University, 52-6. Harry, who wanted to give his teammates publicity and often preferred to stay on the ground with a running game, was 5-for-12, taking B.U. to a 33-0 lead before Donelli made substitutions. Kastan had three long touchdowns, including one for 76 and another for 57 yards.

Donelli wasn't satisfied though. Before the next game against Oregon, rated the fifth-best in the country against passing, he told Harry to start throwing more. "I want you to pass more than you have in the past," he said. Donelli told reporters, "I've been trying to get him to and he's reluctant."

There was a big rally before the game, featuring a float sponsored by Harry's Sigma Alpha Epsilon fraternity. It was called "The Golden Greek" and showed a big picture of Number 33 in a Spartan outfit and gold head plume dropping back to pass. The float won fifteen dollars and second prize in the parade.

These were pleasant times for most college students. The GI bill had allowed many students from low-and-middle income families to go to college, where they could attain the dreams of their immigrant parents. The biggest problem reported was card-playing.

School officials formed a committee to look into it. "I don't like the idea of prohibiting card playing, but neither do I enjoy seeing students, girls as well as boys, losing ten to fifteen dollars a day," one school official said. He said some were playing eleven hours a day.

But there was always football. Oregon coach Len Casanova said he was worried about Harry. Without widespread television coverage of games, coaches had to rely on the media and films and newspaper stories to learn about opponents. Casanova said "That Agganis can throw passes standing on his head. It seems to me he's been passing enough anyway."

Casanova still didn't expect what he saw that Saturday, November 10, at Fenway Park. Harry threw two touchdown passes and had Casanova proclaiming him "the best back I've seen in some years, the best quarterback since Frankie Albert." B.U. romped, 35-6.

It was Dad's Day, and the fathers of B.U. players went wild watching. In the stands, Joseph Schultz, father of halfback George Schultz, who had a 40-yard touchdown run, yelled "That's my boy!"

And John Pappas, Sr., a wrestler for fifteen years and a man who could speak seven languages, was there, proudly beaming as he watched his son, Johnny, a hard-nosed center. Pappas, son of an Albanian Orthodox priest, didn't want his son to wrestle because he thought it was too dangerous. James Cahill, an All-Ireland player in Gaelic football had six girls and two boys, including John, a defensive halfback playing that day.

John Kastan, Sr., saw his son set a B.U. season rushing record that day, eclipsing the mark set by Harry's old Lynn pal and 1949 teammate, Bobby Whelan. Harry's father had died in 1946, but there to watch him were his brothers, Phil and Jimmy, seated near Hap Hanson, brother of Lindy Hanson, whose dad had also passed away.

If Donelli was upset with Harry, he got over it in a hurry and leaped to defend his favorite after more attention was being given to Princeton tailback Dick Kazmaier, who had led his team to a 54-13 pasting of Harvard. Despite the national attention given B.U. because of Harry, the Boston newspapers often lead with Boston College or the Ivy League at the time.

"Kazmaier can't hold Agganis' shoes!" Donelli snapped. "Imagine! Here we have the outstanding college football player in the country and everyone is raving about Kazmaier or somebody in the Midwest or out on the coast! Agganis is just a professional playing in college ranks," he said angrily.

"There are passers in professional ranks who don't have the looseness or smoothness of Agganis. Harry never lets you down. Everyone, including me, expects great things and he always comes through," Donelli said.

"There are no comparisons in college to make with Harry," he added. "He's too good." He said many sports magazines ranked Harry as the top quarterback in the country and an All-American.

Harry had relatively little time to practice too, especially his kicking, which was limited to five minutes a week, although he once boomed a kick 80 yards on the fly. He went from classes to his part-time job, and had to study too. Donelli said Harry was better than Kentucky quarterback Babe Parilli, who was garnering a lot of notice too.

One play which showed Harry's versatility and athleticism astounded fans at the Oregon game. Harry was back to punt when the pass from center hit the ground. He picked it up and, while eluding several tacklers, ran to the left side of the field and punted the ball 50 yards while running full speed.

University of California scout Augie Marra, who was at the game, was amazed at Harry's sense to exploit the other team. "I scouted Oregon three times and I discovered three of their principal weaknesses. Agganis found and exploited all of these, in the first quarter," he said.

B.U., after losing the first two games of the year despite scoring 59 points, was now 5-3 and ready to host Wichita. B.U. rolled, 39-6, as Harry threw his eleventh touchdown pass of the season and the team set a new season scoring record of 280 points. That beat the 1949 record of 250 set when Harry was a sophomore starter.

Next came Syracuse, which hadn't forgotten the game two years earlier when Harry, in his debut, led B.U. to a stunning 33-21 upset. But this year, the Orangemen were going to get their revenge, even if they still couldn't stop Harry, who opened the game with touchdown passes to Oates and Kastan in the first 10 minutes.

Even road games were an occasion for gatherings. Many B.U. fans came and stayed at the Hotel Onondaga, where they could eat in the cafe, where appetizers were twenty cents, a baked filet entree at lunch was ninety-five cents, and desserts were a quarter and coffee a nickel. Harry would sometimes be met by Greek-American families on these trips, anxious to be near their greatest athletic hero. But he was all business on the field.

He finished with 12 completions, including three touchdowns, giving him 14 for the year and only one short of his record of 15 in 1949. In the last quarter though, he had two intercepted, and Harry's 104 completions for the season left him only two short of the Eastern record of 106 set by Boston College's Butch Songin, and B.U. lost, 26-19.

Harry finished the 1951 season with 104-for-185 passing and Oates set a school record with 35 receptions for 493 yards, to go along with Kastan's rushing record. But B.U. was 6-4, losing three games by one touchdown each.

Harry was named the starting quarterback on Collier's All-Star East team, but the Heisman Trophy for the country's outstanding player went to Kazmaier, the man Donelli said couldn't carry Harry's shoes.

On November 28, Harry was named the starting safety on Grayson's All-American team, signaling his uniqueness as an all-star player on both offense and defense. He was named to Mr. Z's All-American team at quarterback, a designation by Murray Kramer, the *Boston Record* sportswriter, and was elected to the New England Grid Sports Hall of Fame.

And he won another important honor too, the Bulger Lowe award as New England's best football player.

And when he went to accept it, he brought his old high school friend, Jimmy Kirios, with whom he had often sung playfully. Kirios wanted to become a professional singer in Hollywood and Harry again wanted to make sure his friends got some attention too, and he wanted to push the career of his bashful friend.

After Harry was introduced, he stood up and said "Well, ladies and gentlemen, Thank you for coming, I appreciate it." Then, instead of talking about himself, he looked over at Kirios, who was a budding singer with hopes of a Hollywood career.

"I've got Jimmy Kirios here, a terrific basketball player and he's a great singer. You're going to be hearing about him." An embarrassed Kirios was looking at the tablecloth in anguish. But Harry kept talking about him, until Judge John Pappas jumped up and tugged at his sleeve.

"Excuse me Harry. Harry, Harry, please, we'll let your friend speak for himself later," he urged. Kirios was relieved. In his brief presentation before a crowd of five hundred people, Harry was humble about himself.

He had been cheered at the dinner at the Hotel Lenox, but said he didn't deserve the award and that others were more deserving. "I hope my conduct in the years will come to justify your faith," he said.

His high school coach, Bill Joyce, who was there, was not surprised. "Harry has never lost the common touch," he said. And, although Harry had won his award for football, Joyce said he thought Harry's love was really baseball, but that he had continued to play football out of love and respect for Donelli.

EPITYCHIA ◆ SUCCESS ◆ ΕΠΙΤΥΧΙΑ

Six weeks later, the Cleveland Browns, who had won five professional titles in six years, a span during which their record was 75-8-3, showed how respected Harry was as a football player. The Browns quarterback was multisport star Otto Graham, and there was a powerhouse team including Lou Saban, running back Marion Motley and kicker Lou "The Toe" Groza.

The Browns only title loss was to the Los Angeles Rams, 24-17, when Rams quarterback Norm Van Brocklin threw the winning score to Tom Fears. Graham was still considered the greatest quarterback in the history of professional football, and not yet ready to retire.

But Browns' owner Paul Brown, who had heard about Harry, an opinion reinforced by the Browns' announcer, Ken Coleman, a Boston area native who had broadcast some B.U. football games before becoming a Cleveland broadcaster drafted him number one as a junior, and a likely successor to Graham some day. Brown wanted Harry badly.

Before the draft, Harry was in his room at the Myles Standish dormitory with his roommate, Harry Zingus, when he got a call that Zingus overheard. Harry was mostly listening, until he said, "Well, to tell you the truth, I'm not sure what I'm going to do." It was the Los Angeles Rams, who wanted him as a bonus pick, but they wanted to know if he was going to play for B.U. or try professional baseball.

That let the Browns draft Harry number one and he was a perfect match for their powerhouse, to eventually replace Graham, who had been a star basketball player and was the consummate quarterback of his time.

Harry continued to pick up other honors at the same time. On February 2, 1952 he was given an award by the most influential of Greek-American organizations, the Athens Chapter No. 24 of the American Hellenic Educational Progressive Association, known as AHEPA. It was presented by the chapter president, Harry Demeter, who drove to Harry's dormitory at the Myles Standish to pick him up.

B.U. President Harold Case and Donelli came to the award ceremony too, given to Harry as the outstanding Hellenic-American athlete in the region. Also attending were Donelli, Case, and a young priest from the Boston Cathedral, Rev. James Coucouzis, who saw success in Harry.

The Browns were still chasing him. Paul Brown had offered Harry a $40,000 bonus and was still calling him frequently. One day, while Harry and Kirios were driving through Kenmore Square in Boston, past hotels where many of the Red Sox players stayed, Harry said to him, "Jeep, I've got make a call."

"OK," Kirios said.

"I need to get some quarters," Harry said. They stopped while Harry went into a store to make change, and he came back with two dollars in quarters. Kirios stopped at an outside phone booth, and Harry went in and talked for about ten minutes. Kirios could hear the quarters jingling in the phone as Harry talked animatedly, his arms moving in the booth.

Harry came back and got in next to Kirios.

He smiled broadly. "Jeep, I just turned down $100,000," he said. It was like a million dollars. Kirios couldn't believe what he was hearing.

"Wha, Wha, What did you do?" Kirios asked, wondering what Harry was talking about.

"They want me to take Otto Graham's place. That was Paul Brown I just talked to," Harry said."

Kirios was still perplexed. He didn't know who Brown was. But before Harry could explain, he yelled and pointed outside the car. "Jeep, look! I'll be right back!"

Harry jumped out of the car because Red Sox star Ted Williams had just pulled up in a LaSalle convertible with the top down. He was about twenty yards away and Harry ran over and he talked to Williams for a few minutes. As Harry came back, Kirios saw Williams casually leap over the door of the convertible into his seat without breaking stride.

Harry had been hounded since high school, with everyone wanting to know which college he was going to, and then, as his college career was ending, whether he would play pro basebal or football. The speculation intensified after the Browns drafted him, but Harry kept his own counsel, and didn't reveal himself even to his closest friends.

Kirios was surprised that Harry hadn't confided more in him because they were so close. "Jeep, I'm going to tell you something and I want you to remember this in your life. Whenver you've got something important, don't tell anybody. Do it. Let them read about it. Wait, and when it happens, they'll see it."

Kirios wasn't entirely sure why Harry had said it, until Harry paused a moment and said to him in Greek, his face souring seriously, *"Zeelevounai."* It means, "People are jealous."

Harry thought it was like a curse to tell something before it happened because he thought that meant it wouldn't work and Kirios thought Harry wouldn't even tell his brothers about Brown pursuing him.

In the Spring, Harry had to run from football practice over to the baseball team. He had been disappointed in his performance in the Spring of 1950, before he went up to Maine to play with the Millionaires. But the next year, he had won All-Star awards playing for the Marines, and he was still exuberant about baseball.

It was a strong baseball team at B.U. There was Harry, and Gastall was an outstanding catcher. George Sullivan, a highly-regarded first baseman in high school, came into B.U. with high hopes of eventually playing in the major leagues, but started thinking about playing another position after he saw Harry. Sullivan was only seventeen, and awed at what he saw.

"The way he carried himself was like magic," said Sullivan, who thought Harry looked like he already belonged playing for the Red Sox. He thought only Ted Williams had the same kind of charisma and style. And he was impressed at Harry's modesty and reluctance to talk about himself.

The players had to take a trolley out to Nickerson Field in Weston to practice and one Spring day Sullivan was taking some throws with Harry during a practice, while Harry was waiting to bat. Harry often hit screaming line-drive laser-like shots and the players had to be aware when he was hitting.

Sullivan was reaching for a throw when he heard an ominous sound: it was the booming, unmistakable voice of Harry Agganis, who was taking batting practice. Harry's voice could be heard anywhere on the field, but this time there was a sense of alarm.

"LOOOOOK OUT!" Harry screamed, one of the few times players could remember there was any loud urgency about him.

He had hit a vicious, curling line drive that was hooking straight at Sullivan. Harry had turned to follow the path of the ball, which he had pulled hard. It was heading straight for Sullivan's temple. Sullivan got his glove up at the last second just before he would have been hit.

"It was the best catch I ever made because it saved my life," he said with a sigh of relief.

Harry was shaken too. If he hadn't yelled, Sullivan would have been seriously injured or worse. Harry took a deep breath in relief too, glad his friend was okay.

It was hard playing college baseball in New England. The weather was often cold or rainy and fields were frequently covered with snow or mud or were as hard as cement late into the season. Harry had a terrible slump in the 1950 baseball season, although he was hitting the ball hard but directly at opponents. He wasn't striking out often or hitting poorly.

Unlike college teams in California and Florida and warmer parts of the country, which played forty or fifty games or more, B.U. had only fifteen to twenty games, and getting off to a poor start could skew a player's performance.

But Harry hit the ball hard, for a .322 average and 12 runs batted in. Ten of his 19 hits went for extra bases. That Spring, he was named B.U.'s Athlete of the Year for the second time.

Harry thought a lot of his friends. Once, after a class at a building at the Copley Square campus closer to downtown, a classmate, Ted Lyons, who didn't have much hair, fell and cracked his head, bleeding profusely. While other people weren't sure what to do, Harry picked up his friend with one arm and carried him to an infirmary.

It was not unlike the time Harry went with Bishop Iakovos (James) Coucouzis to Children's Hospital in Boston to visit a young Greek-American athlete, Nick Sarris, who was only twenty-one, but had been stricken with polio while studying at Colby College in Maine, where he starred on the football team.

At a dinner at the Hotel Statler, where he was honored, Harry, always loyal to his friends, again brought Kirios. Kirios, knowing Harry's penchant for embarrasing him, was reluctant, remembering what had happened at the Bulger Lowe award.

When Harry wanted Kirios to get in a photo with B.U. President Harold Case, Alumni President Nick Apalakis and other B.U. officials for the cover of an alumni magazine, Kirios tried to sidestep out the door so Harry wouldn't see him. He went downstairs into a men's room trying to hide. Harry went looking for him.

Kirios was thinking, "What am I doing here? I go to Suffolk," a small college in another part of the city. "What am I doing it at B.U." as he high-tailed it.

Harry came barging in like Hercules. BANG! BANG! Harry came in kicking open the stall doors. "Jeep! Where are you! Where are you hiding!" Kirios was inside a stall, thinking, "Oh please, don't let him find me." He had pulled himself up over a toilet seat so his feet wouldn't show, trying to keep Harry from finding him. He couldn't hold on, but Harry left.

In the late Spring of 1952, Harry played for the Vrees All-Stars again. The team went to Claremont, New Hampshire for an exhibition game. Andy Vrees had gone over to B.U. trying to find Harry to bring him up to the game, in a town about two hours north, but couldn't find him and headed off.

With the game in the eighth inning, Harry showed up at the field, but didn't have his baseball uniform on. Vrees didn't know what to say, whether to be delighted or upset.

"Harry, go put your suit on," he said.

The home team agreed to hold up the game because everyone wanted to see Harry pinch hit. The bases were loaded. On the second pitch, he hit a grand slam to win the game.

That Summer, Harry went to upstate New York to play for Malone in the Northern League. He was easily the best player on a mediocre team, and being watched by scouts eager to convince him that professional baseball was a better choice than professional football when he graduated.

A Red Sox scout, Neil Mahoney, who had been following Harry since sandlot and high school days in Lynn, came up to watch a game in which Harry was easily outclassing other players.

Mahoney had sneaked into the game unannounced. Harry had not played well, because, for perhaps the only time on a playing field, he wasn't hustling.

Harry was shocked after the game to look up and see Mahoney.

"You sure are making a bum of yourself," Mahoney shouted at Harry, who flushed in dismay and embarrassment.

"I'm sorry," Harry said sheepishly. "I'm sorry."

It was the last time, Mahoney said, Harry ever had to say that.

AMPHIVOLIA ♦ DOUBT ♦ ΑΜΦΙΒΟΛΙΑ

Although he was thinking he would play professional baseball, Harry came back for another year of football at B.U. Coming off his strong year in 1951, he hoped for a great finish in his last year, beginning in the Fall of 1952.

B.U. opened with a tough 6-0 win over Wichita in Kansas, a game in which he was 9-of-20 passing, including the game-winning touchdown to Don DeFeudis. Then it was back to Syracuse and another battle with B.U.'s fiercest rival.

Harry was brilliant, completing 23-of-37 for 264 yards, breaking both the records he held for the school then. He scored the first touchdown and almost single-handledly kept B.U. in the game against a superior team.

Syracuse won, 34-21, but *Boston Globe* sportswriter Tom Fitzgerald gushed "This show which electrified a crowd of some 15,000 unquestionably boosted Harry's individual All-American chances."

During one drive, Harry completed seven passes in a row, and again was often dancing away from desperate defenders. And he was keeping Syracuse pinned down with long or strategically-placed punts throughout the game.

Donelli shook up his line assignments for the next game against Marquette in Wisconsin. Harry's boyhood idol, Slingin' Sammy Baugh, for whom Harry wore Number 33, would be watching. It would be Harry's worst game as a collegian.

He completed only one of eight passes as Marquette romped, 21-0 and was constantly backpedaling against a hard-charging defensive line. Donelli was so angry he walked back to the team's hotel after the game and cancelled the traditional after-game dinner, keeping his players locked up. The team's most loyal fan, Tommy McGee, who had again trekked from Boston, had to sneak pizzas into the players rooms for them to eat.

Off that loss, there seemed little hope B.U. would be able to beat powerful Miami, which was coming up to Fenway Park to play. Miami was a 14-point favorite. Miami coach Andy Gustafson said his players didn't mind leaving 81-degree temperatures for the 50 degrees in Boston when they came in for a game that Friday night, October 10.

"Cold?" said Gustafson, who had been an assistant at Dartmouth and Army. "This is refreshing." And *Miami Daily News* Sports columnist Stanley Woodward,one of the country's best known sportswriters who had been a star in New York, said "This is nice weather for the boys. They got used to this kind of weather in Pennsylvania and Ohio," where they had played earlier.

Globe sportswriter Jerry Nason said Harry's miserable performance the week before shouldn't give Miami any sense of optimism. "If Agganis' stock has dipped in town this week, it can soar just as rapidly. He came off a sour game a year ago to put on one of the greatest all-around backfield performances ever witnessed at Fenway Park, against College of the Pacific.

It was a prognostication that would have made legendary gambler Nick "The Greek" Dandolos, who made and lost more than $500 million in his life-time, think twice about betting.

But the *Globe* headlines the next day, on page one instead of the sports pages, told the story. It was another banner day for Harry in the headlines: "B.U. UPSETS MIAMI, 9-7 AGGANIS PASSES, KICKS'

Harry's passing set up B.U.'s only touchdown in the first period and his booming punts preserved the lead into the fourth quarter when he booted one 64 yards down to the Miami 5-yard line to set up the game-winning safety with 2 1/2 minutes to play. It took a bit of acting, too.

Harry opened the game with four consecutive completions to Mario Moriello, Tom Lavery, Gastall, and Lavery again as B.U. marched 65 yards downfield. DeFeudis ran in from seven yards out on a pitchout from Harry, who faked the Miami line off balance and fed DeFeudis, running rapidly the other way.

B.U. held the lead until there were only four minutes to go in the game, but Miami scored on a 69-yard touchdown pass when end Frank McDonald caught the B.U. secondary coming in and got behind them.

But Harry, who already had punts of 57 and 65 yards go out of bounds near the Miami goal line, kicked another for 64 yards, down to the goal line, before it back-flipped to the 5-yard line, setting up the safety.

After the game ended, Harry came running over to his brother, Phil, who was sitting in the stands but had jumped onto the field in excitement. With his right hand, Harry picked his brother up.

"We did it! We did it!" he smiled in glee.

Before the B.U. touchdown, Harry punted and was hit by a defender. He fell to the ground, appearing to be badly hurt, drawing a key penalty. After the game, Kirios went down to the locker room, but couldn't get in. Harry looked up and saw him. "Hey, let him in. That's my buddy!"

He got in and Harry smiled at him. "Hey, Academy Award, Academy Award, you like it?" he laughed, describing the play on which he was hit while punting and fell down. Harry had faked the injury to get the penalty which allowed B.U. to keep the ball and score.

"I fooled you, I fooled you," Harry laughed, delighted at the ruse which had fooled everyone in the park, including his brother, Phil, and Kirios and all his friends, who were unused to seeing him go down. "I was faking," Harry snickered.

Kirios had trouble laughing. "You scared everybody, Harry," he said.

After the game, Gustafson came into the B.U. locker room and asked Donelli to introduce him to Harry. He shook Harry's hand and said "You're the greatest all-around football player I've ever seen," he said. Harry also had two interceptions and 14 tackles on defense.

Miami's defense was designed to stop his passing, but he continually rolled out with the ball on his hip and evaded would-be tacklers, and then he tore apart the secondary with his passing. It was a familiar scenario when teams played Harry, like hounds chasing a wily fox, but a fox who could turn on them with savage suddeness and unleash fury.

When Harry was trapped, he would often stick out a straight arm that would level an opponent, but he preferred to keep ducking and dodging and twisting to have them come up with only air in their arms. It was the kind of performance that had football great Benny Friedman say, "This kid is better than Sid Luckman, Sammy Baugh and Frankie Albert," the great quarterbacks of that era.

Harry had leveled B.U. at 2-2 and, of the remaining six games, only powerful Maryland, anchored in the defensive line by Dick Modzelewski and several other 230-pounders, and Villanova, would be prohibitive favorites against the Terriers.

In every game, Harry was a marked man by defenses eager to show they could sack the number one draft choice of a professional team. Adding to the pressure on him, Harry was featured in a long article the week after the Miami game in the *Saturday Evening Post*, this one also written by Hirshberg.

Under a photo of Harry in his backyard, stooping to hand a football to his nephews while his adoring family looked on from a porch, the headline asked "Is He College Football's Greatest Passer?"

Hirshberg called Harry, "A tall, curly-haired, dark-eyed Greek-American youth with an elastic left arm and an educated left toe," who seemed ready for

All-American recognition. It brought him even more national attention from one of the country's most respected magazines, and not just for a sports audience. His devotion to his family was cited.

Then William and Mary, the team that Harry had befuddled the year before two days after his discharge from the Marines, came into Boston for a rematch. In those days, William and Mary was a strong team. But Harry responded again, dazzling with dancing retreats into his backfield before passing off at the last moment. Nason wrote, once again, Harry set new standards at quarterback, this time with four touchdown passes to lead a 33-28 B.U. victory.

"The genius of Harry Agganis was written all over the game, for the Golden Greek towered over the first half and bailed B.U. out midway through the final period with a one-shot pass for the winning touchdown," Nason wrote. It was a 17-yard bullet to Gastall.

William and Mary had gotten off to a 7-0 lead before Harry led the Terriers to four consecutive touchdowns in the second period, including a 41-yard Agganis pass to to DeFeudis. Harry hit Gastall and Tom Lavery for scores too. But William and Mary, down, 27-7, came storming back in the second half and took a 28-27 lead.

But Harry, always with a flair for melodrama on the football field and cool poise, struck with the game-winner halfway through the final period, and B.U. held off a furious last-minute march to win. Harry finished with 14-for-22 passing for 187 yards, and intercepted two passes, had two runs of more than 30 yards each and kicked for a 43-yard average, including a 58-yard punt.

"After this one last night, there is even a faint spark of hope burning in the local breasts in connection with mighty Maryland," which was coming into Fenway Park in two weeks, Nason said. But a week later, Harry checked into the B.U. infirmary, suffering from a heavy cold that led Donelli to say his star wouldn't play against Lehigh that weekend.

And Harry's fellow defensive secondary mate George Schultz, whose dad had been the loudest supporter on the Dad's Day game against Oregon the year before, would be out too, with a broken leg suffered against William and Mary.

Gastall was slowed by a shoulder bruise. That meant Donelli had a quarterback problem. Without Harry, he would probably have to go with either Nunziato or O'Connell. And Nunziato was feeling the pressure of being the likely one to replace Harry.

Despite his strength, "Nunzi," as his teammates called him, was described as looking more like the equipment manager than the quarterback. But he was capable and crafty and a good runner too. But the game was away and Lehigh had won two straight, and was feeling buoyant about its chances with Harry not playing.

From his sick bed, Harry tried to cheer his teammates. He sent a telegram to the team in Pennsylvania, directed at Nunziato and O'Connell. "I know you two fellows are more than capable of doing the job. My heart is with you all the way. Keep the boys thinking and relax under pressure. Please help me get well by doing a good job." It was signed, "Your teammate, Harry Agganis."

Nunziato said he didn't know how Harry could be so cool with so much pressure every game he played.

"This was one game," he gulped, and he knew he would have to perform on game day. "You can't be an All-American Monday through Friday, you have to do it on Saturday too," he said. And it would be Lehigh's Homecoming Day that would be waiting for him.

Harry also took some time to write a letter to a young Lynn Airman who was stationed overseas. Ernest Larson was in the Air Force and had never met Harry, but admired him, and that was passed on to Harry by a friend who knew the Larson family.

Harry had several fan clubs and was receiving a couple of dozen letters a day. He tried to answer every letter, either himself or through Donelli's secretary, Themis Stoumbelis, with whom he had become friendly. But Larson hadn't written a letter, although he got one from Harry.

"You'll probably be surprised getting this kind of letter, but I just couldn't resist writing this one. I heard about you through a friend who knows all about you. I want to tell you that I feel flattered about how you have kept your interest in my athletic career. And what makes it greater than that, you are a Lynner."

Harry talked about his own bout with tonsilitis and a cold, and how he wanted to be ready for the big Maryland game. "Take care of yourself and I hope the service is treating you well," he finished.

Harry wasn't ready for the Lehigh game, and although he was hampered by fumbling, Nunziato led B.U. to a 29-20 win with DeFeudis scoring three touchdowns. But that was against Lehigh, and Maryland, winners of 22 consecutive games was coming into town.

HETA ◆ DEFEAT ◆ HTA

The game was so big that temporary stands were going to be put against the left-field wall at Fenway Park to accomodate an expected crowd of more than 40,000.

Maryland hadn't played B.U. since the 1949 game when B.U. narrowly lost, 14-13, a game in which Donelli bitterly complained poor officiating had cost his team the game. Harry had performed brilliantly in that one, an emotional affair that ended with the Maryland fans pouring out of the stands at Fenway

Park to mob the B.U. band and tear down the goal posts.

In 1952, Maryland was the second-ranked team in the country with a big, powerful defense and an All-American candidate, Jack Scarbath, at quarterback. They hadn't lost since early in the 1950 season and were a 27-point favorite, the odds boosted because of Harry's illness that left his ability to play well uncertain. Donelli was even more worried than he had been the year before against Pacific.

"Maryland is one of the best, if not the best team Boston University has ever met on a football field," Donelli said. "Our problem is to get the ball often enough to make a game out of it," he said. Maryland coach Jim Tatum said the odds were overstated, simply because Harry's presence on a football team made his team so dangerous at any time. "We've got to get the football away from Agganis and those other boys," he said.

It was Saturday, November 1, Homecoming Day for B.U. and 70-degree Indian Summer weather brought out a big crowd, including 3,000 Maryland supporters. The stands would be packed. The game program being sold for thirty-five cents had a feature on Harry by *Boston Daily Record* columnist Murray Kramer, who came to be one of his good friends.

"He's no superman, nor is he superhuman, but he is the greatest all around quarterback in football today. He's amazin'. The feats of Harry 'The Golden Greek' Agganis border on the unbelievable. Visiting coaches scoff before they see him. Opposing players laugh at yarns of his wonders. But once they see him operate, his legion of boosters increases," Kramer put it.

Syracuse coach Ben Schwartzwalder, whose first team in 1949 was beaten by Harry's brilliant debut game in a fierce rainstorm, had been asked recently to compare him to other T-formation quarterbacks.

"I can't compare any of them to Agganis as football players for nobody even comes close to that guy. He's an old pro." Schwartzwalder said what made Harry so dangerous was his ability to run as well as pass. "He can take off ... if he goes into pro football, he'll be a sensation," he said.

In the November *Sport*, Harry was on the cover in esteemed company: New York Yankee pitcher Allie Reynolds, SMU and Detroit Lions football star Doak Walker, and Brooklyn Dodger Jackie Robinson, the man who broke the color barrier in professional baseball.

Harry was in full uniform, a scarlet jersey and white helmet, and his gleaming teeth shone in resolution. He looked like a man who couldn't be stopped. The magazine was polling readers to choose their top athletic performer of the year, before Harry's big games.

It would prove to be a fateful game for Harry, one that would alter, and affect the rest of his life. Maryland's captain, Ed Fullerton, had a dislocated elbow and wouldn't be able to play. He broke down and cried in the locker room before the game and the Maryland players, already pumped, came out lusting for a win.

"That was all the inspiration my team needed," Maryland coach Jim Tatum said. "I just pointed to Fullerton and there was no fear of a letdown."

And even before that, Tatum warned his players how dangerous Harry was. Modzelewski, a 6'1", 235-pound son of a West Virginia coal miner was nicknamed "Little Mo," despite his size, because his older brother, Ed, who was slightly smaller, was the fullback on the 1949 Maryland team.

"Agganis has a hell of an arm and he's a great athlete," Tatum warned his team. "We've got to stop him and and his passing. We've got to put the pressure on him,!" Tatum yelled. Modzelewski would shadow Harry.

Before a screaming crowd which packed Fenway Park, B.U. fumbled on the third play of the game and was sent reeling. Before halftime, Maryland led 34-0. Harry had one receiver in the open for an easy touchdown, but the ball was dropped. He boomed a 65-yard punt into the wind.

But, as Nason wrote, "The rest of the time harassed Harry spent trying to comb 235-pound linemen out of his hair as he retreated and zigged and zagged trying in vain to detect at least one pass receiver which Maryland's defensive secondaries had permitted to even peek at daylight. Harry, rarely sacked, had nowhere to turn."

He was being pummeled on play after play. And, just before the end of the half, three big Maryland linemen, led by Modzelewski, came rushing through on a broken play and crushed him. Harry fell, landing on Nunziato, and staggered up, holding his side. For the first time in his career, the man thought to be an indestructible player was badly hurt.

Nunziato had come into the game to call a play in which the ball would be snapped between his legs to Harry, who had already been hit so hard on several plays he had trouble barking out the plays. But the play was misread and B.U. linemen went off on another direction. The Maryland linemen came through unmolested and pounced on him.

Sitting in the press box, Harry's old friend Dick O'Connell, the former head of the Lynn Red Sox, who was now working for the parent club, winced at what he saw. "The Maryland defense was 'Get Agganis.' That's all it was, to do anything they could to hit Agganis ... this was one team playing one man and you could see what was going on," he said.

In the dugout, Harry's teammate on the Augusta Millionaires baseball team, Ted Lepcio, now with the Red Sox, also grimaced at the hit. "The line ganged up on him ... he was hit pretty bad," he said.

Harry, holding his side, went to the sidelines, and tried to throw, but he couldn't lift his arm. Donelli was worried, but Harry didn't want to stay out, even if he couldn't throw. "Coach, I can play," he said, offering to go in at halfback, end or tackle. Donelli said no.

Harry was in agony, struggling to stay in the contest, but Donelli was worried and didn't want him getting hurt any more. He wanted to play. He had been hurt even before the big hit. On the play before, he tried to throw to DeFeudis, and crumpled to the ground.

Despite the pounding, Harry was still able to see holes in the Maryland defense. On one play, Terrasi flared out and was open. Before he even got back to the huddle, Harry looked at him and said "Joe, we're going to run the same play only you get the ball this time." They ran the same play for a long gain to the Maryland 3-yard line but a penalty brought the play back.

A short while later, Terrasi was even more stunned when, after a bad snap, Harry picked up the ball, and, on the dead-run, kicked it about 75 yards in the air with Maryland linemen bearing down on him.

B.U. center Frank Giuliano wasn't surprised though. B.U. used to practice a play where he would snap to Harry and linemen would charge him unmolested to see if they could block the ball before he got it off. They couldn't.

It was Giuliano who made the bad snap and he said he was relieved when Harry got the kick off, just before he was going to be pushed out of bounds for a big loss.

At halftime, Harry had a big sponge taped to his ribs. Toner, the assistant coach, said, "Harry can hardly breathe, let alone do any passing," as Harry paced and winced. Nunziato would have to replace him and the little guy was ready. While he was nervous against Lehigh the week before, this time he was stamping the ground, anxious to get in.

It was an odd sight. Nunziato could barely see over the big, burly Maryland linemen. Tatum, meanwhile, was surprised to see an even odder sight. Harry was sitting alone on the bench, and Tatum wondered where his teammates were. The game was over at halftime, but B.U. was responding to Nunziato, and, in the fourth quarter he moved his team down to the Maryland 10-yard line.

Tatum had taken his starters out, but they wanted to go back into preserve the shutout. The capacity crowd booed. Maryland held and it looked as if B.U. wouldn't even score.

But then Maryland had to punt and Joe Terrasi ran it back 55 yards for a touchdown to avert the shutout. "I loved it because it shut him up and he was going wild on the sidelines," Terrasi said. B.U. felt Tatum was trying to rub it in.

In the broadcast booth, Curt Gowdy was describing the savage beating taken by both Harry and B.U. Some critics scoffed at the Terriers offense, describing them as "The Confetti Line," but Maryland was a vastly superior team that even Harry couldn't hold back.

Even Scarbath, who was battling Harry for All-American honors, didn't like what he was seeing. "The poor guy didn't have a chance. He didn't have a chance to get his feet set." Harry was chased out of the pocket on virtually every play. "It's hard to throw on your back," Scarbath said. Even Harry couldn't do that.

Harry was taken to the hospital where the team doctor, Ken Christophe, examined and X-rayed his side. There was no break, but the ribs were severly bruised and Harry had trouble breathing. Lepcio came to see him, and Kirios and some of Harry's friends were there to take him home.

They had trouble getting Harry flat into the backseat of a car because he was so stiff. "He's like a slab, a board," Kirios said, worried about his friend. Kirios, now a student at Miami, had flown back to watch the game.

"He's hurting," he said, "He can't walk." When they got him home, they walked him gingerly up to the second floor apartment of his house on Waterhill Street.

Red Smith of *The New York Times*, the nation's pre-eminent sports columnist, came to Boston for the game, but he said even Harry couldn't stop Maryland. "An avalanche of meat rolled over him whenever he reached out a paw for the ball," he wrote later.

"Once, hoping either to find a receiver for a pass or just to escape total demolition, he fled back and forth, around and about, ducking and writhing for what seemed five full minutes. What looked like dozens of clamoring carnivori harried and pursued him. He was hounded back 20 or 30 yards but managed to get one Maryland delegate knocked senseless in the chase. Four yards from his own goal line, he vanished as through a trapdoor, flinging the ball away as he disappeared."

Another New York sportswriter at the game called Harry "An elusive jackrabbit pursued by hounds." On Monday, two days after the game, Donelli was left trying to defend putting Maryland on the schedule, and stumbled to explain.

"First, there's the money that a game like that brings in. You can't overlook that," he said. "And secondly, I think we ought to see these good football teams in New England. Show the fans here what is good. If New England wants that kind of a football team, they can get it. We have a team just as good at B.U. And why schedule just the teams that you can lick. If there isn't any competitive angle to this game of football, it's no good," snapped Donelli, who wasn't about to back down from any challenge.

Tatum was ecstatic about his team's play. "My defensive team played Harry just the way we planned it. We wanted to contain Agganis, keep him going back on attempted passes. Harry gives a lot of ground and I told my defensive line not to get to him too quick. When he was tackled, it was for a sizable loss," he said. And a rare exception to Harry's ability to dance away from trouble or stiffarm it away.

Fullerton said "Maybe it's not a fair observation, but it seemed to me that B.U. showed more desire to play football under Nunziato than under Agganis," and Tatum added to the immediate controversy. "Man, did you see the zip and fire that B.U. had coming out of the huddle when the little guy was in there?"

Speaking before an association of New York football writers, Tatum said "Agganis is one of the best athletes I've ever seen for coordination and ability, but there's something wrong. When he's hurt, nobody goes over to him and when he returns to the bench, nobody goes up to him."

The next day, there was an immediate response from sportswriters, and Harry's teammates were angry over the assessment. Harry never complained about injuries and Nunziato said he was showing the same Spartan stoicism this time. "We didn't know he was hurt that badly," he said of his friend and team-mate. Harry had just walked to the sidelines.

Globe sports columnist Harold Kaese said Harry had always been reluctant to pass, even in high school, and had an imperial stance that sometimes made him seem a little distant.

Nason said he had spoken to one of Harry's coaches, who didn't want to be named, and was offered an explanation. "He likes to do the unexpected. He thinks the other team expects him to pass, so he wants to cross them up by running. If he ever plays for the Cleveland Browns, Agganis will not be able to call his own plays. Then people will see what a great passer he really is, because when it comes to hitting his mark, there is nobody better."

Harry had his own explanation. "Sure they hurt me," he said, lifting his shirt to display bandaged ribs. "Four of them were on top of me. But I walked off the field ... didn't want to give them the satisfaction of knowing they'd hurt me," he said. And, he sniffed that the 1949 Maryland team that had narrowly beaten a team laden with World War II veterans on B.U., when Harry was a twenty-year-old sophomore, was better than the 1952 version.

"They wouldn't have any trouble beating this year's Maryland team ... listen, in the last half of that game with us, they didn't do too much," he said. Donelli noted that he had a half dozen other key injuries to his team too.

After the Maryland beating, Harry was still hurting, but Donelli said he nonetheless expected him to play the next week against Temple, a tough team which had upset B.U. the year before. But his ribs were still hurting, so it was up to Nunziato again, and he sparked B.U. to a 14-14 tie.

Harry didn't play the next week either, against New York University, which the Terriers barely won, 14-7, in a game which ended weirdly. With the score tied, 7-7, Titus Plomaritis, a high school star in Lowell, kicked a field goal to give B.U. a 10-7 lead.

But NYU was offsides. Donelli wanted to keep the field goal, but a visitor on the Terrier's bench, Vermont coach Ed Donnelly, said the penalty would give B.U. a first down on the one-yard line, so Donelli changed his mind and took the first down.

And, with 3:20 left, B.U. went for the touchdown, only to be assessed a 15-yard penalty for an illegal shift, and time was running out. It looked like Donelli would be stuck with one of the biggest boners of college football history, but they scored a touchdown to win.

After a glorious collegiate career, but a senior year wracked by illness and injury, it looked like the great Harry Agganis would wind up ending his playing days on the sidelines, unable to even lift the left arm that brought him acclaim.

The last game of B.U.'s schedule would be Saturday, November 22, against Villanova, and a couple of days before the game, Harry still didn't know if he would be playing or watching.

There was already conjecture about whether Harry had already played his last football game ever, as Harry said he was thinking about playing professional baseball instead. "Honestly, I don't know what I'm going to do. If I'd spent as much time thinking about my studies as I have about this matter I'd have the highest marks of all time around B.U.," he said.

It looked like an ignominious end. His body wrapped in a protective harness that left him barely able to lift his arm to the famous stance of dropping back and cocking his left-arm behind his head while his right arm pointed downfield, like Zeus throwing a thunderbolt. Harry was hobbled.

Harry had opened his collegiate career in a rainstorm so loud it seemed like the gods were howling, and he ended it the same way, in a driving rain and mist at Shibe Park in Philadelphia. But even before the game began, Harry's teammates wanted him to know how they felt about him, especially after the criticism from Tatum.

In a secret meeting in which even the coaches were barred, the players gathered and lineman Len D'Errico from Rhode Island stood and read a prepared statement of support for Harry.

Later, he wouldn't reveal the details, but said, "In my book, Harry Agganis is tops. And I'm not saying that just because he's a number one pick now,' he said.

Harry played the first half and connected on nine passes in a gallant effort. But Donelli, seeing the pain he was in, took him out after that because Villanova was running all over his offensive line again on the way to a 51-6 pounding that was so maddening that one B.U. player, Mario Moriello, couldn't stand it any more.

After being ejected for fighting, Moriello was walking along the sideline,when he saw a Villanova player who had intercepted a pass heading for an unmolested touchdown. He dashed onto the field and knocked the player cold, before bewildered referees who'd wondered from where he had come.

Even the cool Gowdy, already one of the country's most-noted broadcasters,was flabbergasted as he called the game. "Wait a minute, wait a minute! We have a penalty," he said. "I guess we have a double penalty," he said, unsure what was going on, before finally uttering in exasperation, "I don't know what's going on here."

After the game, Gowdy went into the referee's room to ask just what had happened because it occurred so quickly. The Villanova player was awarded a touchdown, but there was no replay to review.

Harry went out throwing. With Villanova players cloaked all over him, his arm in agony, he had to resort to throwing underhanded passes sometimes, line drives that went for completions. But it looked like it would be the last game for Harry.

Nunziato said he knew Harry would try to finish by playing in upcoming bowl games, the North-South game in the Orange Bowl on Miami on Christmas Day—the same place at the same day where he had led Lynn Classical to the 1946 national high school championship on Christmas Night. "I just don't like leaving on a sour note, Nunzy," he told his friend.

But then it seemed like he might not be able to. On Thanksgiving Day, Harry went back home to watch the annual Classical-English game in Lynn, and was photographed sitting in the stands watching his old school, pondering his future. He looked pensive.

PHEME ◆ FAME ◆ ΦΗΜΗ

Harry was being wooed hard by the Detroit Tigers, who'd signed his old high school football and baseball teammate, George Bullard, for a $35,000 bonus, and by the New York Yankees, and especially the Philadelphia Phillies, who thought they were ready to sign him.

But Donelli reportedly tipped off the Red Sox, and Tom Yawkey, who didn't want to lose a hometown hero whose football exploits had filled Fenway Park for him already.

"I've been torn between baseball and football for a long time, but have finally made up my mind to concentrate on baseball. I received a letter from the Browns, but it contained no mention of salary," he said.

On November 28, in a quick ceremony that surprised sportswriters wondering what he would do, Harry signed with the Red Sox for a $50,000 bonus. The son of Greek immigrants, who'd struggled through the Depression and poverty, had a major league contract.

After signing at Fenway, he left the park and couldn't be found for two hours, until he showed up at the B.U. athletic offices where a press conference was held. But first he had to drive to a Boston hotel to personally deliver the news to officials of the other teams, who tried to increase their bonus. Harry wouldn't be swayed. He had already turned down a $100,000 bonus from the Cleveland Browns to play football.

Harry couldn't resist the challenge. Although he had been a budding star at age fourteen on the sandlots and in semi-pro baseball, in college and in semi-pro leagues in New England and New York, and, as a teenager, had batted before Babe Ruth in New York, there were some skeptics who doubted he could make it in major league baseball.

"I've already proved myself in football. I don't know if I can make it in baseball, but I have the confidence that I can," he said. "I expect to be farmed out to a minor league club for a year, regardless of how well I do in the South," at the Red Sox camp in Sarasota, Florida in 1953 Spring training, he said.

"I always wanted to be a baseball player, but I never wanted to say it until my college football days were over," he said. His high school football coach, Bill Joyce, who was president of the Red Sox former Lynn Red Sox farm team, influenced him to choose baseball, Agganis said.

"I want to find out how much I have to learn. No, I probably won't make it right off, so I'd like to go to the minor leagues, if that is necessary," he said. As for being a left-hander playing in Boston, he laughed, "Are they bringing in the right field fence at Fenway?" In Lynn, the story was so big, *The Lynn Item* devoted an eight-column wide story to the signing.

The next morning, Harry dashed over to Kirios' house, bounded up the stairs and into his friend's house, past his startled mother, who was always glad to see Harry. He had a copy of the morning paper in his hand showing he had signed with the Red Sox. Harry was kiddingly delighted he had done it before Kirios had signed a professional singing contract.

"Ah-ha!" Harry laughed. "Beat you." And they both laughed.

Red Sox manager Lou Boudreau was elated at the signing, especially with Ted Williams serving in Korea. "Since the departure of Ted Williams, we haven't had a left handed batter who can drive the ball any distance. This makes it difficult for us to win games on the road," he said.

During the summer of 1952, Harry worked out at Fenway Park and hit against veteran right-handed pitching star Ellis Kinder. "That boy looks as though he might develop into a good power hitter. He seems to have good wrist action," Kinder said.

Although he wouldn't be getting his bonus money for a while, Donelli had a suggestion on how Harry could spent part of it. "Now you can send your mother to Greece," he said.

Harry looked crestfallen. He hadn't thought of that. She didn't want a new house yet, which he offered to build for her in the neighboring affluent town of Swampscott. Lynn was her home and Waterhill Street was her neighborhood, and she didn't want to leave.

The next day, he came bouncing back. She didn't want to go to Greece, he told Donelli. She wanted to stay with her family. Soon, part of the bonus would go to landscape around St. George's church in Lynn, and an offer to help set up his brothers in businesses, which they declined.

Although Harry was going to play professional baseball, he had thought about a career in coaching if it didn't work out. Donelli said he talked to Agganis near the end of his B.U. career and told him, "I don't think you'd ever make a good coach because you do everything so easily and naturally I'm afraid you'd never understand that other fellows have to learn a lot more, try a lot harder and then won't be able to do it as well, or as easily, as you do. I doubt you'd have enough patience, or maybe enough understanding of the problems of the ordinary player who's really not very good, but whom the coach has to use because that's really the way most of them are."

But Donelli said later, "I want to take it all back. I was dead wrong in your case. I've never seen more patience or understanding or a better job of teaching. If you want to coach, go ahead. You've got what it takes."

He did indeed. While sports occupied much of his time, when he wasn't studying, Harry dated a number of women in college, including Thalia Valhoulis, a young Greek-American woman from Haverhill, whose father owned a shoe factory. They dated steadily and Harry's mother adored her. One time, she brought nearly fifty pair of shoes to the house of Mary Raimo, Harry's sister.

With his B.U. football career over, Harry's collegiate career in football was over, except for upcoming appearances at the North-South game and in the Senior Bowl, which was scheduled for January 3, 1953 in Birmingham, Alabama.

Harry decided to accept the Florida game instead of going to the East-West game a day later in California because he didn't want to have to make the East coach decide on playing time between him and Holy Cross' Charlie Maloy, who won the 1952 Bulger Lowe award. Maloy's coach, Dr. Eddie Anderson, would be an assistant in the East-West game.

Before that, Harry's idol, Sammy Baugh, retired on December 9, and Harry was featured in back-to-back stories in *Sport* again, coming after a special article in *Football Stars* in which a poll of 500 sportswriters picked him the best quarterback in the country, ahead of Scarbath and Babe Parilli at Kentucky.

Donelli said he was surprised because he didn't think B.U. would get noticed.

But he said Harry was the right choice. "He is virtually a one-man team. He saves games by knocking down enemy passes and tackling dangerous runners, wins them with his slashing runs and his own supremely accurate left-handed passes," and how his punting kept opponents trapped in their own territory. But it was in the December *Sport* where Harry was really glorified. The article, by Ed Fitzgerald, had a full-page photo of Harry and others of him playing football and baseball, including as a schoolboy at Lynn Classical, detailing his illustrious career.

"One-Man Team Hits The Big-Time," it said, echoing Donelli.

He had said before too that it was easy to overlook how fast Harry was. "I had halfbacks who could run the hundred in ten flat and while Harry didn't look fast I've seen him beat them in practice. He could run, pass, kick, punt and he had everything on defense, natural instinct that only seems to come in the great ones," he'd said. With proper training, Donelli said, he thought Harry could have been an Olympic quarter-miler.

The *Sport* article said Harry had carried his team. "Without Agganis, B.U.would be a 'minor-league team,'" Fitzgerald said, not giving enough credit to the players around him, such as Kastan, who had been the Pennsylvania state athlete of the year when he came into the school as a freshman with Harry.

Joyce, his old high school coach, said Harry in high school was a better quarterback than the famed Johnny Lujack, who was at Notre Dame then.

Harry said he had a wide field of split vision which let him see each side. "When I'm going back like that, it's as though I can see everything at once. I see the fans, all worked up, I see the coaches worrying on the bench, I see the expressions on the faces of the guys trying to get me, and I see the guys on my own team trying to get out in the clear."

Kirios knew that even before then. When they were driving together he said Harry, even when he was behind the wheel, would sometimes say to Kirios, "Did you see that guy with the red jacket over there?" or point out a woman with a plaid skirt who seemed to be out of his range of vision too. And Harry was lucky too, he said, almost never failing to find a parking place close to where they were going.

The Fall articles created a furor over Harry, who had been getting sacks of mail a week at B.U. anyway. Now he was getting fan letters from across the country, and all of them, it seemed, wanted an autographed picture or more.

The articles brought him a lot of fan mail, especially from youths, across the country: the letters poured in from Iowa, Missouri, Texas, Washington, New York, Georgia, Ohio, Hawaii, Illinois, and one from Roy Hughes of Queens

Park, London, who wrote that "The only football I see of yours is in the films, but I must say it looks very thrilling."

And a youngster who didn't give his address, Bob Vander Wilk, wrote, "I would like an autograph. Are you going to be a pro player or not? I have read a lot about you."

Corky Coburn of Brady, Texas asked for an autographed photo and said, "If you were on a better team, you would really be an All-American. Anyway, you're an All-American." And Harry even got one from Jim Heilman of Maumee, Ohio, the home of Princeton's Dick Kazmaier, who had beaten Harry for the Heisman Trophy in 1951. The Heilman family lived one street away from the Kazmaier family.

Sometimes, the letters were requesting personal appearances and Harry tried to make as many as he could, although he had to turn down Joe Cerretani and the Dad's Club of Melrose on December 15, 1952, because he had already scheduled an appearance at a youth organization elsewhere.

Frank DiFabbio of Plattsburg, New York said he'd seen Harry play baseball that summer for the Malone Bakers. "If you can play football as good as you can play baseball, you're really good," he said.

Perhaps the most curious letter came from Dan Donovan of the Bronx, New York on November 8, 1952, who said he had been inspired reading about Harry, and was very much interested in the Greek Orthodox church and Greek-Americans. He knew a lot about Harry's hometown.

"I trust you belong to St. George Greek Orthodox Church in Lynn, Mass. It is a very nice church. Always be proud of your Greek people and beautiful church. I have come to love the Greek church very much even though I am not Greek." he said. "I am glad to see young Orthodox youth in the world of sports and all professions today. It helps to make the importance and beauty of Orthodox culture be realized."

Joel Myer Samuels of Revere was the most delighted though. "Boy, was I happily surprised and thrilled to get that football from the team," he wrote. "My uncle had told me someone special was coming to see me but I never expected the best football player in the nation."

He may have been, although Parilli was selected ahead of him as the quarterback on the All-American team. It looked like injuries and illness had forged an unpleasant end to a great collegiate career, although he was still in demand.

One of the letters, on November 3, was a job offer, from Nick Pappas, a cafe owner in Saskatchewan, Canada.

"We are paying good money for players like yourself and I mean good money. We could also get you a good position if you care to take one. Your money is sure, the club has money and the people connected with it are all money men. The game is going big up here." The Canadians allowed eight Americans on each team.

Pappas, who said he had won the AAU wrestling championship in 1910, tried to convince Harry to come by pointing out there was a big Greek-American community in the area. "We are well thought of by the people and share their respect as good citizens," he said.

Harry responded that he'd been drafted by the Cleveland Browns and said at that time he was still playing at B.U. "I am certainly not going to pass up any opportunity to play ball regardless of where it is if it is worth my while." He said "I would appreciate hearing from you or your club on what I can expect if I came to Canada."

Harry finished at B.U. by setting sixteen records, including:
- Yards passing in a season, 1,402 in 1951.
- Touchdown passes in a season, 15 in 1949.
- Touchdown passes in a game, 4, (Scranton, 1949, Wm. and Mary, 1952)
- Touchdown passes in a period, 3, (Wm. and Mary, 1952)
- Yardage passing in a game, 264 (Syracuse, 1952)
- Passes completed in a game, 23, (Syracuse, 1952)
- Punting average, 46.5 (1949)
- Total three-year passing yardage.
- Interceptions in a season, 15 (1949)
- Career interceptions, 27

Many of these were records in New England as well. At B.U., his passing records stood until Jim Jensen, who played four years, broke them 28 years later. Nearly fifty years after he began his career at B.U. and helped establish passing as a formidable weapon in college sports, Harry still held the school records for interceptions, and best career punting average (39.6.) He also averaged more than five yards a carry when he was running.

Harry had led the Terriers to an overall record of 17-10-1 against the likes of Syracuse, West Virginia, Maryland, William and Mary, Wichita, Oregon, Miami and College of the Pacific.

In his three varsity years, he was 226-for-418 passing for 2,930 yards and 34 touchdowns. He scored six touchdowns and averaged more than fifty minutes per game at a time when many All-Americans were one-way players. And Harry set many of his records in three years of play, without having a four-year varsity career as athletes later did.

Besides winning the Bulger Lowe award, he was named to several All-American football teams offensively and defensively and was selected to New England's Football Hall of Fame by the Boston Post. He was an All-New England selection in baseball in 1949 and 1952, and and already won the school's Athlete of the Year award for 1950, and 1952, and was a favorite to do it again at the end of the school year in 1953.

The year ended quietly for Harry. He went to the North-South game in Miami, but, with a Big Ten coach playing Big Ten players, he saw limited playing time in a 21-21 tie, although he had a long punt to the South five which showed his kicking ability.

The next day, his New England rival, Charlie Maloy, didn't play at all in the East-West game. In a few days, Harry would meet Maloy again.

ARETE ◆ **EXCELLENCE** ◆ APETH
1953

Although he had already signed a contract with the Red Sox, Harry kept an obligation to play in the North-South Senior Bowl on January 3, 1953 in Birmingham, Alabama, where he would be coached by Paul Brown, who had drafted him number one the year before to replace the legendary Otto Graham.

The game would also be a chance for Harry to again face Maryland quarterback Jack Scarbath, a rival for All-American honors, who had piloted his team to the crushing 34-7 win over B.U. a few months before in the game in which Harry had been the target of gang assaults by the Maryland team.

He was smiling and happy during workouts, posing with other All-Americans, and teammates, including B.U. lineman Len D'Errico. Harry was undaunted by the competition.

He was chosen the starting quarterback, and would kick off, punt, kick extra points and field goals and play safety, having been the consensus All-American defensive back after his career at B.U., where he had a record 27 interceptions in three varsity seasons.

Besides his uncanny ability to pick off enemy passes, Harry was almost impossible to get around in the open field, with his long, loping strides and the fearless way he would throw himself into opponents. One of B.U.'s most famous photos showed Harry leaping to defend against a pass receiver, soaring several feet off the ground like a hawk descending on a pigeon, causing the receiver to throw up his hands.

The game would be one of his greatest and would erase memories of an injury-plagued senior season that had been his most disappointing since he started playing football in the back yard of his Lynn home as a young boy. The Senior Bowl would be big-time redemption against the country's finest players.

After sensational sophomore and junior years, Harry's ability as a football player was being questioned for the first time, criticism which made those who knew him laugh in anger.

When he signed his baseball contract, there was some head-nodding he had made the right choice. But friends and college teammmates like Joe Terrasi, who played halfback at B.U. for Harry's last two seasons said Harry knew he could have dominated in football and took on baseball because he had been challenged in that game.

"People told Harry he was a football player, that his sport was football,and that he was going to play professional football," Terrasi said. "The more they told him that, the more positive he was that he was going to play baseball for the Boston Red Sox, and there was no question in his mind that he would make it," he said.

Indeed, making the major leagues in baseball was a formidable task in 1953. There were only eight teams each in the American and National Leagues and only two hundred players in each league. Most teams had three or even four top-flight pitchers and there were few relief pitchers. Players were expected to do what they were told, keep quiet, and play hurt.

Harry had the Senior Bowl to think about first. Before he headed onto the field on a windswept day, he walked over to Scarbath.

"I'm glad we're meeting again. This time it will be on more even terms," he said. Scarbath would remember the way Harry said it.

This time indeed the sides were almost even. The difference between the two great teams was Harry. He started the game the way he had as a young boy many years before when, before a sandlot football game at Barry Park in Lynn, he was allowed to tee up the ball a little closer to the opposing team after they had been told he was only a young kid.

To open that game, Harry kicked the ball deep over the heads of the receiving players. In this All-American game, he did the same, kicking the ball almost out of the end zone, causing receiving players to look behind them in wonder.

At quarterback, he dazzled, dropping back to look over the field like a general behind battle lines picking out easy openings. When cornered, he danced away lithely, leaving All-American defenders to come up with armsful of air and disbelief.

In the first period, after Scarbath had been trapped for a safety, and after a fumble was recovered on the South 21, Harry threw a 14-yard pass to Gene Gedman of Indiana to set up a touchdown run by Fred Bruney of Ohio State.

In the second period, Harry threw an 11-yard touchdown pass to Ernie Stockert of UCLA to give the North a 14-0 lead at halftime. He had totally outplayed Scarbath. In the third period, Harry hit Gedman again, for a 14-yard scoring pass, and then kicked the extra point to put the North up 21-0.

In the fourth period, Harry engineered a 33-yard scoring drive and kicked another extra point. Watching helplessly for the South was Dick Modzelewski, the All-American from Maryland who led the gang tackles on Harry a couple of months before.

While the crowd of 15,000 was predominantly from the South, they were cheering a Northern boy with an ethnic name. Harry was 9-for-17 passing and had been an elusive runner. He kicked extra points—with Charlie Maloy of Holy Cross as his holder—and deliberately punted one kick out of bounds at the South 5-yard line to pin them down, had a 68-yard punt and kicked for 10 yards more than his counterparts, despite a strong headwind. He also intercepted two passes and made 14 tackles.

"That Agganis is all over the place," said an amazed Red Barber, who was calling the game, won by the North 28-13. Barber was the premier announcer for college football's greatest games in an era when the sport dominated the media.

He had an easy-going, almost laconic style that was more philosophical than sensation, and was not given to gushing. But he found himself yelling like a rooting fan at Harry's play.

He interrupted his play-by-play often to talk about Harry. At one point, Harry pitched off to a halfback who was about to be trapped for a loss. But he threw to a second back who was about to be stopped too when Harry, sensing something behind him, whirled and threw a block which permitted the ball carrier to make a substantial gain.

"Agganis has a football instinct. He just seems to know what to do even without looking," Barber said. "It looks like the Red Sox are going to lose a ballplayer. Paul Brown is over there on the bench drooling."

Football legend Red Grange, "The Galloping Ghost" from Illinois was as awed as everyone else, especially at the ease with which Harry had dominated some of the greatest college players in the country.

"He's the best college football player I've seen this year. He can pass. He can run. He can kick. He is tremendous on defense. What more can you ask of any football player?"

New York Sports Editor Stanley Woodward was impressed too, calling Harry "The greatest collegiate player I have ever seen." Fred Russell of *The Nashville Banner* wrote that "Agganis proved his greatness on the field." Harry so dominated the game that the sportswriters scrapped their voting and just nodded their heads in acclimation in naming him the Most Valuable Player.

He again became the most highly sought pro prospect in the country, even with the Red Sox contract in his hand. Some quipped the game should have been called "The Harry Agganis Bowl" because of his dominance. Brown wanted him even more now.

As they left the field, Brown made a last entreaty to Harry.

"You can be my quarterback any time you want," he said.

"Even ahead of Otto Graham?" Harry laughed. It was a joke, for Graham was considered one of the greatest quarterbacks ever to play professional football, and had been a great two-sport athlete himself, also playing basketball.

Brown wasn't kidding.

"Yes," he said.

It was Harry's last competitive football game ever. He walked away from the Browns and a $100,000 bonus, a fortune at a time when established major league baseball players were paid $18,000 a year in many cases. To Harry, the issue of making it in professional baseball was more important than money.

Red Sox Manager Joe Cronin was counting on Harry's temperament as much as his ability. "Harry's already had plenty of plaudits and plenty of pressure on him. He's been in tight spots in front of large crowds in football and it hasn't bothered him. He's got that advantange starting out in major league baseball," Cronin said.

But there was more to do before he would even get to Spring training. Acclaimed as one of the greatest athletes in college history, there were clamorings for his time. Still humble, and even a bit shy, Harry was reluctant to have so much attention still. But, at the end of January, 1953 there came a night when even he would be overwhelmed with awards.

The B.U. Varsity Club honored Harry at a dinner at the Hotel Continental in Cambridge where he and E. Ray Speare, a former football star, captain of the 1892 B.U. football team, and a boxer and wrestler, were going to be the first inductees into the school's athletic Hall of Fame.

Harry was also supposed to receive an automobile and gifts from his friends. At the same time,he would receive a crown, an olive wreath dipped in silver, a special gift from Queen Frederika of Greece.

People were sitting in wooden chairs, and across the stage where the head table was located was a B.U. banner and two pictures in front of the stage: one of Speare and another of Harry. B.U. President Harold Case, who had grown close to Harry, was there too.

So was Harry's old marketing professor, John Alevizos, and a young priest from the Greek Orthodox Cathedral in Boston, Rev. James Coucouzis, with whom Harry had become friendly. Curt Gowdy, who had broadcast some of Harry's B.U. games, was the master of ceremonies.

For America's most-honored schoolboy athlete, and now a collegiate star, this evening was the pinnacle of achievement. The olive crown, the highest honor given to the victors in the Olympic games of ancient days, was sent by the Queen to the Greek Consul-General in Boston, Basil Calevras, who placed it on Harry's brow. He had achieved the Greek ideal of *arete*, which meant excellence, virture, skill, prowess, valor, nobility, and was the goal of every citizen in ancient Greece.

And Harry had something to give back. He declined the car and gifts, amounting to $4,000, which were going to be presented from B.U., and by Tom Pappas, whose family had steered Harry to B.U. With Case looking on, Harry asked the cash equivalent be used to set up a scholarship for Greek-American students whose families could not afford to send them to B.U.

"Because while I was a student at Boston University, several students of the Orthodox faith had to leave school because of lack of finances. I suppose if they were athletes like myself, they may have been able to stay on and get their education, so, please take these gifts you have in mind and establish a fund to help needy and deserving boys and girls of the Greek Orthodox faith so that this sort of thing will not happen again," he said.

The scholarship fund was set up, headed by Alevizos and James Henes, who were to help the Greek-American community build it to $10,000. Harry's Number 33 was retired by B.U. too. He had been elected a member of the Scarlet Key at B.U., for outstanding work in student activities, and that night gave out the Harry Agganis Award to the outstanding schoolboy athlete, Billy Donlan of B.C. High.

But Harry wasn't through giving back to his community yet.

Two weeks later, on February 13, he was honored at a farewell dinner given by the Logganiko Society, the group named for his parents' village of Logganiko in Sparta, many of whose families had come to settle in the North Shore area of Boston, around Lynn, Peabody, Swampscott, Danvers, Beverly, and Ipswich.

Tickets for the dinner at the Hotel Edison, where Notre Dame coach Frank Leahy had tried to recruit Harry, were five dollars and the society wanted to present Harry with $1,000, but Harry turned it down again. He asked instead the donation go to the village of Logganiko to buy soccer equipment for the children there, so they could play sports too.

It was a festive night for friends and family and exuberant celebration, and Harry was in his element. "Take the money and send it to Greece to the village for them to build an athletic field and to buy uniforms for the soccer team," he said.

It was a room full of people like Harry and his family: humble immigrants who had worked hard to improve their lives and for their children, and they appreciated what Harry had done to make Greek-Americans proud.

It was a time when there was still discrimination against Greeks and other immigrants from Mediterranean countries, but Harry, as it was often said by his own people, "Helped put us on the map."

Then there was dancing, yells of "OPA!" as men and women with their arms around each other in a line circling around the room, kicking up their heels in the rhythms of the traditional Greek dances like the *kalamatiano*, and the proud *tsamiko*, with clarinets clapping a beat.

It was a joyous occasion for the families from Logganiko. Harry had a lot of his family there, including cousins from his father's side, and from the Pappalimberis family, from Harry's mother's side.

But Spring training was coming up fast now, and Harry would have to make the team before he could sign a major league contract. Before he left, he won the award as B.U.'s Athlete of the Year for 1953, for the third time in his career there.

ELPIS   ◆   HOPE   ◆   ΕΛΠΙΣ

Billy Consolo was a $60,000 bonus baby for the Boston Red Sox when he signed early in 1953 as an infielder who had been the two-time California player of the year in baseball, and team officials hoped he would be part of a new youth movement that would include Harry and Ted Lepcio, Harry's old teammate from the Maine Millionaires.

Since the heartbreak of losing the World Series in 1946 to the St. Louis Cardinals, the Red Sox had been in a cycle of disappointment and failure with their old guard.

Lepcio got his shot in 1952 when Bobby Doerr suddenly retired, but he had been moving around as a utility infielder. Under a change in the rules about giving bonuses, Consolo would have to stay with the Red Sox for two years, but Harry, unless he had a spectacular Spring, could be farmed out to the minor leagues.

And he would have a tough time making the team because Dick Gernert, the big right-handed power hitter whose swing was made for the short left-field distance at Fenway, seemed ensconced in the job, even if he was nervous about all the attention that was given to Harry.

137

Consolo was worried about the rule change that meant he would stay with the team no matter how he performed. "You took the spot of a player. That was a difficult rule," he said.

When he showed up at the Hotel John Ringling in Sarasota, Florida for Spring training, Consolo asked scout Joe Stephenson, who had signed him, who his roommate would be.

"You're rooming with the kid they just signed, Harry Agganis," said Stephenson.

Consolo, who didn't know anything about football or Harry's great career at B.U., said "Who's Harry Agganis?"

"He's a quarterback from Boston University," Stephenson said.

Consolo, a two-time athlete of the year in California, where he played baseball and track in high school, looked at Stephenson and nodded. He figured Harry was probably about his size, 5'10" and 175 pounds. He went up stairs to the room and knocked on the door.

"Come in," he heard a voice say. Consolo, nineteen, just out of high school and carrying some new bags his parents had given him, stepped into the tiny room and sat on a bed. Harry was in the bathroom shaving.

"I'll be right out," Harry said.

A moment later, the door to the bathroom opened and out stepped Harry, wearing boxer shorts. Consolo almost fell back on the bed at what he saw. Harry was twenty-four by now, an ex-Marine with a lot more sports experience, and that toned 6'2", 200 pound body.

"He had a body like a Greek god," Consolo remembered. "He was rippling all over the place and he was big, he looked like he weighed 225 pounds. I said 'Oh my God. He's a rookie?'" Consolo went to the closet, only to find Harry had a complete wardrobe, with shoes to match.

"He was really a finished man," Consolo said.

They became immediate friends. Harry had grown up with and played with a lot of Italian friends, like Silvio Cella, Frank Giuliano, Frank Luciano and Mario Moriello at B.U. More importantly for Consolo, Harry seemed to know everyone, even at the Spring Training camp, where a lot of his followers had come to watch the Red Sox, and him.

"I was a high school kid and he was a man. He took me under his wing," he said. Harry brought Consolo to restaurants, where it seemed someone was always ready to pick up Harry's tab, just like in his B.U. days when he always had nice new clothes and shoes, both of which he often passed on to his family and friends instead of keeping.

"He knew everybody. He could have run for Mayor of Massachusetts. He was a complete hero," said Consolo. When they weren't out at restaurants they often ate in the hotel dining room where Harry was a star attraction, startling for a rookie in a baseball camp where veterans expected newcomers to be awed.

"He had a lot of pressure on him as a kid from Massachusetts. We went to dinner every day and night at the hotel. He'd dress up and he looked like he just got out from Miami. He had white shoes and knew everybody. He was exciting to be around," said Consolo.

Teammates said the respect for Harry came not only because of his reputation, but because of his personality, his willingness to listen and respect his teammates and coaches, and the way he ceaselessly worked at perfecting his game.

"He worked so hard you can't believe what he used to do," said Consolo. "Harry was a workhorse. He was the first guy on the field with ground balls and he never quit. He gave it his all, and he played the same way," said Consolo.

Gernert saw the same thing. On February 28 he said "This Agganis looks like a great athlete but until someone decides he's the better man I'm the number one first baseman on this club." Gernert, a well-respected athlete himself, saw too that Harry had the spark and charisma that few people possess.

"I just want to get a few things straight. I've heard and read plenty about Harry's hustle, ability and spark and now I've seen it the past few days. Harry appears to have the strange thing called color that attracts attention. I guess I just haven't got it. But don't think people aren't aware of me on the field that I'm not hustling in my own relaxed way," Gernert told *Boston Herald* sports editor Ed Costello.

Gernert pointed out that in 1952, he had 67 runs batted in, and 19 home runs, strong numbers for a first baseman.

At the same time, the Cleveland Browns were still trying to get Harry to change his mind and play football. There were reports Paul Brown, desperate to keep his dynasty going, had sent scouts down to check Harry's progress. One fan said he saw a scout climb out on a palm tree to spy on Harry.

Brown got news that it looked like Harry was going to make the major leagues, discouraging him from thinking he could eventually sign him. In response to a letter he had received from Jim Angelos, a young lawyer in Fitchburg, Massachusetts, who was a fan of Harry's, Brown sent back a letter stating he hoped Harry would sign with the Browns.

But Harry was dissuading the Browns and he was emphasizing his concentration on baseball. "I have finally made up my mind to concentrate on baseball. I received a letter from the Browns, but it contained no mention of salary," he said.

Buff Donelli was telling reporters Harry would have been the perfect man to keep the Browns dynasty going. "Harry would have been much better in professional football than in college. He would have been greater than Otto Graham because he could pass as well, and he is faster," he said.

Finally, Brown and the Browns gave up, thinking Harry would not play football. In a major deal, involving fifteen players, they traded his rights to the Baltimore Colts. Harry still didn't tell anyone what he was really thinking about professional football. Except with his family and closest friends, he rarely revealed his deepest feelings.

PHILIA ◆ FRIENDSHIP ◆ ΦΙΛΙΑ

Donelli remained close to his favorite player. On March 5, he sent Harry a letter and enclosed a sheet of stationery, a clue for a reply. "I'm sorry I couldn't enclose a pencil, but maybe you can borrow one from one of the fellows," he joked.

Harry had only been in camp a short time but already was causing a flurry of notice in reports back in the Boston newspapers. "The papers have been reading very well up here about your work," wrote Donelli, who joked he could give Harry some tips on fielding and hitting too. He apologized for not making Harry's going-away party because his mother was ill.

Donelli wrote the press was treating him well. Indeed. As one sports writer noted, "BU's Harry Agganis has become the talk of the camp." Another noted that "If the fans aren't arguing his possibilities to stick with the Red Sox this year, they're digging into his football background."

There was another inescapable element about Harry too. Besides the killer smile and wining personality, he had a gorgeous, well-toned body that made him irresistible to women. Sportswriter Bill Cunningham of *The Boston Herald*, said Harry and Consolo were turning heads off the field.

"They're good looking boys too. If this were a beauty contest instead of a baseball camp, Agganis would be a candidate for top honors. Both lads and *Herald* sports editor Ed Costello were in my room when the Remsens (fans from the Boston area) and my madam arrived from New Orleans late this afternoon and both ladies remarked in a large way upon the handsome phizz and physique of the celebrated Golden Greek," Cunningham said.

Although he was still technically a rookie, Harry attracted other players to his room where he and Consolo would talk with veterans easily and naturally. One night too, a television set in the hotel lobby didn't work right, upsetting some elderly guests who were trying to watch the circus. Harry fixed the TV and smiled. He had some new fans.

Despite the constant attention, he remained unflappable. Back home in Boston and Lynn, his fans read the papers voraciously and listened intently on radio, the same way they had when "The Golden Greek" was the conquering athletic hero on the home fields.

He still had some convincing to do. One sportswriter, Walter Foley, sounded a contrary note as the Agganis publicity built. "It makes good reading, I'll admit, to pick up the morning paper and see flashy headlines about how Harry Agganis bashed a few pills over the distant barrier," he wrote.

He added later in the article that "The other day I picked up a Boston newspaper and was reading an article written by one of our top-notch writers and a good friend of mine, and before I got into it very far I started asking myself how much the Red Sox were paying him on the side to keep them in the limelight. He all but had Dick Gernert's bags packed and labeled 'Louisville' and had handed the first base job to Harry Agganis. It's a wonderful thing to get behind the hometown boy solidly—but there's such a thing as overplaying one's hand and my personal opinion is that Harry Agganis stands as much of a chance as grabbing that first base job away from Gernert as a snowball would in h—. Fenway Park was made for the likes of Gernert, not Agganis..."

Harry had an influential fan in Cunningham who had a lot of power in his column. "Everybody has been impressed with two things about Agganis. The first is his poise. 'He's a pro,'" they say. "He's got the look and the motions.' The other is what the trade calls his hustle. He's moving all the time, they tell you. He's never still. He's never late for practice and he never coasts in any of it," Cunningham said.

And, most importantly, he said, Harry had impressed the most important person of all in the Red Sox camp, someone even more critical than Manager Lou Boudreau.

"It appears that young Mr. Agganis wears the blessing of Ted Williams and, in a way, Williams may have tried to leave him to the Red Sox as his heritage." Harry and Ted had met before at the Sportsman's Show in Boston, and in Miami when Williams was on leave from the Marines, where he was serving in Korea as a fighter pilot, the same duty he had done in World War II..

Cunningham wrote "Williams was much interested in Agganis and his problem of trying to make the majors straight from college, and he gave the young man what amounted to an old coach's lecture on what to expect and what to do. He told Agganis to hustle every minute he's in uniform, to bear down all the way, to make the most of every minute ... Agganis must have taken the departed star's advice, or maybe he naturally always did hustle. At any rate, he's hustling now. He's a big boy with a lot of power, and judging from what I saw today, he's easy and natural around first base. The percentages figure to be heavily against him, but at least they haven't gotten him down."

While he wasn't a bona fide major leaguer yet, there was a harbinger of what was to come when the Louisville Slugger company came out with the Harry Agganis signature bat, a 38-ounce model that had a Babe Ruth handle, a

Chick Hafey knob and a Vern Stephens barrel. The way it was swung though was all Agganis, a hard, stiff swing of powerful shoulders that rolled through a ball.

The Red Sox were impressed by his poise, but columnist Gerry Hern expected it. "Why shouldn't he. He's been a star, a headline attraction and center of attention ever since he was in high school. This is all old stuff to him."

With Harry catching everyone's eye, Gernert was sounding anxious, despite Boudreau's constant couching. After the first ten days of training, Boudreau said it appeared Harry was already ahead of the veteran. "Harry is a better fielding first baseman than Gernert was at this time last year ... the only question on Agganis is his hitting. He has all the life and spark anyone would want. He is tireless in his work and he looks as if he might be able to hit. As yet he has taken it easy at the plate, just concentrating on timing, and he has looked good."

Harry hit a pair of tremendous home runs off George Susce in a rookie camp. Harry was so pleased that when asked about pro football, he said "Look. I'm a baseball player. I don't even want to talk football. I never said it before, but I always liked baseball better than football. I was recognized in sports as a baseball player before I ever got a nod as a football player. I don't want to think about anything else now but playing baseball and making this team. This is the team I want to be with and this is the sport I want to play. Let's forget about the football, okay?"

In batting practice, Harry didn't try to show off. "I'm just trying to meet the ball. I'm not trying for distance. I want to be sure of my timing before I try for the long ball. There's another reason too," he added with a grin. "I've had a pair of pretty tender hands. I've been bothered with blisters until the last couple of days but I guess I'm getting tough. They're all right now."

In his first game against another team, Harry got to bat for the first time in the twelfth inning of a game against the St. Louis Cardinals on March 11. This was the team of Stan Musial, who, with Lou Gehrig, was the first baseman against which all others had been measured for decades.

With two out and nobody on, Harry spanked a hard single and scored on a triple to lead the Sox to a 5-3 run. Cards Manager Eddie Stanky wasn't surprised. "I saw Agganis really dominate that Senior Bowl," he said.

Harry posed with Haywood Sullivan, a football star from the University of Florida. On the team too was Jackie Jensen, "The Golden Boy" of California, who had been a star in the Rose Bowl and was a feared hitter and runner. The Red Sox had three former college football stars, and Jensen signed a picture to Harry: "From one gridder to another."

Donelli knew Harry's persistence would pay off, and the way he said Harry always followed the Greek philosophy of Socrates that "An unexamined life is not worth living." Once, when he asked Harry do so something, Harry asked why.

"What do you mean why?" Donelli snapped.

"I've got to have a reason for everything I do," Harry said.

Donelli continued to follow Harry's progress closely. On March 18, he wrote him that that "Everybody's watching you very closely and listening with an ear to every game. I'll say for Curt Gowdy, he keeps everybody posted very well when you're coming up to bat and just what you are doing," he said.

Gowdy was an important ally for a rookie because he was the voice of the Red Sox. But he had called the B.U. football games too and seen Harry's Spartan stance on the field, and was even more impressed with Harry's easy going manner and the way he wasn't intimidated.

Gowdy had come to Boston in 1951 to do baseball and was asked to do the B.U. football games, an assignment he didn't relish at first because he had been doing Oklahoma football, which was among the powerhouses in the country then. But then he met Donelli, and Harry.

"I was very impressed with Harry as a football player. Paul Brown doesn't draft you number one unless you are good. He was a terrific kid and always had a great smile on his face," said Gowdy.

After Harry signed with the Red Sox, Gowdy knew he had someone who could put color into the game, and a role model as well for the community and fans. "He had a great personality. My wife was very fond of him and said he always had such a nice smile on his face. He was a smooth, high class guy."

Gowdy said when Harry first came up with the Sox in 1953, he had two weaknesses at bat. "A high fast ball got him. I remember Pinky Higgins telling me it was all that pounding he took in football up in his chest and shoulders, and he had trouble picking up a low throw at first base. But he would go out and practice at first for hours picking up low throws. And he kept working on his hitting. He was one of the greatest athletes New England ever had and I grew very close to him," he said. Gowdy's word was gospel for Sox fans.

But the Sox, with Consolo and Lepcio already signed as bonus babies, had few roster spots open, even with Harry's outstanding performance. He played in thirteen Spring games and hit .243, including playing six games in the outfield.

In a letter to Donelli, he even acknowledged some trepidation, not about his own performance. "Well coach, I don't feel too good today, since Gernert hit two home runs. But to me, that's a battle I like. Believe me, I've been playing better ball. I'm leading the club in hitting and hustling as usual," he said.

Harry said he wasn't sure when, but felt he would become the regular first baseman. "But not until I hit 1.000," he said, knowing how much was expected of him. "I have to do twice as much as my competitor to even be considered. But

I'll make it, if it takes the last act of Congress to do it," he said.

The Sox decided to send him to Louisville, a Triple-A franchise in the American Association. It was a sign of their confidence in him, although his former professor at B.U., John Alevizos, said Harry should have gone straight up to the majors.

Harry was still worrying about his friends and family too. Donelli's mother had passed away and Harry quickly wrote back a sympathy letter. "I just wish I could do something to comfort you or to be of any assistance at a time like this," he said.

He asked Donelli if he saw the story about the Colts acquiring his rights, and told him "I just hope I improve in my baseball so I can stay with the Red Sox. If I don't do it this year, I'll do it next year," he said.

On April 1, Donelli wrote him a letter of encouragement and advice, which followed Harry's letter of sympathy on the death of Donelli's mother. "I have been following you as closely as possible and hope things are going well with you. Don't let this trip to Louisville bother you. You have always been big enough to stand up to any reverses, and I don't expect you to do any differently at this time."

"Don't express any ill feelings about going to Louisville. As you know, some of these newspapermen will make a lot out of nothing, as a few have tried to do already," he cautioned, worried about the potential for backlash about a big home town hero trying to make it big in the big leagues.

About the same time, Harry wrote Alevizos, "I really miss all of you at the university. I wish I could be around and discuss matters over a cup of coffee like we used to do in the cafeteria," Harry wrote. He asked about his friends too, including his Lynn classmate, Nick Sentas.

"Good Greek boys never fail," Harry wrote in jest, adding in Greek, "*O Theos eene mazi sou*," which means "God is with you." He thanked Alevizos for that phrase and kidded that Alevizos probably didn't think Harry knew what it meant.

"Not bad for a rookie. I didn't ask anyone what it meant either. Since there aren't too many Greek people here in Deland, how could I?" he asked.

Harry said he thought he was doing well with the Red Sox, but said Boudreau and club officials "thought it would be best if I would go to the minors and play baseball, rather than sit on the bench and play once in a while." Harry was not deterred.

"I feel in my heart that I can make the grade. It really is too bad that I couldn't make the Boston trip, just so I could see my mother," he wrote.

"Well," he added, "that's life. As you say again, '*Apo kathe kako erhete to kalo*,' or 'Out of something bad, something good will come.'"

And, as Harry added about the designation to Louisville, "I'm hoping something good will come from it."

Typically, when the Red Sox had told him, he didn't gripe. "I don't mind going because I know I'll be playing regularly to make good and it didn't look like I'd be able to play regularly on the Red Sox right now."

Out of something bad, he knew, something good would come.

TAPEENOTES ◆ HUMILITY ◆ ΤΑΠΕΙΝΟΤΗΣ

Louisville had never seen a player quite like Harry Agganis. The team had several players who would become major leaguers, like left-handed pitcher Frank Baumann and right-handed pitcher Ike DeLock. But Harry came in with the kind of charisma seen in the big leagues.

He was handsome, dashing, but with the kind of politeness and manners Southerners liked. That endeared him to his teammates and club officials too, but especially to the flocks of women that soon came to the park in waves.

DeLock said "He was a popular guy with the players, and with the girls as well. But he realized he was a babe-in-arms, so to speak, because there were some ballplayers in that league and some guys on that club who were major leaguers, and he was just an average player when he came down, although he had talent."

Harry started off like he would be the MVP of the league. In 1953, Triple-A ball was not far removed from the major leagues and many of the minor league clubs were stocked with major leaguers, and those who soon would be.

At Indianapolis, a young infielder named Don Zimmer got off to a tremendous start with his slugging, and Harry's competition for honors included Bill "Moose" Skowron, with whom he had played in the Hearst All-Star game at the Polo Grounds in 1947.

In his first six games with 24 at bats, Harry had 10 hits, including a homer and eight extra base hits and 10 RBIs. He hit safely in 20 of his first 23 games and by May 13, he was hitting .389 after flirting with .400.

Uncharacteristically, Harry talked with his roommate Joe Tanner, a Texas star, about his hitting streak—and then the next game went hitless, prompting him to stop talking about hitting. And hitting against Triple-A pitching was tougher than the semi-pro and college pitchers he had been facing.

"In college, sometimes you'd go up to the plate sort of mechanically and wouldn't give too much thought to it. I find myself now saying to myself up there at the plate 'You got to fight. You got to fight. It seems to do something to you. It seems to work," he told a sportswriter, before quickly veering off with "But say, let's talk about something else.'"

One of Harry's closest boyhood friends, Mike Frangos from Lynn, was

145

stationed at nearby Ft. Knox, where he was recuperating from a serious auto accident. He came to the park often and said Harry's personality took over the place. "He was always laughing and tossing the ball around," and getting the crowd involved, he said.

Frangos was used to seeing adulation poured on his friend, but even he was amazed at the attention Harry was getting in the South. "They loved Harry in Louisville, they packed the stadium every game," he said. One day, Harry was photographed shaking Frangos' hand while he was sitting in the stands.

Harry loved to kid around with his friend, and used to mimic one of his favorite comics, Jimmy Durante, when Harry was talking to Frangos. "Hi, howaya," he'd say, trying to make his voice sound like Durante's gravely big-nosed bite. They used to sometimes hang around with Delock and another team-mate, Al Richter. Sometimes, they'd go to Ft. Knox, and would go to the Greek Orthodox church in Louisville to worship.

In late May, the Red Sox asked Harry to accompany the scout who had signed him, Neil Mahoney, to Newburyport, Massachusetts to try to sign a high school phenom, another Greek-American, Angelo "Junior" Dagres, who was a basketball star who averaged 36 points a game, and who had hit .679 in baseball that Spring. A lot of teams were after him, but the Sox thought they had an ace in Harry.

Although they had asked his dad, George, not to let anyone know Harry was coming, word got out quickly and neighbors around the four-family Dagres house came by, including Rabbi Yellin, who lived next door, and Father Crispo from the Roman Catholic church, and Father Papadimitrios from the Greek church.

Inside, in front of Mahoney, Harry urged Dagres to sign with the Red Sox, and talked about the advantages of being near home and family. The Red Sox wanted to assign him to Louisville, where Harry was starring.

But, as they left and Mahoney had walked down a flight of stairs to his car, Harry turned back to Dagres' father, outside of his son's hearing, and said, "*Pes to pethee, na pai sto skoleeo ke that paree pio pola lepta.*" It meant, "Tell the kid to go to school and he'll get more money."

The team had offered Dagres only a $6,000 bonus and Harry thought his education was important. He had told his father, in Greek, to tell his son, "Go to school and you'll sign for even more money." Dagres went to the University of Rhode Island instead of signing. His dad hadn't told him what Harry had said.

Back at B.U., Harry's former backup at quarterback, Tom Gastall, who was a two-sport star in football and baseball, was in some trouble.

He had been involved in a water-throwing incident after some horseplay at his dormitory and fined twenty-five dollars, and admonished by a disciplinary committee. "Your case will be dealt with severely," if there is a recurrence, said

Elsbeth Melville, secretary of the disciplinary committee.

It was a minor incident, but even tomfoolery was taken seriously in 1953. Gastall wrote Donelli from his Fall River home asking for help. Donelli paid for it out of his own pocket, upbraided him, and told him to repay it.

"You know the rules and regulations down there, and regardless of how much that would be an imposition on you, I think that, by golly, it's your problem and you ought to take care of it." Even star athletes weren't coddled on campus. Gastall repaid the money, but complained the committee had acted too harshly over a minor incident.

In Louisville, despite Harry's quick start, the rumors about pro football wouldn't abate. Boston sportswriter Tap Goodenough wrote there was a chance Harry would still shift to pro football, especially since the Colts had acquired his rights and were desperate for a quarterback.

A report in *The New York Times* said Harry and his Louisville fans were enamored of each other. "The people of Louisville have the highest regard for Harry and have taken him into their hearts. Over the weekend in Louisville, the folks talked about Agganis as much as Native Dancer," the champion race horse, the paper said.

A headline soon appeared in Louisville calling Harry "The Lion of Louisville." He was the subject of a four-part series in the *Louisville Times*. Attendance was soaring, and Harry was everywhere in the town when he wasn't playing ball. But he adhered to the advice Donelli had given him earlier in the year, counseling him not to show too much braggadoccio.

Even the apartment he shared with Tanner was clean and orderly and he was pictured doing some cooking. His teammates called him "Bananas," for a reason they didn't explain.

Eddie Lyons, a veteran minor leaguer who played with the Washington Senators, described him as exceedingly modest. "He never says anything unless you drag it out of him. He's always concentrating on his hitting." It sounded like what Harry's brother-in-law Tony Raimo had said about him, that "He never knocked anybody. If we tried, he'd always stop us."

The Red Sox, floundering again, were watching as well, especially after one early game when Harry hit a pair of long home runs and Louisville coach Mike "Pinky" Higgins started praising him.

Mahoney, who'd scouted Harry back in 1946 when he was a seventeen-year-old schoolboy starring in high school all-star games, said it was the uncharacteristic incident while Harry was playing for Malone, New York in the Northern League that provided further impetus for success.

In Louisville, watching Harry tear up Triple-A pitching, Mahoney told sportswriters about that time he had reprimanded Harry for taking it easy. "Maybe he learned something that day. I like to think maybe I helped him with that scolding. He's not stopped hustling since," said Mahoney. Harry didn't forget.

Before one game at Louisville, where Mahoney was watching, Harry smiled at him and said "I'm getting good wood on the ball. I'll show you. I'll hit one out for you."

And he did. Harry stroked a long home run and as he trotted around the bases, paused a little to glance over at Mahoney and give him an "I told you so look." Mahoney smiled back.

In 1946, when Harry was playing semi-pro with the Lynn Frasers, Mahoney said he was startled at the young man's poise and ability. "Harry fitted in even then. At sixteen or seventeen he could hit the ball well and hit it long. We scouts look for a lot of things in a young ball player ... I leaned to Agganis, over some who looked better because of his attitude, determination. You just couldn't keep him out of prominence. Agganis will fight you, he's always in there fighting," Mahoney said.

He had seen Harry on leave from the Marines in 1950 too, at Fenway Park when he was in a hitting contest with some of the Boston Braves. Harry hit three home runs into the bullpen. "He fought them," Mahoney said of the major leaguers. "He was simply determined to out-hit them."

"He was as cocky a kid as I've ever met, but without being overbearingly conceited," he said. For all his stardom and ability, Harry was forever humble, an attribute that was as foremost in his personality as the smile that never stopped. And he was tearing up the league with his bat, too, and was a leading candidate to be the most valuable player.

Zimmer suffered a serious beaning in July, when he had more than 20 home runs, but his start would carry him to the MVP of the league, by one vote over Harry, who would play every inning of all 155 games for the Colonels. Attendance rose from 132,000 the previous year to 175,000.

Harry finished the season at .281 with 111 RBIs and 23 home runs, and nine triples. He was selected by *Look Magazine* to the American Association All-Star team as the outstanding first baseman. On September 25, he was asked if he thought he would be brought up to Boston in 1954. "The chances depend entirely upon the judgment of the Red Sox, and I am sure they know what they are doing," he said.

Meanwhile, scout Ted McGrew, who saw the American Association play-offs in which the Colonels were eliminated by the Braves' Toledo Farmers, said Harry was the best player in the series. "He was great. He hit well and fielded well. He can hardly miss being a regular in 1954."

DeLock, who was called up to the Red Sox earlier in 1953, said he knew Harry would make the big time. "He was an excellent Triple-A ballplayer. When they have to make the extra step, a lot of them don't make it, but he did. He was a hard worker, he was good fielder, and he was fast with good hands."

Richter, who played for the Lynn Red Sox in 1947, said "Nothing seemed to bother him. He had a big reputation as an athlete, especially in football, when he came to Louisville. But there was nothing stuffy about the guy. He had that certain kind of confidence who inspired others who played with him.'"

"Even on a bad day, when things weren't breaking just right for him, he just kept smiling. He shrugged off all his troubles. I marveled at the way he would come up smiling." He said. "He looked as if he had four or five years experience. Hit hit the long ball and he was always good in the clutch.

Colonels President Eddie Doberty said "I never saw a first year boy do so well in Triple-A. He's a high-grade kid with his first thoughts for his mother. No lollygagger and he doesn't read his press notices. His cap was too big for him when he got here and it was the same size when he left. When you get a kid like that, you know you have a pro."

After the season ended, Harry came back to Lynn to be with his family, and work as an assistant coach for his alma mater. Another assistant was Charlie Maloy, the former Holy Cross star quarterback who came to law school at B.U.

In the first game of the year, against Syracuse in New York, the first tragedy affecting Harry's B.U. teams struck.

His former center, John Pappas, grandson of an Albanian Orthodox priest, was excited about playing. He was a big, tough 220-pounder who was also a shotputter on the school track team. He loved football, and his father, a champion wrestler, didn't want him wrestling because he thought it was too dangerous.

As Johny headed into the game, he turned to his parents and said "This is my last year—to do or die."

During the game, he suffered a head injury and was taken to a hospital, where he fell into unconsciousness and died before his parents could see him.

Harry went out to Worcester and was a pallbearer. Pappas' mother thanked him. She would see Harry again later.

MOIRA ◆ **FATE** ◆ MOIPA
1954

In January, Harry told *Boston Traveler* Sports Editor Arthur Siegel he thought this was the year he'd make the big leagues. "I feel I belong up here. I've worked hard for it. I put in that year with Louisville and I had trouble getting going. But I worked hard. I put in an awful lot of work before the games. I knew I belonged, but I had to prove I could belong. Honestly, I don't see how a player can just sit back and do nothing when things aren't going right," he said earnestly.

"I've found," he said, "I could cure troubles with work."

"I can make the plays. There were reasons why things went wrong, but I won't name them because they may sound like alibis. I know there is a place for me on the Red Sox and I'll make it," he said.

Harry said he was going South early, at his own expense. "All I want is a chance to work out. Trying to get in shape here in the North isn't enough. You can't do the right kind of work," he said.

"I'll work and prove that I belong on first base. I don't care who will be battling me for the job. I belong as a starting player. I'll make it."

Harry decided to fly to Spring training. He had narrowly missed winning the Most Valuable Player award in 1953 in Louisville, where his personality and charm had him touted as "The Lion of Louisville."

It was an especially apt description because, to the Spartans, *Leonidas*, which means lion in Greek, was the king who had taken three hundred Spartans to the Pass of Thermopylae in 480 B.C. and held off the entire Persian Army for days. He represented the epitome of courage and fearlessness.

On February 6, Harry was honored at a dinner at the Brown Hotel in Louisville, where he was named the Number One Louisville Colonel as the team's most valuable player.

At the head table too was Red Sox General Manager Joe Cronin, Lefty Gomez, Pee Wee Reese and Cincinnati Reds outfielder Gus Bell, who was being honored. While he was back in Louisville, Harry went over to the University of Kentucky to watch his old Classical basketball teammate, Lou Tsioropoulos, star in a game against Georgia Tech.

Harry, no matter how well he had played—even at the Triple-A level right after college—still had to prove himself in the major leagues. There were plenty of Agganis fans who thought he should have made the Red Sox off his strong showing in 1953s Spring training, including $60,000 bonus baby Billy Consolo, who came into camp and said he was awed by Agganis' physical presence and work ethic.

And 1954 was going to be a big year for Harry. Because he had spent a year in the Marines in 1950, he had kept going back to class at B.U. to obtain enough credits to graduate. Education was as important to him as athletics, his family had stressed, and Harry had not forgotten the lessons of his home, no matter where he went or how far. As Plato had said, "Knowledge is the food of the soul," and Harry knew it.

"I want nothing to serve as a diversion while I am down South. I want to devote all my efforts, mental as well as physical, to baseball and a place on the Red Sox squad," he said while heading to the Hotel John Ringling in Sarasota, an old-southern style hotel where the team was training.

His friends knew that for all the ebullience he showed, he was an intense competitor whose drive was as much inner as extroverted. Although he almost always played before scores of thousands of people, Harry did not like crowds.

And for all the natural ability he showed in sports, Harry worked constantly on his game. He was almost always the first to be out to take hitting and fielding practice, and usually the last to leave the field.

Although he didn't have to be in camp until March 1, he arrived a day early—paying his own expenses to get there. And he didn't even take his new car, a light blue Lincoln, he had left behind and let his brother Paul's wife,

Bessie, use to take her driving test. The car was only a few months old, and Bessie was reluctant to use it.

"I'm afraid something will happen, Harry," she said.

"So what," he said. "It's only a car." He had traded in his red Mercury, but kept the license plate he had been given by Gov. Christian Herter. It was H3369, the "H" for Harry, and number 33 for his football idol, Sammy Baugh. The 6 was his number, and the 9 was for his baseball idol, Ted Williams.

"I want to concentrate on baseball. I'm aiming for a regular job. Therefore, all I want to do is eat, drink and live baseball. A car might offer some temptations to play golf or take a fishing trip or something. I don't want anything on my mind except baseball," he told writers.

"I've set baseball as a career and I want to be successful. I'm convinced I can make it. I can field my position—and I can make that 3-6-3, from first to short to first, play—and I can hit. The year at Louisville helped me tremendously," he said, being careful not to show up the executives who had decided he should spend a year in the minor leagues.

After all the equipment was packed at Fenway Park, Harry was talking to John Alevizos about Rev. James Coucouzis, who was the pastor at the Greek Orthodox Cathedral of the Annunciation at Parker and Ruggles Streets in Boston.

They decided to go there for a blessing. Father Coucouzis, a humble man, was impressed by Harry's humility too. "He was rather humble and very kind, and he liked to converse with everyone, especially the young, to lead an example of excellence in sports. He was an example to the young athletes of the time. He was grateful to God for his parents who were church people and who were very humble. He was proud of them, and they were proud of him." Father Coucouzis would sometimes come to Fenway to watch Harry play later that year.

As the year before, when he was trying to make the club, Harry's main competition would be Dick Gernert, the 6'3", 210-lb. power hitter whose swing seemed tailor-made for Fenway Park's short left field line, which was little more than 300 feet away, even if the Green Monster, a 32-foot high formidable wall, often turned screaming line drives that would have been home runs at other parks, into careening singles. Harry, for all his strength, was a left-handed hitter and had to contend with a 380-foot right field line.

And Gernert was a good athlete as well, having starred at Temple in basketball. In 1952, he had hit 19 home runs for the Red Sox and in 1953, when he bumped Harrry to Louisville, Gernert had hit 21 home runs and had 88 RBIs. He still had boosters among the sportswriters.

Harry was undaunted. The confidence that had made his grizzled college football coach Buff Donelli smile in wonder was still with him. Harry noted that in the last month at Louisville in 1953, he had hit close to .400 and although his club had been eliminated in the American Association playoffs, several scouts said he had finished as the best player in the league.

"Dick Gernert is a good player. But I believe I can win the job. If I don't, then it won't be because I've loafed on the job. I'll give it everything I've got," he said. It didn't take long for him to start earning praise from Red Sox Manager Lou Boudreau, who in 1947 had coached a sandlot team at Fenway Park which had opposed another all-star sandlot team on which Agganis had played as a teenager.

Louisville Manager Mike "Pinky" Higgins, who had seen Agganis play every inning for his team, said "He's got a good shot at it, at sticking this year ... he did a tremendous job for us at Louisville. You take any kid stepping out of college and into Triple A ball, batting .285 and leading the club in RBIs (111) and you've got a real prospect. Harry learned a lot of baseball with us. He played every day, every inning of our season (155 games.) That's what I think helped him as much as anything we did for him. If he had faults, we worked them over. Harry's hitting will tell the story for him. He hit well for us and he's taking a big step up to the majors. The pitching will be good every day, every time he steps to the plate."

The years of competition had made Harry almost immune to getting down on himself. He was instilled with the Greek sense of *zoe*, of life, the word used to explain the sense of joy that was felt by facing each day with great expectations, and of overcoming adversity, as his parents had. And, after they did, there was time for laughing and dancing in the family, where they always found time to sit down and eat together.

Plato had said, "Nothing in human affairs is worth any great anxiety." And Harry was the epitome of confidence, in a quiet way.

Spring training wasn't all work, especially in Florida, where there were a lot of fans from Massachusetts, who liked the easy manner of watching games and being able to walk right up to the players and talk. Even some of the sportswriters and those who made their living covering baseball brought their families.

Boston Herald cartoonist Vic Johnson, who liked Harry immensely, brought his daughter, Anne, a young woman whom Harry liked to kid with. One day they were talking about college.

"Why not go to college during the summers too? That way you'll be done in three years instead of four," he laughed.

"Why rush?" she said.

"Oh, you just might have some crazy old plan in your head by then. Marriage or some silly thing. You never can tell," he said, and they both laughed so loud the hotel clerk peered over his desk, trying to shoosh them so the ladies playing scrabble in the next room wouldn't be disturbed.

Later, at breakfast, Harry was trying to persuade his teammates and friends to go see a movie he was delighted with: "Demetrius And The Gladiators," with Victor Mature playing a Greek slave during Roman times who became a famous gladiator.

"Don't miss that Demetrius either, he's a real hero. You know, he was a Greek. Just think, there never would have been any book or movie either if he hadn't held onto that robe," Harry said, talking about the robe worn by Jesus on the cross, and which was saved by Demetrius.

"In fact, there probably wouldn't have been any Christian religion," he said. For the next few meals, the waitresses called him "Demetrius."

One midnight, when the hotel band was playing the rhumba so loud he couldn't sleep, Harry jumped out of bed and ran to the door, opened it and yelled loudly, "Shuuuuttt Upppp!" a sound which reverberated through the Spanish courtyard. He needed his sleep to play well.

Anne remembered seeing him later in the same courtyard, and she was taken with him. She recalled soft lights bouncing off the palms in the room, lilting over his white sport coat, which wasn't as bright as the smile. "He was always the most alert, the most alive," she said.

Harry couldn't resist jibing her father, Vic, about a pink tie he had worn one day to please her mother. "Hey everybody, look at the pretty butterfly! Look out, Vic! It landed on your shirt," Harry laughed.

In his first appearance in a Spring training game against another team, on March 8, he singled in the tying run off lefty Bob Kuzava of the Yankees, who had struck him out in the first inning. Southpaw pitchers were toughest on lefty hitters, but Harry's ability to bounce back would soon make him a favorite of Yankee manager Casey Stengel, who said he was amazed Harry could come back to the plate and make a clutch hit.

It didn't take long. The next day, March 9, he went 2-for-4 with a triple as the Sox beat the Yankees, 5-4. Boston Herald American Sportswriter Dave Egan, who was called "The Colonel" and had a reputation of being harsh on ballplayers, especially Ted Williams, was immediately impressed.

He wrote that Harry was already a good big leaguer and "in two or three years will be a supremely great one." And, he lashed out at some of his own colleagues who were being hard on Harry, who was under immense pressure as a local hero playing for the home town team.

"Fortunately for him, it seems to roll off his back without even touching him and the day is coming when he'll make them love him, when they'll be

154

leading the choir in its rendition of 'I'm just wild about Harry.'"

Williams, who had a career-long feud with Egan, was out with a broken collarbone and Egan was optimistic that a one-two left-handed slugging punch of Agganis and Williams would lift the Red Sox from their 1950s doldrums.

The team had been built on a vision of slugging, but not speed, and Harry had both. He could hit for power and average, was a hard-working slick-fielding first baseman who led the American Association in putouts, and had a deceptive, loping speed that made him a base stealing threat. Plenty of would-be tacklers during his days at Boston University had been befuddled trying to stop him and finding themselves holding air.

"This is a team that will blaze with color once Williams returns, and the glitter of The Golden Greek on first base will add to the vividness of the panorama," Egan wrote. He said the 1954 Red Sox were an intriguing team, with a blend of veterans like Williams and Mel Parnell, and bonus babies like Consolo, Agganis and Harry's teammate with the Augusta Millionaires, Ted Lepcio. But, said Egan, "Agganis alone would make them worthy of interest."

EUKAIRIA ♦ OPPORTUNITY ♦ EYKAIPIA

Harry's high school coach Bill Joyce, who quit coaching when Harry left Lynn Classical, dropped by the hotel to see him early in Spring training because he wanted Harry to think he still had doubts about whether he had made the right choice in selecting baseball over football.

For all his talent in baseball, Harry's presence at quarterback made him the dominating player in virtually every game in which he had played.

Joyce called Harry aside one day. "Look Harry, if you can't make this Red Sox club, turn in your uniform and get yourself one of those football contracts they've been dangling at you the last couple of years," he said. Harry, who loved Joyce like a father, didn't want to show any disrespect, but felt challenged. It was what Joyce wanted.

"Look coach, I'm in baseball for keeps. Just watch me when I get into that lineup. That's all I want, the opportunity."

"He took the burn just the way I wanted him to," a delighted Joyce told sportswriters, because he knew Harry would be motivated even more if he had been told he could not make the grade in baseball.

Egan's colleague on the *Herald American*, John Gillooly, who quickly became one of Harry's great admirers, wrote "The bathing beauties around Sarasota will start whistling when they get a glimpse of the Avenue Apollo, bachelor Harry Agganis, strolling on Lido Beach." But, he advised them not to even try to take him away from baseball. "They will be wasting their Listerined breath, for Harry is totally devoted to baseball."

Not totally. When Harry was at Spring training, he was being picked up by a wealthy Greek businessman, known as the Florida lumber king, whose daughter was attracted to Harry. She was a striking woman and she and Harry dated. Her father liked Harry so much, he let him use a Cadillac. A lot of Greek fathers wanted their daughters to marry Harry.

Harry's disarming smile, but his penchant for working hard, made him admired by even hard-nosed veteran sportswriters who disliked prima donnas. They saw him take the extra batting and fielding practice and not be swayed by his reputation as an All-American football player who at age fifteen had been touted as one of the nation's best high school baseball players too.

Even Boudreau was impressed at Harry's poise and progress. "You wouldn't believe the tremendous improvement this boy has shown in twelve months time," he said. Gernert started wilting under the pressure, and the attention Harry was getting. Writers said Harry's experience in big-time college games was making him the favorite, and Boudreau thought Harry had shed some of his football muscles and was more limber at first base too.

Gernert said "Harry was getting most of the publicity being a local guy. I thought I was doing pretty well." But he was worried Boudreau was leaning toward Harry.

On March 17, St. Patrick's Day, Harry's pinch-hit single with the bases loaded lifted the Red Sox over the Washington Senators, 10-6, and his Spring average was looming at .400. Boudreau had been hedging, but was leaning toward making Harry the regular first baseman. Philadelphia A's players said Harry was the best looking player they had seen.

On March 18, Donelli wrote him that "The reports coming out of Sarasota about you are very good so far, but nobody has predicted who would be the first baseman. I know you have a feeling in your mind who will be first baseman."

He advised him too that despite some glowing articles, to be wary of the Press. "The less you say at this point, I think the better off you will be. Above all, don't let them know your feelings about anybody or anything!" he wrote. Harry, a laconic son of Spartan ancestors, already knew that.

Gernert had a good game March 22 in Bradenton against the Boston Braves where he hit two home runs, and said he felt encouraged when Boudreau gave him a good word. But management and public opinion was quickly shifting toward Harry, putting pressure on Boudreau.

By March 31, Boudreau said he was planning to platoon Gernert and Harry, which would give Harry most of the playing time since most of the pitching the Sox would face would be right-handed.

Boudreau though said if Harry was 'hot,' he would keep him in even against left-handers. Globe sportswriter Roger Birtwell wrote on April 4 that "Judging from the form the two players have shown in Spring training, however, it would not be surprising if Agganis eventually eases Gernert out of the picture. For Agganis' promotion seems richly deserved. He has outhit Gernert down here by a hundred points. Agganis also has consistently outplayed Gernert in the field."

On April 4, before a game against the minor league Atlanta Crackers—where Harry would play against his old Lynn mate Billy Porter—Boudreau said Agganis had made the team and Harry signed a major league contract. He celebrated by driving in the tying and winning runs, after writers told him he had made the parent team.

Trying to downplay the news, Harry said "Gee, thanks a lot. Gosh, that's wonderful news for me. I've worked hard to stay with the team. I'll keep on working. It's what I've always wanted," he said. He was hitting .323.

Because of the deep right-field fence, there had been only two left-handed hitting first basemen as regulars with the Red Sox in the previous two decades. A former Sox first baseman, Walt Dropo, said "If Boudreau uses Agganis, he has less right-handed power, which is what you want at Fenway. But if he uses Gernert, his defense is not so good," he said. The reviews on Agganis were so good there was talk about trading Gernert.

It was a good day, and night all around.

Harry's close friend from Lynn, Jimmy Kirios, was in the Army, stationed at Ft. Jackson, South Carolina, and he wanted to see Harry play, but he had to convince his commanding officer to let him go to the game.

"My buddy is playing for the Red Sox over in Atlanta and I'd like to see him play," Kirios said.

"I'll tell you what," the commanding officer said. "Bring me back a ball and I'll know you were there." Kirios thought he was doubting his story, but he went to Atlanta and found Harry staying at the Hotel Statler and knocked on his door. Harry was delighted to see him and got him tickets for the game right behind the first base dugout.

"Harry," he explained. "I have to bring a ball back to prove I was here," he said.

That night, the game ended with a screaming line drive right at Harry. As he caught it, Harry spun around gleefully, waltzed over to the stands and, smiling broadly, flipped the ball from his glove directly to Kirios.

And there was a bonus. Because of rain, the Red Sox couldn't fly to their next game and had to take a bus instead. That meant Harry would miss a date with Miss Atlanta, so he asked Kirios to pinch hit for him and take her out instead.

She was a Southern belle beauty. And as he stood in front of the hotel with her, the Red Sox bus came passing by. Suddenly, Jimmy Piersall, Ted Williams and the rest of the team came running to where they could see her. They were whistling and hooting. "You lucky stiff!" one yelled.

Harry was laughing. "Take care of her, Jeep," he said.

Kirios smiled back. "I'll do just that," he said, as the bus pulled away. They went for a walk in the park. It was a wonderful night. The woman was on his arm, and the ball was in his duffle bag.

Harry got a letter from Donelli, who had been keeping up a correspondence with him. "It was very good to read you had been signed to a Red Sox contract,and have made the grade as a major leaguer," he wrote. "I know you don't need any pep talk, but I want you to know that I have gone on record as saying you would be on first base against left handers before long," he wrote. Harry was being followed by his home town fans and admirers, especially from B.U. and in Lynn, and the Greek-American community which adored him.

Donelli knew Harry didn't need any advice at being humble, but warned him that he was stepping into a major league world of even more intense scrutiny than that to which he had been subjected at B.U.

"You know you will be undoubtedly be interviewed by everybody and his brother when you get home. Give it a little thought and still be the guy trying to make the majors. Don't let anyone trick you into being an expert regarding either yourself or anyone else on the club," he wrote.

For Harry, making the Red Sox was the fulfillment not only of his lifelong dream, but of the family and community from which he had come and had made so proud. Harry had long admired Williams and now was going to be on the same team, and before long would be hitting in front of the game's greatest hitter.

It would be Ted-and-Harry for the next ten years, thought Sox broadcaster Curt Gowdy, who said major league observers would soon predict Harry would be the first-baseman for the American League All-Star team for the next decade.

But Gernert had rallied on the trip North and was playing better too, hitting A's star pitcher Bobby Shantz hard. It was too late though. "Things seemed to deteriorate with Boudreau and it looked like Harry was getting the publicity and the upper hand," he said.

Gernert, who came from the small town of Reading, Pa., met Harry at B.U. through Lepcio. "When he came to the Red Sox, we were battling each other. I come from a small town and everything is competitive when you get to the major leagues," he said.

"Harry was a good player, but when you're competing against someone you are fighting each other," he said. Harry loved the competition, but felt the camaraderie more than did Gernert.

Harry was now only a few days away from playing in the major leagues.

He had a last chance to meet with his old high school friend and baseball and football teammate George Bullard, who was as highly regarded as a baseball prospect and had signed a contract with the Detroit Tigers, but was not faring well, admitting he was frittering away his chance at the big leagues with a lackadaisical attitude.

Before a late Spring game with the Phillies in Montgomery, Alabama, where Bullard was playing for the Montgomery Rebels, the two met on the field and were photographed together. It was one of the many photo sessions the two had endured over the years and always made them uncomfortable, said Bullard.

Bullard looked unhappy. One writer noted he "had a rather odd expression on his face. There was a reason for that expression. While watching Harry bat with the plush major league Red Sox, he knew he would be batting in the twilight and the bushes with the Montgomery Rebels."

Bullard often wished he had gone to B.U. to play football with Harry. He said he had to sign to play pro baseball because he had dropped out of high school once and gone back in at age 16. After the 1947 Lynn Classical season, Harry's last, Bullard wouldn't have been eligible to play high school sports in his senior year, because he would have been nineteen.

Ironically, the Red Sox were interested in him because of his glove, and his speed. He had played with Harry on the Vrees All-Stars, and against him when Harry was with the Augusta Millionaires in Maine.

"I got a little more money from the Tigers, but the main reason I didn't sign with the Sox was Junior Stephens," who was playing shortstop. "He had a great year with a flock of home runs and runs batted in. I thought he'd be there a long, long time," Bullard said.

And then he said something he said he'd kept in for several years, about an injury he said had held him back. "I never told anyone this before," he told a sportswriter, "But I believe it was a football injury that caused the chips in my right elbow. I lost one year after signing because I had to have an operation. Then the next year I had trouble getting back into shape and then I was in the Marines," he said.

Bullard briefly opened a deli in his home city of Lynn with his bonus money and after the Marines, he went to the Tigers minor league team in Little Rock, Arkansas. He played behind Harvey Kuehn, who would go on to a long career with Detroit. From there, Bullard would go to Buffalo, where his minor league career would end.

Harry was sporting something new on the trip back. It was the pink tie Vic Johnson had worn, and about which Harry had given him so much grief.

Before the team returned to Boston, Vic gave Harry the tie for good luck. Harry blushed lightly and thanked him softly.

Before the season started, Harry collected signed photos of all his team-mates, including Ted Williams, who had broken his collarbone and would be sidelined. "To Harry, All American on the baseball, football in every way," Williams wrote. Harry's rookie baseball card came out, Topps Number 152, showing his grin, and another photo showing him in a long stretch at first base. Harry would wear Number 6.

He brought the photos to his sister, Mary Raimo, who had been keeping a detailed scrapbook of all his clippings, which were now in the thousands, dating from his high school days. Back at B.U., his former backup at quarterback, Johnny Nunziato had been named the school's athlete of the year for 1954.

On April 13, Harry made his major league debut in Philadelphia, pinch hitting for his old roommate, Consolo, and fouling out in the eighth inning.

But he was coming home to Boston, where thousands of fans, from B.U., Lynn, and his family, were waiting for his first game at Fenway Park, where he had starred so often in football, and played high school all-star games in baseball, showing the promise of things to come.

Harry's Fenway Park debut on April 15, 1954 was typical New England spring weather: cold, raw and windy, but it didn't stop busloads of fans from Lynn and B.U. from coming to see him start against the Washington Senators. Despite the weather, more than 17,000 fans turned out.

There were even bands heralding his return. "What with all the bands and all, it felt like a football day," he laughed later. In the stands were seven members of his family, including his mother, and Harry leaped into the stands to help her take her seat. There were also four hundred rooters from B.U., including Donelli, and they were all yelling for Harry.

"I was a little nervous at first. Not much, though. I wanted to do a good job for the people who were out there cheering for me," he said.

Boudreau was not surprised at Harry's demeanor. "Football has helped him.He has been under greater pressure than this and once the game started he was right at home," he said. Starting for the Senators was Bob Porterfield, who had been the major league's shutout leader in 1953, and hadn't allowed a run in the last 22 innings of that season.

Porterfield started off. strong again. In the fourth inning, slugging third baseman George Kell started off with a single. Up stepped Harry, who was batting fifth.

With a 1-1 count, he screamed a line drive over the head of right fielder Tommy Umphlett into the deep, arching corner of right field. Umphlett was playing short and the ball caromed around, giving the fleet Agganis time to head into third with a triple with an eye toward the rarest of Fenway feats, an inside-the-park home run.

But Harry, looking ahead, saw the lumbering Kell and started to slow rounding second. By the time he reached third, he was almost up Kell's back and he had to settle for a triple, to the delight of thousands of his fans in the stands. The smash had just missed being a home run by inches, and Harry thought it was gone when he hit it.

"It felt awfully good when it left the bat, but the wind must have caught it," he said. Later, the ball was given to him and he had it signed by his teammates. "I thought it was gone for sure," he said.

Harry, trying to protect Kell from criticism, said, "I think George did too. He slowed down near second. Yes, maybe he could have tried for home (sooner.) I don't know for sure."

Kell, sitting close by in the locker room later where Harry was mobbed by reporters, said "I looked back and saw the ball curving around the foul pole. I didn't question but that it was gone." Then, he laughed too.

"I hoped nobody noticed me slow down. I really didn't mean to." Kell said "Harry's going to be all right. You can't play as much football as Harry did and be too concerned even today. There's pressure in every game. I'm nervous out there all the time and I've been around a few years."

After the triple, Harry scored on a Sammy White home run, crossing home plate for the first time at Fenway as his family and friends watched, freezing in the 40-degree temperatures. Red Sox Assistant General Manager Dick O'Connell said if not for Harry and promotions to fill the park, there would have been perhaps only 5,000 fans there.

Harry's mother had only seen Harry play baseball once before, with the Augusta Millionaires, but she was there for his opener. She said she prayed half the time Harry would get a hit, and the other half praying the Senators would not get hits. She would not watch football because she didn't want to see Harry get hurt.

Harry's hit gave the Red Sox a 3-0 lead, but Boudreau showed how much he would depend on his rookie first baseman later in the fifth inning. Washington Manager Bucky Harris replaced Porterfield with left-hander Bunky Stewart. Boudreau, who said he would let Gernert hit against lefties, kept Harry in the game against the southpaw.

He responded with a perfect bunt on the first pitch to move Kell, who had singled after a double by Jackie Jensen, over to second base.

The 1954 season would pair two great college gridiron heroes, Jensen, "The Golden Boy" from California, who led his team to a victory in the Rose Bowl, and "The Golden Greek," the All-American quarterback from B.U. Harry later had a sacrifice and what would become a trademark, a laser-beam like line drive single.

"Two hits a day will keep the minor leagues away," he laughed.

Former Red Sox all-star second baseman Bobby Doerr was among Harry's instant admirers. "There is a fellow who seems to have the heart," he said. And Hall of Fame pitcher Lefty Grove chimed in after the game, "There is a fellow who stands up at the plate as though he expects to hit," he said.

A *Boston Globe* headline on page one the next morning, under a photo of Harry and former Red Sox all-star first baseman Jimmy Foxx posing together on the dugout steps showed the optimism of fans: "AGGANIS GIVES PROMISE OF LONG STAY WITH SOX"

Although he had brought life to the Red Sox, Harry was characteristically modest in the locker room. "I don't want to say anything. Heck, I'm a newcomer here. All these fellers have been around a long time so I wouldn't want to take any play away from them," he said softly, just a little embarrassed at the attention.

The Red Sox won, 6-1, and Harry's performance left Boudreau with a pleasant dilemma. He said he would platoon Harry and Gernert. "The people are going to be yelling 'We want Agganis' in every game played at Fenway Park if he continues the way he started. And it will help at the gate if you say he's the regular first baseman," he admitted. "That's my problem," he said. He said he would still platoon the two.

In the stands watching was Foxx, who had been one of the game's great first basemen. They had met before. It was 1948, when Harry had just graduated from high school and Foxx was playing in an exhibition game at Fraser Field in Lynn against the Vrees All-Stars. Foxx's professional career had ended and he was trying to earn a few extra dollars. Bullard was on Harry's team.

It was a hot Sunday afternoon. Foxx, overweight and out of shape, walked his first time up and was forced at second. His second time up, he hit a hard grounder to Bullard, who threw him out. On his third at bat, he hit a long fly out. It was his last at-bat in baseball.

Globe sportswriter Hy Hurwitz, noticing the coincidence, wrote "What star of destiny decreed that Agganis should have been present at the absolute end of Foxx's playing career, and that Foxx should be on hand - nearly six years later - when Agganis started a Red Sox career that promised to be both long and exciting."

The Greeks believe *"E Meera eene gramenee."* It means, "Fate is written."

CHARIS   ◆   GRACE   ◆   ΧΑΡΙΣ

Harry had again mesmerized the city where he had been a schoolboy and college hero, and it didn't take long for him to increase the drama that had filled his life. A few days after his Fenway debut, on Easter Sunday, April 18, he had two hits in the opening game of a doubleheader against the Philadelphia A's. During batting practice, he had the A's standing around watching as he whacked low pitches on a line deep into right field, causing them to murmur in admiration.

In the second game, he really brought some thrills. In the third inning, he hit a 380-foot three-run homer, his first in the major leagues, to give the Sox a 3-1 lead. They won, 4-3 in the 13th inning on a homer by Jensen, but the day belonged to Harry, and the press quickly picked up on an old nickname, calling him "Hairbreadth Harry," and talking about the Agganis-Jensen gridiron connection again.

The home run came on a high fast ball, a pitch apparently designed to keep him away from the low pitches he was smashing in batting practice. The home run landed in the grandstands where a former B.U. football teammate, Sam Pino, whom Harry was coaching during his off-season part-time assistant coaching job with his old school, retrieved the ball from a serviceman who had gotten to it.

Pino pleaded that the homer was hit by his friend and told the serviceman he would get him two signed balls if he could bring Harry the home run ball.

"He said, 'OK, I'll give you the ball.' I couldn't wait until the game ended so I could tell Harry I had it for him." He told sportswriters he would be waiting outside the gate where the ball was hit. When he was told, Harry beamed, "'Good old Sammy. Always was a good kid. I'll meet him outside and tell him what a great guy he is."

The double header was necessary because of a rainout a day earlier, as a bad stretch of weather was plaguing the team. Williams, still with a pin in his shoulder because of the broken collarbone, came into the clubhouse the day before the doubleheader and gave one of his impromptu clinics on hitting.

Harry was listening and saw something unusual as Williams held a bat in hand. They both used the wrong side of the bat to hit.

Most hitters held the bat so that the Louisville Slugger label and their autograph on the bat was showing because the grain was stronger that way and would protect against breaking the bat. Williams said, "When I look down at the bat, if I can see my name or the Louisville label, I know I'm not holding it right … I don't want to see anything on the bat as even your own signature on the label can be very distracting," he said.

Agganis, who idolized Williams, was delighted. "They used to kid me down in Louisville because I was swinging with the wrong side of the bat," he told a gathering of writers and teammates. One of those listening was Charley Maxwell, who played with Harry in Louisville. "Why, Harry used to break so many bats we always claimed he kept the factory in business," he said.

The next day, against the Yankees in the second game of a Patriot's Day doubleheader at Fenway, Agganis broke up a no-hitter against a former Lynn Red Sox pitcher, Jim McDonald, whom he had seen play at Fraser Field in 1947, with a handle hit on a tough curve ball.

The Yankees won the one-hitter, 5-0, but Boudreau said he thought pitchers were already trying to decipher how to stop Agganis, who seemed poised for a rookie, albeit one who was twenty-five-years-old and had so much competitive experience already. Harry had seen major league pitching when he was fourteen and playing semi-pro baseball for the Lynn Frasers, of course, and gone against some top flight hurling too when he was playing for the Augusta Millionaires and Louisville Colonels, including several who would be major league stars.

When he wasn't playing, Harry was back home in Lynn, where he would stop old friends on the street and talk. His brother, Paul, had moved back from California, where he had built up a clientele of celebrities in his hairdressing salon, and Harry made a point to stop by and personally drop off tickets for his brother to help him attract customers to his new salon in the Hotel Edison on Exchange Street.

Whomever he met, Harry shook their hand. And after he did, "I'm never going to wash my hands again. Harry Agganis shook my hand," was a frequent refrain.

Harry liked to show off his record collection too, especially Frank Sinatra and Dean Martin. He had all their albums and loved to listen to them for hours, sometimes trying to hone the singing skills that his friend Jimmy Kirios had. Bessie would listen with him and they would debate who was a better singer.

"Sinatra is a master in every aspect of music, Bessie," he said seriously. Music and singing were as important to Harry as was sports. It was one of the central themes of his life and he would love to sing with Kirios.

In his tiny room when he was younger, Harry and Kirios liked to sing along to the musical "Oklahoma," and they would burst into laughter when Harry's mother would walk in smiling, trying to follow along, and sing, in broken English, "Okahoma!"

His mother and Mary lived in modest homes, but Harry loved to entertain there. One night, Harry brought B.U. President Harold Case and his wife to his house on Waterhill Street. Mary was there with the best silver and china.

There was no formal dining room, and everyone sat at an old wooden table they had used for years. As they were enjoying a sumptuous dinner Mary had made, Harry laughed and said to Case, "Look at the table."

Harry lifted his knees to balance the table an inch off the floor, and pulled out one of the legs, which was broken and had kept a tedious balance for the diners.

Harry laughed uproariously and said, "The china belongs to Mary too," he said. His sister was embarrased, but Harry wanted to make a point: we are what we are, and he was proud of it.

The families were growing now, and Mary had several children who adored Harry, as did his other nieces and nephews. Harry would spend a lot of time playing with all of them when he was back in Lynn. Harry would sometimes go up to his brother Phil's house in Hamilton, an affluent suburb about ten miles from Lynn, and take his friends and teammates to grill steaks and share food and talk.

It was a good summer for Harry. He was playing major league baseball, he was an idol to sports fans, especially the young. And then, one hot day while he was walking Lynn beach, near his old high school hangout of Christy's, he saw an attractive young woman coming out of the water.

He was standing there waiting and smiling.

"Hi. I'm Harry," he said innocently.

She knew who he was. Everybody did. Jean Dallaire had just graduated from Salem State College but had seen him play against Salem, where she lived. She was flattered, surprised, and not sure how to react. "I couldn't believe he was talking to me," she said.

Dallaire, whose dad was French and mother was Irish, wanted to be a teacher. Her father had been a star quarterback at Loyola of Baltimore and Fordham, so she knew athletes and liked sports. She was a dark-haired woman with a quick smile, but was a little reticent around the famous figure in front of her.

They made small talk, but she didn't see him again until later on the same beach. And then one day he showed up at her house. Waiting in his car, laughing, were his friends Jimmy Andrews, Lou Tsioropoulos, his nephew Jimmy Orphanos, and George Maravelias. He fidgeted on her front steps trying to talk while they waited. Then he left.

He came a couple of more times, always with a carload of friends, shy and waiting for a chance to ask her out. And then she said the magic call came. He telephoned her and asked her to go out. She was breathless.

They went to Kimball's Starlight in Wakefield, an outdoor dancing pavilion. She was dancing with Harry Agganis. Dallaire was working the three to eleven shift at General Electric in the summer and would have to take a bus from Salem to Lynn and another there to get to the plant. A lot of times, she didn't have to wait too long. Harry would show up and give her a ride.

And he would be waiting at 11 p.m. to take her home.

They dated all summer, going to Varley's diner for a quick bite, or over to his old high school coach's house, Bill Joyce, where they would join with Joyce's wife, Sandy, to play cards.

Sometimes they would go over to the Swampscott home of former Red Sox star Johnny Pesky, to play whist, or to a Chinese restaurant, China Sails, near the General Edwards bridge for dinner. Harry always ordered Egg Foo Yung.

ERGON ◆ WORK ◆ ΕΡΓΟΝ

Harry had baseball on his mind too, though. He told his family he wanted to concentrate on his career. Boudreau had already decided though that he would play Harry against lefties too, and not platoon him with Gernert, after Agganis knocked in the winning run in a game against the Senators early in May, hitting southpaw Dean Stone hard.

"They're trying him with low balls, fast balls, sliders and curves. They're feeling him inside and outside, close to the fists and off the corners," he said. What impressed Boudreau more was not when Harry was hitting well, but after he had been called out twice on strikes that the manager felt were balls.

Harry came back to the dugout to tell Boudreau he had been called out on pitches that were out of the strike zone, where pitchers were trying to bait him. That gave him even more confidence in Harry. "He's a good man up at the plate. He's going to do all right," the manager said.

Yankee Manager Casey Stengel agreed, maybe because Harry was killing Yankee pitching. "He's got natural moves and he never looks like a patsy, even when he's taking a third strike," said Stengel.

Before long, Gernert would be sent down to Louisville, where he was struck ill with hepatitis, and would have to compete there against slugger Norm Zauchin, who was back after spending the previous couple of years in the Marines in Korea. Gernert would be moved to the minor league team in Buffalo and be called back up to the Red Sox at the end of the year, but not for long.

Harry's legions of admirers believed in him, although some took a little coaxing. After his opening day performance had won him headlines in his home town papers, there was jubilation and expectation he would quickly become an all-star.

But in the 20th Century Barber Shop in Lynn, where owner George Blackjohn was a big Agganis fan and had followed him to Spring training to report on his progress, one customer, attorney Ben Stone, wasn't as convinced yet that Harry would be a big star.

Stone was sitting in a chair arguing that Harry had gotten lucky on his triple because Umphlett was playing in so close. That was heresy in Lynn, but Blackjohn's shop was a gathering place where conversation sometimes got heated, if friendly. As Stone argued his case, Blackjohn laughed and swiveled Stone around away from the mirror.

"Tell that to this guy," Blackjohn said, laughing.

Sitting and waiting his turn was Harry Agganis.

George Stephanos, a close friend of Harry, said when Harry would come back to Lynn, he would stop to shake hands with elderly Greek women in the streets, whose smile was as broad as his when they met.

They would walk away with one hand often still in a fist. "Harry had put a five dollar bill in there," to help them out, said Stephanos.

The Waterhill Street neighborhood would see a lot of Red Sox players coming to Harry's house for dinner, including Ted Williams, who sometimes would have a car pick up Harry.

They used to delight in big plates of Greek food. Harry reveled in Ted's company and Williams was perhaps the only person of whom Harry was in awe. Occasionally, they would go to the Wonderland Diner in Revere, owned by Harry's uncle, George.

Harry liked being around home when the Red Sox were in town, although he was still battling Gernert. A stretch of bad weather and rain cost the Sox eight postponements that Spring, including five games in a row.

After only seven games though, Jensen, who had a fear of flying, and Harry showed signs they would be stars for years. Both were big and fast and tough and had the football background that gave them unusual poise. Kell had stopped hitting, as had Jimmy Piersall, and even Mel Parnell, one of the team's greatest pitchers ever, had started off 0-2 with a 5.33 ERA.

By May 12, Harry was hitting .310. Two days later, he had two RBIs in a game as the team awaited the return of Williams, who came back to play the next day and went 0-for-2 against the Chicago White Sox, while Harry raised his average again with a 2-for-3 performance the first time he and Williams played in a regular season game together.

White Sox General Manager Frank Lane saw brilliance in Harry. "He's a real athlete. He never gives up. Fights all the time," he said. Like Boudreau and Stengel, he was as impressed with Harry's failures at the plate.

After Harry had twice struck out in one game his first two times up, Lane said he wondered how the rookie would handle his next at bat, and whether he would be tentative or timid. "Not this kid," admired Lane. "He gets up the third time and really lays into the ball," smacking a triple.

"This kid doesn't quit. He stays right in there at the plate. You can fool him once, or even twice, but then he gets hold of one for you," he said. Like others who had seen Harry, Lane came away shaking his head in wonder.

But it would be the next day, May 16, that would make Red Sox fans sigh at the possibilities of years of a Ted-and-Harry lineup. In a double header against the Tigers, Williams went 8-for-9 with two homers, a double, and seven RBIs.

Only Williams could have overshadowed Harry, who had been the center of attention all his athletic life. Hitting against left handers, Harry was on base nine times, went 5-for-9 and scored five runs, each time driven home by Williams. Harry was batting second with Williams hitting fourth.

A month into his rookie year, Harry was hitting .359. In the first game, he hit a double off the right-field screen which missed by a few inches of being a home run. He was helping fill the stands too, as nearly 35,000 people packed Fenway to watch the twin bill.

Harry continued his torrid pace against the Yankees a few days later at Yankee Stadium, leading a six-run sixth inning with a three-run homer off Whitey Ford into the right field grandstand to give the Red Sox a 6-1 win.

The hit gave 6'7" pitcher Frank Sullivan the win and thrilled him, he said, because his dad was a semi-pro pitcher. Sullivan had been used in relief until facing the Yankees.

After the game, Harry admonished reporters to talk to Sullivan. It didn't surprise the pitcher, who had seen Harry get unusual respect for a rookie, perhaps because of his strong showing in the 1953 Spring training camp when Harry had shown he wasn't a prima donna.

"He was treated pretty good because everyone knew of him as a football player who was a hard working guy. He was no nonsense and put in a good effort every minute," he said.

But Harry wasn't done with the Yankees.

A week later, at Fenway Park, he hit his third home run of the year off fireballer Allie Reynolds, with whom he had appeared on a cover of Sport magazine a couple of years earlier.

After a 5-0 Red Sox lead had been pared to 5-3, Harry opened the sixth inning with his shot into the right field bullpen. An inning later, his friend Lepcio hit another home run. Harry was now hitting .311, and was still at .300 by Memorial Day, when he again homered in the second game of a doubleheader against the A's, after a bases loaded double in the first game drove in three runs.

The next day Williams told *Globe* sportswriter Bob Holbrook that Agganis was a "comer" who could be a star in the league. "He has good form at the plate. He doesn't overswing," said Williams. "He has a good eye and he's going to get better. I haven't seen any pitches yet that Agganis can not hit. I'd say he's a good hitter ... a darned good hitter."

For Agganis, the praise from Williams was like a blessing from Mt. Olympus. Williams cautioned Harry would be tested even more later in the year, and especially the next year.

"It's not the first year in the majors that's the test, it's the second year. That's when they start bearing down and working on a hitter. The first year they don't know whether you can hit an inside pitch or an outside pitch, high or low. At least in the second year they remember that here's a guy who hurt me last season. Then they really start to operate," he said. Williams though said Harry had all the tools: eye, power and ability.

And even as Harry's average began to slip a little, he still remained a feared clutch hitter, and Williams said baseball people admired Harry's determination. "He has the willingness to learn," Williams said.

Cincinnati Reds Manager Birdie Tebbetts, who had managed the Indianapolis minor league team in Triple-A which played Harry's Louisville Colonels, had said earlier in the season he had seen the same qualities.

"Agganis may look bad the first few times he comes to the plate. But watch out that fourth time. That's when he murders you, just when you don't want him to hit." Pitchers were already trying everything on him, from fork balls to palm balls, knucklers and junk pitches to get him out of synch.

Baseball and sports were one thing to Harry, but family and friends were another, and just as important. He never forgot his friends. When the Red Sox were in Washington for a game against the Senators, he called back to Lynn to find out where his old Classical and B.U. teammate, Nils Strom, who was in the Army, was stationed.

Strom got a phone call in the barracks. It was Harry.

"Do you have Sunday off?" Harry asked. He wanted to leave a ticket at the box office in Washington so Strom could see him play.

Strom said he had made plans with his friends and felt funny leaving them behind. "How many guys are you hanging around with?" Harry asked. Strom said six. "I'll leave six tickets for you at the box office," Harry said.

And, he added, "Please show up early."

When Strom and his six Army buddies showed up, Harry took time out to meet and talk with them. Strom was dumbfounded, even though he knew Harry well."Here he was in the major leagues and he had to take time to call my parents and find me. He was not too busy to do something for his friends," he said.

On June 2, a group of Greater Boston Baseball League College All-Stars came to Fenway Park. His old backup quarterback at B.U., tiny John Nunziato was there, along with Joe Stoico, who had also played football and baseball with Harry for the Terriers. Harry, at 6'2", posed for a photo in *The Boston Globe* which showed him with his right arm cradling a rapt Nunziato around the right shoulder as Nunziato looked up.

Stoico got more out of the meeting: it was Harry's first baseman's mitt. Harry invited his old teammates into the locker room and asked Stoico if he had a good glove for the upcoming college all-star game at Fenway.

"You're just awed by all these people," said Stoico. "You go into the locker room and see these Big Leaguers, but Harry just had us over there talking and wanted to know what was going on at B.U. and he gave me the glove. I was dumbfounded, but he was that type of guy. I knew him well and we played together but he didn't have to give me that glove," he said.

The name "AGGANIS" was marked on the glove. Stoico used the glove in a tournament along with a cap owned by Harry, which Stoico sheepishly admitted he took off a bench during a football practice a few months later where Harry was assistant coach.

One night, when movie stars Tony Curtis and Janet Leigh came to a game and talked with Harry, they invited him out to a party that night. He declined because he had promised some friends he would go out with them instead.

When the college players visited, Harry was hovering around the .300 mark and Globe columnist Harold Kaese said "Harry Agganis is doing everything they feared in Spring training he could not do, which is, a) hit home runs at Fenway Park, b) hit left-handed pitchers, c) keep from chasing bad balls."

That came a day after the Sox, who were again falling apart as a team despite the strong seasons being put together by Harry and Jensen, had lost to the White Sox, 9-6. Harry had hit his fifth homer, nearly tying the game in the eighth inning.

With Billy Goodman and Jensen on base and two out, Harry blasted a pitch to left center that looked like it was going to hit the left field wall at Fenway. But fleet Minnie Minoso raced over and speared it after jumping into the wall.

For the Red Sox, who still had no black ballplayers, Harry was a needed home town attraction during a tumultuous time in American society. J. Robert Oppenheimer, who had overseen the Manhattan Project that developed the atomic bomb in World War II, was being banned from further nuclear work, and Wisconsin Senator Joseph McCarthy was leading hearings he said would root out communists.

But GI's could buy homes with no money down and tract development houses were becoming popular, especially since they could be bought for as little as $13,200 and be affordable at $66.89 a month for principal and interest. Back Bay apartments in Boston were going for $65 a month. For now, people were still coming to Fenway, even as the Red Sox were slipping again. The mix of bonus babies and veterans was not working and Boudreau was anxious.

On Friday night, June 4, it was B.U. Night at The Boston Pops, and Harry went with Case and Mrs. Case, and got a standing ovation, in rhythmic time, when he walked down the aisle into Symphony Hall, and was later photographed singing along with a tune, standing in front of the first row, holding a music program. It was the start of one of his greatest weekends.

The next day, Saturday, Harry hit another homer, joining with Jensen and Lepcio, who had two-run shots, to give the Sox a 6-0 win over the Tigers at Fenway. It was the start of one his most rewarding times in sports, and in his life.

The next day he was scheduled to graduate from B.U., which was only about a mile up Commonwealth Avenue from Fenway Park. The graduation was going to be at the old Braves Field, now owned by B.U.

But the Sox had a 1 p.m. game and the graduation was scheduled for 4 p.m. It would be close whether he could make the ceremony. Because of his time in the Marines in 1950 and signing with the Red Sox in 1952, Harry had to go back to school to make up missed credits, in between playing for the Red Sox. He would be the first one in his family to graduate from college. His older brothers had to work to support the family. Harry, the youngest, had been allowed to nurture his love for sports.

"He had to be in two places," said his brother Phil. "We were very elated, he was the first one from a poor family to graduate and my mother was very excited. We were all so proud of him," he said.

Harry didn't want to miss the graduation, and had put his cap and gown in the locker room. He had tickets for A Tier, Box 53. B.U. President Harold Case would be waiting.

By the fifth inning though, the Sox and Tigers were tied, 4-4, and a potential extra-inings game loomed, which could keep Harry from getting to Braves Field for the graduation ceremony.

In the bottom of the fifth, Jensen opened with an infield hit. Harry came up and, as Globe sportswriter Hy Hurwitz wrote, hit the game winning home run "with one summa cum laude swing of his bat." It was pure Hollywood.

At game's end, Harry dashed into the locker room to shower and change into his size 7 cap and size 48 graduation gown, taking a ribbing from his teammates.

"A lot of good that degree will do you Harry," kidded Consolo, his roommate from the previous year's Spring training. "You've still got to work a doubleheader tomorrow," he laughed. Del Wilbur said "It's the first time anyone ever hit a home run at Fenway Park and had to go to Braves Field to celebrate."

Harry whirled out, his gown flying behind him, his hand trying to hold down the cap and he headed out, tickets in hand, heading up the one-mile run of Commonwealth Avenue like a man trying to steal second base with a big jump. Finally entering Gaffney Street, he came flying into the field, just making his seat. It was a breathless entrance.

The next day, Harry was on the front page of *The Boston Daily Globe* again, this time in a two-panel photo showing him crossing home plate and being congratulated by Jensen in one picture, while in the adjacent photo he was in cap and gown being congratulated by Case. He received his bachelor of science degree in education.

The smile was bigger than ever. In the same day, Harry had achieved the ancient Greek ideal of "A sound mind in a solid body," or, as it was said in Greek, *"Nous E eyees en Somatee Eeyee."*

The headline in the Globe, which cost a nickel to buy, said it all: "HARRY'S HEYDAY"

There was some Rookie of The Year talk and former Red Sox infielder Johnny Pesky said Harry would hit 30 home runs at Briggs Stadium in Detroit if he played for the Tigers, which had a shorter right field than Fenway.

Sportswriters in Boston said Harry had already hit at least a dozen shots for outs that would have been home runs in other fields. His versatility made his name appear in trade talks too, including with the Yankees.

The Sox though continued to slide, perhaps because their pitching was among the worst in the league. The Cleveland Indians were enroute to stopping the Yankees from winning a sixth straight pennant, bolstered by a pitching staff of Early Wynn, Mike Garcia, Bob Lemon and Bob Feller, one of the best rotations in baseball history.

After Harry's game winning homer against the Tigers, the Red Sox went on an eight-game losing streak, ending it with a 3-2 win against the Tigers in Detroit when Harry opened the seventh with a single, moved along to third on a Jensen single, and dashed for home on a Lepcio hit, taking a chance that proved good when third baseman Freddie Hatfield's throw hit him in the back. It was Harry's speed that had given the Sox the victory.

ATECHIA ◆ ADVERSITY ◆ ATYXIA

By now though, Boudreau was desperate to stop the Sox slide into the basement of the American League, as attendance dropped too. Fans had other outlets, and the big sports story was the upcoming heavyweight boxing fight between Brockton's Rocky Marciano and Ezzard Charles. Marciano won.

By June 17, Boudreau decided to bench Harry, whose hitting had fallen, and who was getting shaky in the field. It was an uncommon time for "The Golden Greek," who had known mostly sensation and success in his life. He didn't complain.

"Lou knows what he is doing," Harry said. "Everybody goes bad sometime or other. But I just don't like to go bad." The newspapers reported he took the benching "without whimpering."

A few days later, Boudreau tried to analyze what was going wrong with

172

the team, and said he was moving Harry back to first base. He told sportswriters he had a dilemma because utility infielder Billy Goodman's best position was first base too. Gowdy asked Boudreau if Harry knew he was being benched for only a few games.

"Yes," Boudreau said. "Agganis said to me, 'I'm glad that happened. Now I have time to think.'" During his visits back to Lynn, where he would always stay with his mother on Waterhill Street, or over at his sister Mary's house a few blocks away, Harry talked to his brother Phil about the slump.

"I'm learning. It looks like I'm going to get the handle on this," Harry said. Phil remembered, "He was not down on himself, just a little disappointed and thought he could do better."

Boudreau was moving the young players around in the infield too, switching Consolo from third to second base, and Lepcio from second to third. "It looks to us that with these kids you can go along with them so far. Then you have to take 'em out and give 'em a rest. Otherwise you'll ruin 'em. I'm thinking of Agganis and Consolo," he said.

Lepcio had become impatient with Boudreau too, and felt he was not being given a chance to prove himself. Consolo had hit only .215 the year before and was under pressure to produce.

The three young players were good friends too, and Harry had brought them both back to Lynn to eat at his mother's house and at his sister Mary Raimo's house, where they would eat and laugh as Harry got his white shirts covered with tomato sauce and gulped meat balls stuffed with raisins for sweetness.

Lepcio used to laugh that they both liked singing so much, they would call each other "Enzio Pinza" after an opera singer. But Lepcio mostly called him "Aggie," as did some of his other teammates.

Harry started off at a torrid pace. After one game, in which Harry had tripled off the center field wall at Fenway against the Yankees, he kidded Consolo, his teammate on the road about it.

Consolo came back. "I'm not taking anything away from you, but Mantle should have caught it. He over-ran it," he said of the Yankees' great center fielder, Mickey Mantle, who already had injured knees, a problem that would plague him all his career.

"You know why," Consolo said. "His knee. When he gets going, he can't stop."

"He should have caught it?" Harry cracked back. "It wasn't a hit? Maybe I should play for the Greek Red Raiders, so I get some legitimate hits, huh?"

"I'm not taking anything away from you, Harry. The ball was hit good. All right, you hit .500 against the Yankees," in the series, he said.

"What did you hit?" Harry asked. Consolo laughed back.

"That series? Zero-zero-zero."

But now, Harry was starting to fall off a little, and there was some veiled criticism of Harry's ability. On a road trip against western teams, he had gone only 5-for-36 for a .139 average.

Globe sportswriter Clif Keane recalled that Brooklyn Dodgers catcher Roy Campanella had predicted Harry would slump after seeing him in an exhibition game between the two clubs in Miami.

"I understand Agganis was quite a football player," said Campanella. "But you know they don't curve a football."

And that's just what Harry was getting as pitchers were not showing him many fastballs, fearful of that line-drive hitting rip he possessed and which had carried him from semipro games as a teenager through high school and college and many All-Star teams.

Billy Goodman said "Harry's been getting almost nothing but curves lately. And I think it's got him down a little bit. Only rarely do they give him a peek at a fastball, and it's almost always on the outside of the plate," he said.

Goodman though had seen the Agganis work ethic. "Pretty soon he'll have his confidence back again," he said. But it was mid-June and Harry had fallen to .253, a plateau around which he would stay the rest of the season, disappointing him, although he continued to be able to make clutch hits.

He struggled through the heat of July and the Summer, but didn't lose his perspective. On a road trip to Chicago to play the White Sox, Harry left tickets for his uncle, Louis Pappas, his mother's brother, and for an old friend from Lynn, Jimmy Andrews, who was there on business.

After the game, instead of going to a fancy restaurant or nightclub, they went back to Louis Pappas' house. Harry loved him, and often laughed that he saw Louis, wearing a silk suit, following him everywhere in different towns.

Pappas was a prominent political figure in Chicago too, and it didn't take long for word to spread that Harry Agganis was in the neighborhood.

In a few hours, the house was full of aunts, uncles, nieces, nephews and cousins. "That was the environment and we spent the whole night there," Andrews said. "He never mentioned his playing or how he was doing. He kept asking about his friends and family and how they were doing," he said.

But Harry had not lost his penchant for drama either. On August 15 in Yankee Stadium, he again showed why Stengel was always coveting him.

In the sixth inning, with the Sox losing 6-1, Harry rocketed his first major league grand slam, twenty rows up into the right-field seats, off Bob Grim. He would describe the slam as his biggest baseball thrill.

The next day, in an exhibition game at Fenway Park against the National

League New York Giants, Harry had a home run in a hitting contest, matching Willie Mays. Williams didn't connect. Mays and Jimmy Piersall, both possessed of great arms, had a throwing contest with Mays being declared a narrow winner on tosses home from right field. Piersall hurt his arm

Harry went 1-for-2 in the game, won by the Sox 6-5 in the ninth inning, on a Lepcio double which scored Sam Mele, a veteran from New York who moved to Quincy in Massachusetts. He was brought in by Boudreau in a trade with Baltimore to shore up first base. And although he and Harry were competing with each other, he said he knew the job would be Agganis' soon, and for many years, he thought.

"Harry eventually was going to be the first baseman. It was just a question of him honing his skills," said Mele. "He had them, but they had to be a little more fluid, even at the bat he was a stiff hitter, but a good hitter. You could tell he was going to be a hell of a ballplayer. He just needed the experience."

The benching didn't haunt Harry. "He knew what was going on and he was a fantastic competitor. He was just biding his time," said Mele. "He was dedicated and he was tough. You knew he was going to make it through his perserverance and his practice habits," he said.

There were a few more bright lights for Harry in the 1954 season. On August 2, he tripled in the eighth inning of a game with the Yankees at Yankee Stadium, helping his team to a 10-9 win. The hit also hurt the Yankees chances to catch the Indians, who were on a record breaking pace that would see them end with 111 victories in a 154-game season, still the most wins in baseball history.

Harry's triple sent outfielder Gene Woodling running into the center field fence, where he struck his right hand against the wall, breaking his thumb. He remained in the game until the twelfth and last inning. Stengel would be left to grumble again about Harry hurting the Yankees. Harry finished the year hitting .369 against the Bronx Bombers.

A few days later, Harry batted in the tie-breaking run to help beat the Tigers, 5-3, putting the two teams in a virtual tie for fourth place in the eight-team league. Harry's hit was a 400-foot sacrifice fly in the fifth inning that would have been a home run in any other ball park. "I guess I'll have to have an extra bowl of cereal every morning," he said.

As he struggled, the Colts continued to show interest in getting him to change his mind. Some of Harry's teammates also wondered whether he had made the right decision, feeling he would be a very good major league baseball player, but that he could dominate in professional football.

"I don't think baseball came half as easy as football did," said Frank Sullivan, the lanky pitcher. Harry said he was thinking of football as Colts officials watched some of his games.

When the Red Sox were in Baltimore, Harry would have dinner with Colts owner Carroll Rosenbloom, who keenly wanted him, even if it meant Harry would have to play two sports in different seasons.

And Harry continued to stay involved in his community too, setting up the Harry Agganis bowling tournament for teenagers at the Huntington 55 alleys. It was little consolation to Harry as the Sox would finish in fourth place at 69-85.

It was a disappointing year for him and he vowed to do better in 1955. "I know I'm a .300 hitter, " he told friends. Still, he finished with a respectable .251, six stolen bases, and 11 home runs, including eight at Fenway Park, the most there by a left-handed batter except for Ted Williams, in more than 20 years. He led the American League in assists and worked hard on his fielding.

Broadcaster Curt Gowdy was impressed. He said Harry had hit four home runs deep into the right field bleachers at Fenway Park where he said Joe Cronin told him Yankee great Lou Gehrig hadn't hit any.

Stengel said "Against us, here or at Fenway, he's another Gehrig. How do you get him out?" Later, Stengel told Herald sportswriter Bill Cunningham, "He's got that thing, you know, the hustle, the 'ol zizz."

Harry returned to be an assistant football coach at B.U. in the Fall, working with his good friends, Charlie Maloy, the former Holy Cross star quarterback, to help Tom Gastall, a quarterback and outstanding baseball player who was also being wooed by major league teams, especially the Baltimore Orioles.

After B.U. lost a heartbreaker to Boston College, 7-6, a team that didn't want to play B.U. when Harry was there, a co-ed in the stands turned to her date and pointed him out. Harry was wearing a camel's hair coat.

"See that fellow down there? I wish he could have played for us today," she said.

When he wasn't at B.U. or with his friends and family, Harry went to the Lynn YMCA to work out and to try to bulk himself up for the 1955 season, when he said he would improve. It had been a good year in many ways already though.

Harry was selected as Lynn's greatest athlete, ahead of Cleveland Indians catcher Jim Hegan, who was second, and Boley Dancewicz, the All-American quarterback at Notre Dame, who had preceded Harry at Classical, Blondy Ryan of the New York Giants, Bump Hadley of the Yankees, Bernie Friberg of the Chicago White Sox, Tom Whalen of Notre Dame, Georgetown and the Canton Bulldogs, and Henry Toczylowski, quarterback for Boston College's 1940 Sugar Bowl champions.

Later, Harry told a Kiwanis Club meeting in Lynn about the time he broke his leg as a teenager playing American Legion ball as he was trying to score on a hit. "I hesitated a fraction of a second when I found the catcher a few feet up the line, and, as I was attempting to score from third base on a ground ball. The momentary hesitation threw me off stride. The result was that I ran into the catcher, did a complete flip in the air, and you could hear the crack all over the park when the fall snapped a bone in my leg."

His weight had fallen to 189 pounds during his rookie year and he wanted to get up to nearly 220 pounds for the rigors of the major league season when he was expecting to play most of the year as a starter. Gernert had been called back up at the end of the 1954 season, but still had a yellow pallor from his hepatitis bout and was shipped out again.

In 1955, Harry's competition would be the big slugger Norm Zauchin, who was a tough veteran and a great athlete too, having played professional hockey, golf, and been a professional bowler. Then too, the Colts were staying in contact. They wanted to make him a star in two sports.

THARROS ◆ COURAGE ◆ ΘΑΡΡΟΣ
1955

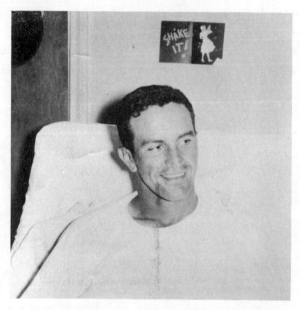

Shortly before he left for Spring training, Harry went to his brother Phil's house in Hamilton for a going-away party. Most of his family was there, and he brought Jean Dallaire. It was a warm, wonderful family night in the finished basement and there was a sense of optimism in the room.

Harry had some concerns about what his future held, and whether he should be involved in personal relationships when he was trying so hard to concentrate on staying in the major leagues. Also that week, Harry showed Phil a photo of the daughter of the lumberjack king in Florida. She was, Phil said, "A knock-out." Harry said, "She's a very nice girl, but I'm going to concentrate on my career."

He knew his competition in Spring training would be even more formidable this year because Norm Zauchin, a big, powerful right-handed slugger who had been in the Marines in Korea before spending the year before in Louisville, was back.

As the party went on, Harry went to a corner of the room and talked quietly with Phil. A few days later, Harry took Jean to Waterhill Street to meet his mother for the first time. Jean was nervous and just smiled a lot as Harry did most of the talking. "She was a handsome woman," Jean remembered. It was a serious step to be meeting her, she thought, and there were concerns in the family about a Catholic girl and a Greek boy getting together.

Inside, Harry was having a conflict with his own words. As perhaps the most famous and premier role model for Greek-Americans, he struggled with wanting to stay within his culture and the rapid way the country was changing and assimilating the children of first generation immigrants of all ethnicities.

He finished workouts at Lynn Classical indoors that winter, in the gymnasium, where his cousins, Stella Agganis and Elaine Demakis, were attending school. The students were delighted too, and a photographer for the school yearbook took a picture of him stretching in a grey sweatsuit, which went into the book for the Class of 1955.

Harry took time to go back to the B.U. Varsity Club in February to present the award in his name by the Greek-American community for New England's outstanding schoolboy to Don Allard.

Shortly thereafter, Jean drove Harry to South Station to catch the train to Florida, and he was in a good mood. And so was she. As he boarded the train, Harry turned and put his Sigma Alpha Epsilon pin on her. She drove home on Cloud Nine, soaring in the romance. "It was a time of innocence, it was the 50s, the last of the innocence," she said.

When Harry got on board, he started reading Dr. Norman Vincent Peale's "The Power of Positive Thinking," and he was looking forward to a full year of playing after having worked hard all winter to improve his hitting.

His coach at Louisville in 1953, Mike "Pinky" Higgins, had been hired as the Red Sox manager to replace Lou Boudreau, who had been fired after 1954's disastrous year, when the team didn't respond to a blend of mixing the bonus babies with veterans. Harry was especially disappointed in his performance, although he had a respectable year and was developing a reputation as a feared clutch hitter.

He had another problem in the rising presence of Zauchin, the big slugger who, like Dick Gernert in 1954, was a right-handed hitter whose swing was made for the short left-field wall at Fenway Park, the 32-foot high Green Monster. Like Harry, Zauchin had a calm demeanor that belied his size.

Zauchin, whose parents were German and Dutch, was a friendly, easygoing man though and he and Harry got along well. Some sportswriters thought Zauchin would win the starting job because of that prodigious swing. Harry told friends the reason he had tailed off in 1954 was that he had gone down to 189 pounds, and he spent the winter bulking up to nearly 220 pounds.

Sportswriter Austen Lake, who had been critical of Harry's release from the Marines on a hardship dependency in 1951, had become friendlier toward him, and came over to him by the batting cage in Spring practice to ask about the first base battle.

"What if you lose your job?" asked Lake, who was always looking for a sharp angle off which he could spin a story.

Harry smiled easily and looked over. "I won't," he said. "The competition is what I need." He said it easily, without braggadocio. Lake later said he could feel the confidence coming off Harry. Zauchin and Harry would battle all Spring, but Higgins would leave it to a barnstorming trip coming North from Florida before deciding who would have the job. It was a tense time around the clubhouse because Ted Williams, who had started the year before with a broken collarbone that sidelined him, was in the midst of a messy divorce that was so complicated and tense that he wasn't even playing.

Harry had been sending letters back to Jean, but he didn't talk about baseball or how he was doing. He always kept those thoughts to himself, and wrote mostly asking how his friends and family were doing. And he sent her a present for her birthday on February 27. It was a yellow halter dress made for the summer, the time when they met. It was embroidered and it fit perfectly.

She wrote back. "I'll wear it for our first date when you get back, no matter how cold it is," she said. She couldn't wait to see him.

Harry had other pressures too. On Sunday, April 3, in Charleston, South Carolina, Zauchin hit a two-run homer off Philadelphia Phillies ace Robin Roberts to give the Red Sox a 4-2 win.

Higgins was delighted, because he had told Zauchin at the end of Spring training in Florida to change his stance, and the results were immediate and dramatic as the big slugger had his first display of power since.

Globe Sportswriter Hy Hurwitz said "As the Sox left Sarasota on Friday Higgins said the first base debate would be a dog-eat-dog affair between Zauchin and Harry Agganis. It looks as if Zauchin is the top dog now."

That was hard for Harry, who had always been the premier attraction in virtually every athletic contest in which he had appeared. Typically, he didn't complain, but vowed to work harder to win the job back. But the pressure on him was intense as the team headed North.

The next day though, in Greenville, South Carolina, Zauchin had two singles and a double to lead a 9-7 win over the Phillies again. Harry wasn't saying anything, but he wasn't playing and Higgins, his manager in Louisville in 1953, was talking about Zauchin now, whom Higgins had also coached at Louisville the year before. Zauchin was happy now too.

"I never was worried about my hitting. I knew I could hit. It was my fielding I was worrying about," he said. Harry had led the American League first basemen in assists in 1954 and was a better fielder than Zauchin. Higgins said the sudden return of Zauchin's power was "just what I expected." The next day, the two of them would have even more about which to cheer.

The Phillies, who had come close to signing Harry in 1952, won a slugfest, 17-12, but Zauchin had three hits to boost his Spring training average to .325, and he was swinging with an easy confidence. The next day, Zauchin again pummeled Roberts, one of the National League's best pitchers. He had a 365-foot homer in a game in Portsmouth, Virginia. Zauchin narrowly missed a second home run when a deep center field shot hit the fence.

With opening day only a few days away, Zauchin was getting most of the playing time now, and had been up to bat 55 times already, while Harry, with 38 at-bats, was hitting a sickly .158. But Harry still didn't seem down. He had immense confidence in his abilities and had been in slumps before, including his sophomore baseball season at B.U. when he started off by failing to get a hit his first 20 times up and still wound up with a .300 average and was an All-New England selection.

The headlines, which had always been the domain of Harry Agganis, were going to Zauchin. The two remained friendly rivals and tried to help each other. "He was always considerate and had nice things to say about other people, and his mom. I never thought there was a bad bone in his body. It was just twenty-five guys trying to do their best and whoever did got the job," said Zauchin.

He was modest, a big man from outside Detroit who, when he was playing for Louisville, met his future wife, Janet, when he was fielding a pop foul that fell into the stands. He fell in with it and landed on her lap. He looked up from his immodest position and she smiled back. It was love at first sight. The event landed them in Ripley's "Believe It Or Not."

But baseball was a business and a livelihood and both men played hard to win the job. Zauchin was hitting .524 on the road trip North and the headlines on April 8 proclaimed "Agganis' 1st Base Foe Nailing Down Hose Job." Birtwell wrote that "The incredible Norman Zauchin has been belting the ball all over Dixie and making a shambles of his so-called duel for first base with Harry Agganis." It was a remarkable comeback because, in Florida, Zauchin couldn't get the ball out of the infield.

The papers played the game too, putting Harry and Zauchin together for a photo of both leaning over looking like they were ready to field a ball.

They were smiling above a photo caption that read: "Who's On First?" Harry was named the best athlete on the Red Sox. His B.U. teammate, Tommy Gastall, who had been compared to Harry, was named B.U.'s Athlete of the Year for 1955.

And Harry went up to Salem to see Jean, their first date since he came back from Spring training. They went to the Continental on Route 1 in Saugus for dinner, but it was a cold day and she didn't wear the yellow halter dress he'd sent. She figured there would be plenty of time for that in the summer when they could go back to Lynn beach when Harry was on home stands with the Red Sox and staying in Lynn. She looked forward to those long, languid days on the beach when they could lie in the sun and talk.

In a final warm-up before opening day, in an exhibition game against the New York Giants and Wille Mays at Fenway Park, Zauchin was again impressive and was named the starting first baseman. Harry would open the season in an uncharacteristic spot, the bench.

He wouldn't be there long.

ANESYCHIA ◆ WORRY ◆ ΑΝΗΣΥΧΙΑ

Zauchin, who had been tearing the cover off the ball, went hitless on opening day while his wife was in Birmingham, Alabama, waiting to deliver their first child. In the team's first three games, Zauchin went 0-for-12. On that Friday, his wife delivered their daughter, Jean, while sportswriters wondered if his worry about his wife was adding to his slump. He was striking out all over the place, but Higgins defended him. "Let's not get too hasty," the manager said. After Zauchin's wife gave birth, Higgins smiled that Zauchin would have to hit now.

"That's it," he laughed. "Those evening dresses cost a lot of money."

Harry got some playing time the next day, going 1-for-4 against the White Sox. The next day, he had four hits and three runs batted in in a doubleheader against the White Sox, but the Red Sox dropped the two games, 14-5 and 12-9.

When Harry wasn't playing, he was back in Lynn with his friends and family, or going out with Jean, sometimes just driving around. Harry would sing along with the music on the radio, especially his two favorite songs, "My Funny Valentine," and their song, "Someone To Watch Over Me." When they were apart and heard that song, she said it always reinforced how close they felt to each other.

And then one day, while she was in her classroom in Lynnfield, she heard the gleeful peals of laughter from children in the schoolyard, and a buzz rolling through the corridors like a stampede of boys and girls in chase. It was Harry.

He was surrounded by amazed schoolchildren, and even teachers who came to see the Golden Greek. Harry stopped to talk and play with the children, who adored him. Jean was astounded to see him, but that was Harry. He was always showing up. He invited her to come to New York to spend a weekend and watch him play the Yankees in Yankee Stadium.

She wasn't sure if it would be proper. This was the 50s, after all. But Harry, always a gentleman, assured her it was an innocent proposal, and she could bring a friend to stay with her at her hotel. She asked her mother, who urged her to go. She brought Louella Cummings of Salem with her.

Jean sent him a telegram in New York she was coming. It was good timing. Mike Frangos was driving through New York and had called Harry, who invited him to stay with him and to go on a double date. After the game, they went to the Black Angus for dinner, but Harry had to get back for a curfew and Jean and Louella returned home the next day. Harry was so surprised she'd come, he had to get an advance on his pay from the road manager to pay for the dinner for all of them. It was, she said, one of the greatest weekends of her life.

Zauchin's single in the ninth inning beat the Yankees, 1-0, on the Sunday game that weekend, but he and Harry were splitting time as Harry began to hit the ball hard.

Harry had more on his mind than baseball though. One Spring day when the Red Sox were on a home stand, he drove up to Salem to see Jean again. He looked worried. As they were driving, he looked over at her and took her hand. But it wasn't for a moment of tenderness.

He took her hand and put it on his right calf. It was the leg he had broken as a boy playing baseball for the American Legion in Lynn. She was startled. There was a big lump there. Neither of them said anything.

"We didn't know what to make of it, we didn't know if it was serious," she said. They didn't talk about it again.

When the Red Sox were home, he would leave a ticket for her in a box seat near first base, where she could watch him play. She would take the train to North Station and then a subway over to the park, and meet him at the players entrance later, and they would often go to the General Edwards Inn in Lynn for dancing, and to Varley's again for a bite to eat later. It was a blissful arrangement.

Jean once bought tickets to see the play "Damn Yankees" at a Boston theater, although Harry had taken sportswriters to see it in Chicago one time, and didn't tell her. The seats were not good, way in the back of the theater. At intermission, a fan recognized Harry and laughed, "Is this the best you can do?"

But always there was baseball and the battle with Zauchin, although they remained good friends. And on May 4, in a game in Detroit in which Tigers fans threw beer cans at Red Sox center fielder Jimmy Piersall, Harry's hit in the eleventh inning, a whining line shot off the right field screen that was hit so hard it bounced back and kept him to a single, set up a Red Sox win and he was starting to ensconce himself at first base.

The Red Sox, picked to finish fourth in the eight-team American League, were falling toward the cellar now though, and fans clamored for Williams to return. On May 8, he finally got an uncontested divorce, but went into seclusion instead of reporting to the club. Three days later, details of the divorce were revealed. Williams had to pay his former wife $50,000 in cash and to turn over their $42,000 Miami home and his Cadillac. Williams telephoned Red Sox General Manager Joe Cronin and told him he would report to the club in two days. He was coming back to play, because he was making $85,000 a year, and loved the game.

Williams signed his contract on Friday the 13th.

On Sunday, Harry had one of his best days in a doubleheader at Fenway Park against the Tigers. In the first game, which the Sox won, 10-4, Harry started a rally with a double and finished a second with a three-run triple, raising his average to .307. "I'm not trying to kill the ball. I'm trying to be a hitter. I'm following the ball better and hitting it where it's pitched," he said. He said he was going to try to stop swinging for the fences.

The year before, in his freshman season, he tried to pull pitches. Now, he was learning his craft and Williams, who had kept an eye on his development, said he saw the makings of a hitter who also had power. "He was just on the verge and he had power and he could pull. He was going to be a hell of a hitter," Williams said. He said Harry's style reminded him a lot of another developing power hitter from the New York Yankees, Roger Maris, who in a few years would set the single season home run record of 61 to beat Babe Ruth.

The next day, May 16, was an off-day for the Red Sox, but Harry went to Fenway Park anyway, where he saw Williams working out. Harry wanted to work out as well, although he wasn't feeling well, and Higgins was startled to see him there because Harry had played so well against the Tigers a day before in a doubleheader.

"What are you doing here at the park?" Higgins asked, puzzled.

"I don't know what's the matter with me," Harry said. "But I couldn't sleep a wink last night. I developed a terrific pain in my right side."

"It can't be anything serious the way you were hitting yesterday," Higgins smiled suddenly. "You usually get a stitch in your side when you miss the ball. You didn't miss many swings yesterday. Every time I looked up you were smashing out a line drive," he said.

Higgins, sensing something wrong since Harry never complained, ordered him to see Jack Fadden, the team trainer. Fadden put him on the table for heat treatements, but, after taking his temperature and seeing a fever, he had Harry sent to Sancta Maria Hospital, a small, Catholic-run hospital on Memorial Drive in Cambridge, along the Charles River on a site which later housed part of the Massachusetts Institute of Technology. Many of the nurses and adminstrators were nuns.

It was a curious assignment, although the Red Sox routinely used Sancta Maria. But Harry's case seemed serious, and some teammates and friends wondered why he wasn't sent to one of the more prestigious of Boston's many teaching and general hospitals. Harry had a history of pneumonia, and was going to be treated by the Red Sox team physician, Dr. Timothy Lamphier, who was not well-liked by some of the team officials.

At Sancta Maria, Harry was diagnosed with pneumonia in his left lung and admitted quickly. He was feeling very poorly. It was a grim admission from a man who never complained, who had been chased all over football fields, often without being hit. But the beating of the Maryland game in 1952, when he suffered severely bruised ribs, had taken its toll.

Still, few thought there were any serious problems with Harry. He had a constant stream of visitors at the hospital, including reporters and photographers and teammates, old friends and coaches and well-wishers. Jean Dallaire was among the visitors, but Harry was not getting much rest, and he was anxious watching the papers—Zauchin was starting to hit well.

Harry wanted to return to the Red Sox as quickly as possible. Zauchin was playing well and, after having worked so hard to become a starter, Harry didn't want to get into a platooning situation again, where he would be alternating with Zauchin.

After a ten-day stay, Harry got out of the hospital—just in time to watch Zauchin have his greatest game ever, on May 27. Zauchin had three home runs, including a grand slam, and 10 RBIs, as the Red Sox beat Washington, 16-0. Harry was under more pressure than ever to return to the team or risk being out of the lineup, but his leg was still hurting.

The next morning, May 28, Harry went to Fenway Park and put on his uniform to pose for a photo with Cleo Sophios, a seventeen-year-old high school student from Medford, who was the first recipient of the Harry Agganis Scholarship to attend B.U. Since he had had turned down a car and gifts from the B.U. Varsity Club in 1953, the scholarship had been built up to $10,000.

Sophios, daughter of Greek immigrant parents, had been selected after a screening process led by Harry's marketing professor at B.U., John Alevizos. She had worked babysitting and at other jobs trying to earn money for college, but would not have been able to go without Harry's scholarship, which was renewed for four years.

She was nervous, a young Greek-American woman from a strict family background meeting the idol of Greek-American youths. Her father came too, but Harry put her at ease, asking questions about cooking, ethnic matters, and her background and family.

"*Pou eene ee metera sou?*" "Where is your mother?" he asked.

"Sto spiti mas." At our home, she said. They laughed.

Sophios said, "You know how the Greeks are. She has to stay home and cook," and Harry laughed again. "My family is important to me and I respected the man," she said.

But something didn't seem right. Harry was forcing his famous smile. "I'm weak," he said on a warm and sunny day. "It's good to be up and out in the sunshine," he said.

His family was worried too, wondering if he'd come out of the hospital too soon, and uncertain about his medical treatment, especially since his father had suffered from pneumonia and Harry had suffered a bout with it in high school.

His mother was anxious as Harry had left the house that day to go to Fenway Park to work out. *"Pou pas, pethaki mou? Na pexeis bolo. Then fenese kala,"* she said in Greek, "Where are you going, my child? To play ball. You don't look well."

Harry responded, in Greek, telling her not to worry, that he was alright and that the doctors wouldn't have let him out if he wasn't recovered. His mother turned to his brother, Paul, and said, *"Pestone, pou pas?"* Where is he going? Paul thought he looked weak too.

Phil came home from work for lunch that day, but Harry had already gone to Fenway for the photo session with Sophios and to work out, and his mother told her other sons she was worried about Harry's health. She thought he was going back too fast from pneumonia, because she had cared for her husband when he was ill. Harry had told Phil he had to get back. "If I don't, they'll think I'm shirking it," he said.

Red Sox broadcaster Curt Gowdy was at Fenway and he saw Harry working out, taking hitting practice with Ted Williams. Harry was sweating heavily.

"What are you doing here?" Gowdy asked, and Harry responded wanly that "The team needs me, Curt." But he didn't look well.

Harry hadn't forgotten his friends either. He spoke to a father-and-son breakfast at Temple Sinai in Swampscott, at the invitation of his friend and former high school assistant coach, Harold Zimman. He had a telling message. "You've got to do the right thing in life," he told the kids. "You can be the greatest athlete in the world, but unless you're a religious person, unless you abide by the rules of the game, it all means nothing," he said.

Zimman was thrilled. He said, "Harry's idea was that a person should know the true value of things, no matter how much success or failure he has." And Harry always did. He was trying to do the right thing by going back to his teammates.

Harry caught up with the team in Chicago on June 1, but he still wasn't feeling well. He said he thought he could work his way back into strength, but was coughing a lot. Lepcio said he was worried about his friend and urged him to see Fadden again and rest instead of playing.

Lepcio was fretful. "Aggie, what the hell's the matter with you?" he asked, urging him to get some medical treatment and not play.

The night he returned, a Wednesday, Harry and *Daily Record* sportswriter Joe Cashman went to see "The King And I" at the Shubert Theater in Chicago. "The Golden Greek on that evening was a happy, smiling picture of health. You would have taken a lease on his life," and he seemed fully recovered from the first bout of pneumonia, Cashman wrote later.

On June 2, a Thursday, Harry leaned over the steps of the dugout to see if he was in the lineup. He did a double take and looked twice. He was going to start. He looked over and saw a forlorn Zauchin sitting on the bench, and went over to sit next to him.

"What's the matter with you?" he asked.

"I'm not hitting the long ball," Zauchin said.

A sportswriter muttered, wondering if the Sox were thinking about trading Harry again, "I wonder if Agganis is in the showcase." Higgins arrived though and said "We'll give them (the White Sox) the left-handed treatment in this park."

The Red Sox lost, 4-2, but Harry, batting cleanup behind Williams, the game's greatest hitter, who was third, went 2-for-4. But after he doubled on a hit that looked like he could have had a triple, Harry simply sat down on second base, too fatigued to move.

Lepcio was even more worried now because Harry had never seemed so vulnerable or weak. But he had moved his average up to .313 and Williams was impressed. He told Lepcio that Harry would be a big hitter who could help the club, especially in clutch situations.

Harry stayed in the game and, in his last at-bat with the bases loaded and one out, hit a screaming line drive into center field that was caught off the shoetops in a diving grab by the fleet Jungle Jim Rivera, who threw back to first to double up Williams, who was running on what looked like a sure extra-base hit.

After the game, *Boston Globe* sportswriter Clif Keane came over to Harry and asked how he was. "I'm tired, just tired," said Harry.

On the train that night to Kansas City, where the Red Sox were going to play on the next stop of their road trip, Harry coughed incessantly and was downspirited, unlike his usual self when he would be leading songs and talking with his closest friends on the team, like Lepcio and Mele.

The next night, Saturday, he went out with Lepcio and Mele, but had to stop on a street corner to rest. That morning, at 2 a.m., he had called his sister Mary. She thought it odd.

Later that morning, Harry went to see the team's trainer, Jack Fadden. "Jack, I'm not feeling well, can you take my temperature?" Harry asked. Fadden discovered a fever, and made an urgent call to the team's General Manager, Joe Cronin and said he was sending Harry back to Boston. It was Sunday.

After a quick packing, Harry was walking through the corridor of the hotel where Gowdy spotted him. Harry walked over to him slowly and said, "Thanks for all the support you've given me. I'm going to be back, but I've got to catch a plane now." Gowdy had an uneasy feeling.

In Boston, Harry was met at the airport by a worried Cronin, who accompanied him back to Sancta Maria. This time, Lamphier wouldn't be treating him. The Red Sox had a trio of doctors, Eugene O'Neill, Timothy Badger, and John Rattigan overseeing his treatment.

It was announced he would probably be out of action for two months. Immediately, there was speculation he came back to the team too quickly. Harry tried to explain.

"I felt weak but I thought it was just due to the fact I had been ill and that I would keep getting stronger. But I just haven't felt right," he said. "Now I know that by hurrying back I'm not doing the club or myself any good. I'll follow medical orders but I sure hope it will be real soon. I still feel perfectly all right but I just seem awfully weak."

O'Neill said that "Harry was a lot sicker than realized when he entered the hospital. His case is a very complicated one and a very serious one. If his condition warrants it, he could be idle all season .. we will take no chances with him. He is too nice a boy and too valuable."

The pneumonia the first time was in the right lung, and now it was in the left lung, and there were complications—phlebitis—a swelling in the leg he had shown Jean Dallaire. Doctors packed the swollen leg in ice and kept him rigidly immobile, a frustrating problem for the athlete.

This time, few visitors were allowed, except for family and Jean and calls from close friends like Shirley Mandeville, whom he had dated and whose young brother Harry had befriended.

Not even Donelli, his college coach, could get in to see him. There was almost no notice in the Boston papers, except for a small story which said Harry had been hospitalized a second time with pneumonia and would be out indefinitely. O'Neill said Harry had returned to action too soon. His family, especially his brothers and sisters and mother, came to see him often.

Columnist Murray Kramer went to see him and said his face was wan and he was coughing a lot, but his spirits were fine. Kramer talked about how he was hitting .313 and slugging the ball. Kramer said just before Harry got ill, he had hit the left field wall more times in two weeks than all the last year.

"I'll do even better when I get back, Murray," he said. "I've got it figured out. I'm basically a left-handed pull hitter and with the deep right field and that wind blowing in so much, I have been flying out a lot. Trying to pull those outside pitches had me popping up a lot, too. But I've got it beaten. I'm using a 38-ounce bat, one of the heaviest in baseball. With this war club, I can hit an outside pitch off that left field wall. And I'm strong enough to still pull that heavy bat if those pitches come inside and the wind is right."

On June 16, Harry was placed on the disabled list so the Red Sox could bring up shortstop Milt Bolling to take his place on the roster, but Harry, who had dominated headlines in the papers for a decade, disappeared from them, except for a cartoon that day, June 7, which talked about Zauchin's resurgence."Long as Norm Clouts, Zauch-In, Agganis Out," it said.

On June 23, Themis Stoumbelis, Donelli's secretary at B.U. and a close friend of Harry's ever since, sent him over a book, "Auntie Mame." She didn't want to frazzle him with a visit, but sent a note that said, "This book is supposed to be good for what ails you."

That night, Donelli was sitting at his home when the phone rang.

"B-36, right!" Donelli heard, the bark of a B.U. football signal. It was Harry.

"Harry, you must be feeling better," a relieved Donelli said. Harry had an unmistakable tone of authority and command when he spoke. "Harry had the sort of voice, well, no one else talked in the huddle while he was quarterbacking," Donelli said.

Harry had told his brother, Phil, that the Baltimore Colts wanted him to sign to play football in the offseason and that he was seriously considering accepting the deal that would have made him a star in two professional sports.

Two days later, on Saturday morning, June 25, Father Charles Mihos of St. George's church, came to see Harry. Except for Harry's mother and sister and direct family, he was one of the few allowed in. Harry had donated money to help with the landscaping of the church, and was financing a $10,000 renovation of his mother's home because she didn't want him to build a new house for her.

"When will the church be landscaped? Are we receiving enough donations?" Harry asked. Earlier, he had come to the church to talk to Father Mihos about the donation Harry had given to the church to help with the work. Father Mihos had talked about a clock and where to put it, a topic which unsettled Harry.

"Clocks do not belong in the house of God, Father," Harry said.

But now, with Father Mihos there, Harry was in a more somber state of mind. "Father, please pray for my recovery," he said.

Father Mihos was worried. Harry was good to his family and the church and always came by the church to light a candle and drop tickets to him for the ball games. He tried to ease the tension. "Do you want me to take care of Zauchin for you?" he laughed.

Harry laughed back. He admired Zauchin and they were friendly rivals, but Harry was confident in his ability. "I'll take care of him myself," he smiled.

Harry told him that on Monday morning the doctors were going to sit him up and let him move a little. He was excited and asked Father Mihos to see if some of Harry's best friends, Mike Frangos and George Maravelias and Harry's nephew, Jimmy Orphanos, could come by.

Jimmy "Jeep" Kirios was in the Army in Germany where, only a month before, Harry's Christmas card had arrived—four months late. He didn't like it. Harry was sending all his friends Christmas cards that were deep black with silver lettering. It made some of them shiver.

Father Mihos left.

And then in he came.

It was Ted Williams.

PROEIDOPOIESIS ◆ WARNING ◆ ΠΡΟΕΙΔΟΠΟΙΗΣΙΣ

Harry's brother, Paul, and his wife Bessie, came in a few moments later.

"You just missed Ted Williams," Harry said.

"How you feeling, Harry?" they asked.

"I feel great," he said. But then he started to cough and spit up.

Paul was very quiet, but he was very concerned. Bessie moved to the side of the bed to sit next to Harry, who was now coughing loudly and spitting.

"What did you just spit up?" she asked.

"Oh, it's nothing," Harry said. "It's just a little blood." It was a Greek act of *tharros*, courage, to spare his family worry.

"Let me see it," she said. "Harry, please, have you told anybody about this?"

"It's nothing," he said. "I've had this before."

They stayed for an anxious thirty minutes and left because Harry looked very tired, although he was trying to be buoyant.

Later that day, the Red Sox team physician, Dr. Lamphier, said he was walking by Harry's room when one of Harry's nurses, Mary Ellen Good, came running out. "We rushed in and his face was bluish-black and he had a red foam coming out of his mouth and his blood pressure was up," Lamphier said. Harry's right leg had been packed in ice to try to alleviate the pain of phlebitis and break up what doctors thought was a blood clot there. There was talk of surgery.

Lamphier called Cronin at the Hotel Cadillac in Detroit and said he warned him Harry had a dangerous clot, but that he was told the doctors treating Harry were aware of all the complications. But some Red Sox team officials didn't accept Lamphier's observations, and didn't want him treating Harry.

That night, Harry felt better, although he was still sweating a lot. John Alevizos visited and saw Harry talking with three young Greek-American women from prominent families who had managed to get in, as had Ted Lepcio.

The next day, Sunday, June 26, Harry's old high school friend, Nick Sentas, came to visit and nurse Elsie Morrow was photographed taking Harry's temperature, and he spent some time watching the Red Sox play the White Sox on TV that afternoon.

The Red Sox swept a doubleheader, and Zauchin had a long home run that made Harry's friend, sportswriter Bill Cunningham, wince for his boy.

Harry though laughed at the story of Luke Hollingsworth, an eleven-year-old Red Sox fan from Elkton, Kentucky, who had gotten into a fist fight with another boy who had said that Ted Williams wasn't as good a hitter as Al Rosen of the Cleveland Indians.

The Red Sox had flown the boy to Boston to watch the White Sox game and get a ball signed by Williams, and he was going to fly to Pittsbugh with the team later for an exhibition game against the Pirates the next day.

Jean Dallaire came by later and spent a couple of hours alone with Harry, sitting next to him on the edge of the bed watching television and talking. He told her he was going to be fine and not to worry. But he had been sweating a lot earlier.

She got up to leave and kissed him goodbye. He had a big grin on his face. She walked to the door and turned around. "I'll see you tomorrow," she said.

In the hall, she met Harry's sister, Mary, who was coming in with Harry's mother.

"I'm worried about Harry," Mary said.

"Oh Mary, don't worry. Nothing is going to happen to Harry," Jean said.

After the visit, Harry's mother, as she always did, went over to him and tenderly leaned over and kissed him on the cheek. Mary went outside where her husband, Tony, was minding their children so they could wave goodbye to Harry at his window. As the children waved and Mary looked up at the window where Harry was waving wanly, she thought she could see a ring of light around his head. It looked, she thought, like a halo.

That night, Harold Zimman, his old assistant coach in high school, came by with his wife, Helen. Harry had especially liked Zimman, who had been close to him in high school, and was glad to see him because they could speak frankly.

The TV was on, and they talked only a little bit about the effect on his career. "It's only temporary," Harry said. They talked about Zauchin, but Harry was not worried and said he didn't think of him as a rival. "There's room for both of us in the major leagues. As a matter of fact, I like Norm, we've roomed together," Harry said.

But he was sweating a lot now, and uncharacteristically complaining of a pain in his leg. Still, Harry tried to dismiss it. "Being sick is an education," he said. "It gives you a better sense of values," he added.

They turned back to the television. Ed Sullivan's Sunday night variety show was on. After they left, Harry picked up a book he was starting to read. It was Somerset Maugham's *Of Human Bondage*. He put in a bookmark and closed it, on page eighteen. Tomorrow morning he was going to sit up and walk.

That night, his cousin, Stella Agganis, who was worried deeply about Harry and couldn't stop thinking about him, had an unsettling dream.

She was dreaming about Harry's house on Waterhill Street. It was falling apart. "Oh my God, What's happening to my aunt's house?" she thought. A moment later, she saw an image inside St. George's Church in front of the altar. It was Harry, standing there, wearing a topcoat and beige suitcoat.

He was in front of the icon of the *Panagia*, the Virgin Mary. He was lighting a *lambatha*, a giant white candle, and placing it into a holder.

He walked to the icon of the Virgin Mary on the left side of the altar and blessed himself with the Sign of the Cross.

Chapter Ten

ATHANATOS ◆ IMMORTAL ◆ ΑΘΑΝΑΤΟΣ
June 27–30, 1955

J oe Terrasi, a halfback for B.U.'s 1952 team in Harry's last year, was in Buff Donelli's office on Monday morning, June 27. Dr. Ken Cristophe, the team doctor who was affiliated with the medical school, was agitated that Harry's treatment had been going on so long. It was starting to look like Harry would be out for the season.

"If he's not better by tomorrow, I'm going to get him out of there," Cristophe said to Donelli, as Terrasi listened, wondering and worried.

Ted Williams was in the Red Sox medical room, talking, as usual about hitting, when Harry's name came up. "Harry's going to be a real good hitter when he gets a little more experience and learns a couple of things. He's a great natural athlete."

Early that morning, about 8:30, Harry got a call in his room. It was John Alevizos, who was calling to talk about the scholarship that had been given to Cleo Sophios. Harry was anxious because the doctors were on their way to lift him out of bed so he could stand for the first time in weeks. Alevizos said he would see Harry later.

It was going to be a big day. Harry's friend from high school days, Jimmy Andrews, who was eight years older, was going to stop by later that day too because his work as a salesman would take him by the hospital. Harry's high school coach, Bill Joyce, was also going to come about noon, and Father Mihos was going to get some of Harry's boyhood friends by. His mother and sisters and family were looking forward to seeing him too.

There had been a sign outside Harry's door, limiting visitors to his family. Of course, that was unless Harry recognized who was outside and he would often wave them in. The doctors had been concerned at the beginning he was seeing too many people and not getting enough rest.

Sometime after 9 a.m., the doctors and nurses came in. The big moment had arrived. They were lifting Harry up, getting him righted in the bed. His first steps were a few moments away. His right leg had stayed immobilized, but the ice in which it had been packed had been removed long before.

Suddenly, he clutched his hands to his breast.

"Oh, I've got a terrific pain in my chest," he said urgently.

It was critical. Something terrible had gone wrong. Harry Agganis, the invulnerable athlete who seemed immune to pain, who had walked off the field with badly bruised ribs in the Maryland game so the opponents wouldn't see he was hurt, was fighting for his life.

The blood clot doctors were worried about in his leg had broken loose and shot into his lung, blocking vital blood flows. It was a pulmonary embolism and it was choking the life out of the Golden Greek.

They were working frantically now, but the clot had gone into his lung and locked like a cork in a bottle. Harry would not give up. He was struggling for survival with the same redoubtable spirit that had carried him through so many battles on the athletic fields. His toes were curled in pain.

It was too late. After a furious twenty minute fight, Harry Agganis had died.

But before he did, he pulled a nurse close to his ear and uttered his last, gasping words. "Take care of my mother .... be sure she is alright."

APISTEPHTON ◆ UNBELIEVABLE ◆ ΑΠΙΣΤΕΥΤΟΝ

Harry's brother-in-law, Tony Raimo, was working, changing gas meters in the basement of a six-family house near the Lynn Hospital. A supervisor came to see him and told him there was trouble with Harry at the hospital and to go home.

When he got there, he found out the awful news. His wife, Mary, and Harry's mother were stunned. He took them on the long, slow drive to the hospital, twelve miles away in Cambridge, on the banks of the Charles River. It was just across the river from Fenway Park. They cried all the way.

They went in the room. Harry's mother walked over and closed his eyes and mouth, delicately, using a handkerchief. Mary and her mother were talking in Greek. Doctors and hospital officials were flustered and could only mutter, over and over, "I'm sorry, I'm sorry." Only Mary, Tony and Mrs. Georgia Agganis were in the room with him after that.

Hospital officials were frantically trying to locate Father Mihos at St. George's Church in Lynn, but he was out. They finally found Rev. Stephen Anthony at Assumption Church in nearby Somerville. "Father, we have a young man here, Harry Agganis, and he is in need of his last rites." They didn't tell him Harry had passed away.

Later, one of the doctors, Theodore Badger, said "It all came, one, two, three. We never expected it to happen that fast." He, along with O'Neill and Rattigan, signed the death certificate. They said death was caused by "a massive pulmonary embolism," the sudden blocking of an artery or vein by a clot or obstruction in the lung.

"Harry Agganis had been making a slow but but apparently satisfactory recovery from a severe pulmonary infection complicated by phlebitis," they stated.

When Father Anthony arrived, only Mrs. Agganis was is the room and he saw that Harry was dead, and she was fighting to maintain her composure. To calm her, he started reading the *Trisagion*, a brief requiem. When he got to the part where he would read Harry's name, he started to say, Charalambos, the usual Greek name for Harry.

Mrs. Agganis stopped him, her strength and bearing back. "*Ochi, Pater. To Christiano tou onoma eene Aristotelees*," she said in Greek. "No Father, his Christian name is Aristotle." She stayed composed, steadfast and stoic.

Father Anthony thought to himself it was fitting. In Greek, Aristotle is a compound name, *aristo*, which means excellence, and *telos*, to the end. Harry was excellent to the end.

He went out to call the Mavris Funeral Home in Lynn, which was directly across the street from St. George's Church. He told the director, Christy Mavris, who owned the business with his wife, Mercy, what had happened.

Mavris didn't believe him. "Give me the number so I can call you back," he said.

Father Anthony put down the phone and a sigh escaped from him. A nun came over to him. She was in tears and started talking about how Harry had died, how the blood clot had broken loose and killed him. "I just can't believe a twenty-five-year-old man can die," she sobbed.

Downstairs in the lobby, a happy Jimmy Andrews was on his way in to see his good friend. He didn't know what had happened upstairs. He saw one of the hospital officials looking grim. "Hi, how's Harry?" Andrews asked.

There was a pause. He couldn't believe what he had heard. He turned around, numbstruck, and walked outside, almost into busy Memorial Drive. He looked up. Walking toward him was Harry's high school coach and mentor, Bill Joyce. Now it was Andrews' turn to deliver the shocking news.

He told Joyce, who almost collapsed and staggered back, dazed himself. It didn't seem possible, they both thought. NOT HARRY! It wasn't believable. It couldn't have happened.

The news spread rapidly. Harry's brother, Phil, was at work at General Electric, looking forward to seeing Harry later. He got a call from a nun at the hospital and could barely catch his breath. He couldn't move. But, finally, he went to a phone booth to call his wife, Helen, at the company's West Lynn plant. No one knew where he was and he couldn't leave the booth, immobilized with anguish, speechless. A company operator, Jean Hegan, sister-in-law of Cleveland Indians catcher Jim Hegan of Lynn, traced the lines and talked to him. "Where are you? Where are you? Stay where you are. We'll come get you,"

Harry's brother Paul, and his wife, Bess, were going to see Harry that morning. Paul was in downtown Lynn near the Paramount Theater on Union Street. He double parked his car and a young man walked over to him. "Paul, I'm sorry to hear about your brother, Harry," he said.

"What do you mean?" Paul said. A moment later, he clutched his hair, pulling at it in disbelief and horror. Bess was in the car, perplexed, wondering what was going on. Paul staggered back and told her. They drove to Mary Raimo's house in a cloud of tears.

In Union Square, the place where thousands of people had gathered on Christmas Night in 1946 to hear the radio broadcast of Harry leading Lynn Classical to the national high school football championship, his high school sweetheart, Joan Fitzgerald, was driving through when someone stopped her. She hadn't heard the news spreading on radio and television.

She was shocked. She was with her daughter. She stopped the car and looked down. When she looked back up, the square was full of people, staggering and crying. "It was unbelievable, it was like VJ day," she said, the end of World War II when people had come out to celebrate. Now they came out to console each other.

Harry's family, his brothers and sisters and cousins came scrambling to 118 Waterhill Street, running up the stairs, bewildered by pain, hurrying to comfort his mother and each other. The news was spreading across New England, and the country.

Stella Agganis, who had the unsettling dream about Harry the night before, heard the news on the radio and wound up at Agganis' diner, owned by

Harry's cousin, in downtown Lynn. She didn't know how she got there, but met her good friend, and Harry's other cousin, Elaine Demakis. They started crying. The diners were in shock.

At B.U., Donelli was sitting in his chair in his office when he got a call. He almost dropped the receiver, and rocked back, tears coming quickly and involuntarily. "I can't believe it, I can't believe it," he muttered. It would be the most often-used phrase that day.

His secretary, Themis Stoumbelis,was coming up a back stairway when one of the players told her. She cried and ran upstairs. Everyone in the office was stopped, like the hands of a broken clock. Outside, on the campus and along the streets, people were standing, staring at nothing, or sitting and shaking their heads.

One reporter came in and asked if there were any special friends of Harry."Up here, we're all special friends of Harry," Stoumbelis said. She had handled all of Harry's fan mail at B.U., and said he responded to them all, with notes on many to young fans.

Anne Johnson, the daughter of Boston Herald cartoonist Vic Johnson, was in a subway car that hot, sticky morning. She had loved bantering playfully with Harry when she was a young girl at Spring training the year before, but her thoughts were dark this day.

All around her, Harry's name was being whispered softly on every lip, and she could see crumpled headlines under the sweaty, weary arms of people too tired to re-read the crushing news. She was seated next to a heavy man who was sweating heavily in the heat, and tried to stop hearing the incessant cacaphony around her ... "Wonderful athlete ... so good looking and strong ...such a fine boy ...."

She wanted to scream, "Keep still, can't you!" hoping if they stopped, it wouldn't have been real. The same scene was repeated on elevators and on park benches and sidewalks, in cafes and offices and along the waterfront. People were stopped, stunned, or talking to each other, as if hoping their words would take away what had happened.

In Oakland, Harry's former Red Sox teammate Billy Consolo, in the minor leagues, was notified by a Boston Globe reporter. Consolo started crying. "What happened? What happened? What happened?" he asked.

Then, he said, "What about his poor mother?" He hung up, unable to continue.

In Lynn, Father Mihos received a phone call from Mercy Mavris, who, with her husband, ran the funeral parlor near the church. "I have some bad news for you," Mavris said. "Harry has passed away." Father Mihos reeled. "You're crazy, I just saw him Saturday," he said.

As he slowly walked across the street from the church to the funeral parlor, Father Mihos was shaken. Harry was the *paleekaree*, the brave young warrior of the Greek-American community.

Before home games at Fenway, Harry would come in to light a candle and always had time for a few words with his admirers, and the old Greek women who would come in to the church.

He walked into the funeral home and saw Harry's body on a table. He still looked golden and strong, but awfully still. Mercy Mavris was crying and so was he. "You can have the greatest faith in the world ... but there comes a day when you say 'Why?'" he said.

Newspapers in the cities were flooded with calls, all asking the same question: "Is it true?" frantic callers asked. Across Boston, newsboys were hawking the early afternoon editions. "Harry Agganis Dies!" they yelled as people rushed off escalators to grab the newspapers, emblazoned with headlines that didn't seem real. HARRY AGGANIS DEAD EXTRA! HARRY AGGANIS DEAD

There would be more the next morning.

ALETHEIA ♦ TRUTH ♦ ΑΛΗΘΕΙΑ

The Red Sox had arrived in Pittsburgh that Monday morning to get ready for an exhibition game that night against the Pirates. They had taken Luke Hollingsworth, the Kentucky boy with them, but he wasn't feeling well and the team's traveling secretary, Tom Dowd, was trying to make arrangements to get him home, when he got a message in the lobby of the Hotel Schenley to call the team offices in Boston.

He went to a phone booth in the lobby, expecting a perfunctory call. He came out grim-faced and ran to have the available players gather in a room of the hotel. Some were already out for lunch, but Norm Zauchin and Ted Lepcio and a few others were there.

"This is the most awful news I've ever had to announce," Dowd said. "Harry Agganis is dead."

There was incredulity in the room. No one could believe it. Infielder Billy Klaus, who had been sitting on a couch with Hollingsworth and a couple of reporters, opened his mouth wide, but couldn't say anything. Hollingsworth put his head down sadly and wouldn't look up.

In his hotel room, Red Sox Manager Mike "Pinky" Higgins had gotten a separate call and said the same words so many others had that day. "I can't believe it. I can't believe it."

Jimmy Piersall came in to the lobby a little later. "I watched as he helped other fellows this year even though he was battling for his own job ... he was one of the best, that's all," said Piersall, who had often gone to charity banquets with Harry.

The Red Sox played their game that night, although none of them wanted to. "I don't know what to say or what to do," said Jimmy Piersall. "I don't even feel like playing, but I have to. It's taken something out of me." The Pirates won, 8-2.

During a moment of silence before the game, a lone voice yelled out, unable to hold the pent-up grief. "God bless you, Harry Agganis."

The news resounded everywhere, across the country and even overseas. In Worcester, on WNAB radio, sports broadcaster Bob Gallagher said "Today is a black day in sports ... How great would he have been? He might have gone on to break, set or tie many major league records ... but as a man, he couldn't have been greater."

Harry's former B.U. baseball teammate, George Sullivan, a newlywed just back from his honeymoon, had started working for *The Boston Traveler*. He was going to go to Baltmore to do a story on Harry's old teammate, Tom Gastall, who'd signed with the Orioles.

Sullivan went to a bank in Cambridge to withdraw some money when a teller who had gone to B.U. and knew him came over and said, "Is it true what I heard about Harry?"

Sullivan looked at him. "Not that stuff about Harry being traded?" he said.

"No, no, no, I hear he's dead," the man said.

Sullivan still didn't believe it. "Where do these rumors start?" he said. "My God! Harry Agganis dead," he said. "Impossible, tell me, anybody, Harry Agganis the most finely conditioned athlete in the flower of his youth dies, come on," he said.

But he was enough of a newsman to call his editor, Arthur Siegel, and he called him from a pay phone at Billings and Stover's drug store. "I just heard this ridiculous rumor," but got no further. "It's no rumor," said Siegel. "You're writing his life story, page one for the next four days." He hadn't even used Harry's name. It was understood.

Sullivan drove to Lynn, looking for reaction. He went to the funeral home as it was getting dark. He headed for Waterhill Street and the neighborhood where Harry had grown up, and saw a stark image. It was dark, but there were so many people out it seemed like the middle of a day. But they weren't talking.

What struck him most though was the sight of immigrants who'd lost their hero, a first-generation son who'd achieved the American dream of fame and success. They too couldn't believe he was gone. He saw elderly Greek men, veterans of Balkan wars and life's worst adversities, sitting silently, blankly in rocking chairs on the porches of their homes, rocking back and forth, their deep, proud eyes looking out at nothing.

VASSANISTERION ◆ ORDEAL ◆ ΒΑΣΑΝΙΣΤΗΡΙΟΝ

On the morning of June 28, as the Red Sox were flying out of Pittsburgh, eventually en route to Washington for a scheduled June 30 exhibition game against the Senators to benefit the Red Cross, a stewardess walked along the aisle, smiling, looking for someone special.

"Where's the ballplayer from Lynn?" she asked of ashen-faced players. She had been to stewardess school with a neighbor of Harry's from Lynn, and promised she'd look him up if the team was ever on her plane. She'd heard a lot about him.

"She asked me to be sure to say hello to him if I was ever on a flight with him," she smiled. She hadn't seen the newspapers yet.

HARRY AGGANIS DEAD
HARRY AGGANIS DEAD
HARRY AGGANIS DEAD

No matter how many times you looked at the headline, it didn't seem real. It didn't seem possible, the most perverse oxymoron, the most awful juxtaposition of contradictory words. The invulnerable athlete was gone. In a column that day, *Boston Daily Record* sportswriter John Gillooly said what seemed so awfully ironic was that Harry seemed to be what the Greeks called *athanatos*, immortal.

"He appeared indestructible; he'd pop up unpunished from under a pile of bruisers who had plummeted into him from all directions and shout fresh, crisp signals; he seemed invulnerable," Gillooly wrote. "Agganis had the physique, the demeanor, the superman qualities which placed him on an Olympus all his own."

"AGGANIS DIES" said *The Boston Globe* in forty-eight-point Bodoni bold type, over a set of four photos that showed Harry kissing his mother at a Red Sox game, with former Red Sox great Jimmy Foxx in Harry's Fenway debut the year before, kidding with TV star Sid Caesar, who was trying to figure out a bat, and with former manager Lou Boudreau on the dugout steps. Every shot showed a radiant, healthy man with a beacon smile.

"HARRY AGGANIS DEATH SHOCKS SPORTS WORLD" was the front page of *The Boston Daily Record*, over photos of Harry with his mother and, as a schoolboy looking over some of the awards he had received as the most-celebrated high school athlete in America.

New York Times sports columnist Arthur Daley, one of the most esteemed in the country, wrote that Harry seemed to be one of those men whose death was inexplicable, especially at an early age. "He seemed to be made of whipcord and pressed steel. He was vibrant and alive, bubbling with energy and vibrant spirits. He had admirable character and he was a matchless competitor."

His old friend, columnist Murray Kramer wrote "He was the greatest football player I ever saw, and I've seen them all." Gillooly wrote starkly what many men felt: "A guy could bawl over this one." And many did.

Joe Cashman, who had gone to a play with Harry in Chicago on June 2, wrote "Odds never meant anything to the Lynn boy. The tougher the obstacles confronting him, the more he enjoyed a contest. We can still see him on the Fenway Park gridiron, a marked man who was being charged and hit by a half dozen of the Mainliners on almost every play, taking it all, neither asking nor giving quarter and never seeking 'out.' He appeared immune to pain, plague,pox or virus and that's why the death of Harry Agganis yesterday pierced the heart of the city, plunged the entire sports world into deep grief."

At Fenway Park, grounds crew member William J. Hynes looked up at the flag at half-staff tearfully and said "He was my kind of guy." At his South Carolina plantation, Red Sox owner Tom Yawkey said he was stunned and saddened. Boston Mayor John Hynes said Agganis "epitomized the strength of the old Greek warriors."

The weight of Harry's death crossed religious lines. That night, the day after Harry had died, Boston Mayor John Hynes had scheduled a field day at Fenway Park, where the powerful Roman Catholic Archbishop Cardinal Cushing, a strong orator, captivated a stunned crowd with a tribute.

He welcomed them to the event, but said in a stentorian tone that "There nevertheless hangs over the park the pall of sorrow. Here a great athlete won fame. He was loved by his teammates and admired by competitors. He was an inspiration to hundreds of thousands of young people. He is no more an athlete to grace this park. Harry Agganis is dead. He has been in many a contest and won great laurels in them all. Who will say he did not win the great battle of life? Who will say that death was victorious over him? A character such as Harry Agganis never dies. He is perpetuated in the hearts of everyone who admires a good man. He has been called to eternity at the time of great promise in his career. Death did not claim a victory over him. Life has been changed for him. He won the greatest contest of all, the battle of life. He will wear a crown of everlasting glory."

It was little solace to those closest to him, however. His high school coach and mentor Billy Joyce, who'd become like a surrogate father to Harry, was lost in bewilderment. "Harry was the finest boy I ever knew. He was the greatest athlete I've ever coached ... but more than that he was the most loyal friend any man ever had." He added, "There will never be another Harry Agganis." He added, "Something dropped out of life, never to be replaced, when Harry died."

Judge John C. Pappas, who'd guided Harry into B.U., given him a part-time job and helped get him out of the Marines, was driving with his young son,

Jimmy, when the news came on the radio. He had to pull over and stop to compose himself. He was, his son said, thunderstruck.

Later, he said "We've lost a wonderful boy. I'm really shocked and my heart goes out to Harry Agganis' mother and family. I looked upon the boy as though he were one of my own sons. He was a great kid with plenty of heart, determination and courage. I'm heartbroken."

Zauchin was still reeling, stuck in Washington with the team that couldn't get away to come to the funeral. Later, he would say, "There was no rivalry between Harry and me. A rivalry, yes, but just in the word. That's as far as it went. We were friends, pretty good friends. ... we weren't fighting each other, more in the sense of fighting together to make the Red Sox better." Lepcio was livid. He thought the team shouldn't play the June 30 game, which was scheduled to start at the same time as Harry's funeral Thursday.

As Harry dominated the headlines again, the reaction continued, and it was more of the same. Donelli was dumbfounded. "I don't know what to say. There was never a more loyal kid. He was a great competitor who loved a challenge."

B.U. President Harold Case was softly eloquent, trying to assess not only the loss, but the measure of the man Harry was and how he'd influenced so many people with his own humility, and passion for life.

"He loved competition and played best when the odds against his team were the most serious. Anyone who saw him prepare to pass a football, find himself rushed, drop back ten, twenty, thirty, forty yards and then pass with precision to a teammate far down field recognized this rare inner poise ... He was religious in the real way: that is, he was not ostentatious about it, but he supported his own church in Lynn, and when he was on a trip, he went to church for worship. He possessed an amazing personality, with such outreaching dimensions that he had more genuine friends than any young man of his age which I have ever known."

"In his short life, Harry Agganis taught us some important things," he said. "We must remember them."

Red Sox General Manager Joe Cronin, who had come to the airport in Boston to meet Harry on June 5 when he came back ill from Kansas City, said "Everyone connected with the Red Sox is grieved and shocked." He also said, "Harry Agganis was a great athlete, a grand boy, a great credit to sports."

There were hundreds of telegrams, including one from New York Yankee Manager Casey Stengel, who coveted Harry the ballplayer and loved Harry the man. "We were all deeply shocked and saddened at the passing of your son, and wanted you to know how much all of us on the New York team thought of him. He truly was a wonderful fellow and a great credit to our game. We certainly shall miss him," Stengel said.

Western Union Boston Manager Turner Berry said an avalanche of telegrams had poured in. "It's the largest one-day volume in the twenty years I've been with the office," he said. One came from Lou Pollack, who played baseball with Harry at Lynn Classical and was in the Army in the Bavarian Mountains in Germany. He heard the news on overseas radio and telegraphed his wife in Saugus to send flowers for Harry.

Suddenly, the young Father Mihos, who was presiding over one of the largest Greek churches in New England, found he would have to have a leading role in the arrangement and eulogy for Harry. The wake and funeral would draw thousands of people to the church and make the community the centerpiece of attention throughout New England, indeed, in many places around the country where they wanted to mourn The Golden Greek.

It was an exhausting time, especially because of the grief felt by so many. Father Mihos too had to prepare for the involvement of the church hierarchy, including the head of the diocese in New England, His Grace Athenagoras, Bishop of Elaias. Also, Rev. Archimandrite Christopher Argyrides, pastor of St. George's, the Rev. Peter Kyriacos, deacon of the Greek Orthodox Cathedral, the Rev. Kallistos Samaras, chancellor of the New England Diocese and Father Anthony of Somerville, who came to the hospital to preside after Harry died so suddenly.

And the funeral would take place on the Feast of the Twelve Apostles, a solemn religious holiday in the Greek Orthodox Church. Father Anthony winced at the irony. "What a day for a *paleekaree* to be buried," he thought to himself.

There would be enormous logistical problems handling the crowds, even though St. George's was relatively new. Some of the landscaping outside had been done with a donation from Harry. Church officials decided to let Harry's body lie in state from 7 to 11 p.m. on Tuesday and from 1 p.m. on Wednesday, until the funeral at 2 p.m. on Thursday, June 30. And it was getting hot. Mrs. Agganis arrived long before the church doors opened.

A heat wave was underway and the church would be crowded with the maximum of 1,000 people. St. George's, fronting the long stretch of Lynn Common, and almost directly across the street from Lynn Classical where Harry had gone to school, was a beautiful and elaborate church, but many of those who would come would be unfamiliar with the rituals of a Greek funeral.

The open casket was in front of the altar, parallel to the pews so people could walk by and pay their last respects. Harry was dressed in a navy blue suit, a new tie and a watch his mother had given him. Many of his trophies were by his side. An olive wreath presented to Harry in 1953 by the King and Queen of Greece was inside the casket, in a small glass box.

A crown of apple blossoms purchased by his grandparents, Aristotle, who was also called Harry, and his wife, Connie Visvis, was placed on his brow. They had also purchased a wedding ring that was placed on his finger, the symbol of the marriage to God for an unmarried man. His head would rest on a pillow of roses, some of which would cover him. An apple blossom was in the lapel of his suit coat, part of his marriage outfit. A silk handkerchief was placed in his hands, and would be used to cover his face from midnight to dawn, and during the service at Pine Grove Cemetery, where he would be buried beside his father.

In front of the casket, many of his awards and trophies stood, a testament to his mortal greatness. And there were many photos of him too, although it was hard to look at anything except the still, fallen athletic hero who only seemed asleep.

Mrs. Agganis donated the trophies to the church as an inspiration to youth, and gave the church most of his photos too, except for one. Harry was wearing a homburg hat and pretending to smoke a cigar and laughing. She wanted to remember him in good humor.

PONOS ◆ PAIN ◆ ΠΟΝΟΣ

Harry's mother, stoic and silent, decided she would sit by the casket for the entire twenty-five hours his body would lie in state, from Wednesday through Thursday. She would greet all the mourners. She was comforted by her family, her daughter Mary Raimo, frequently at her side, as were her other sons and daughter, and her family, including her brother, Louis Pappas from Chicago.

But even her Spartan strength would leave her momentarily when she first saw Harry. She screamed involuntarily, before composing herself. "Who am I to fight with God?" she told her anguished family.

As she sat by the coffin, the first streams of people who had lined up outside St. George's, stretching around the corner, began to come into the church. An estimated 30,000 of them would pass by Harry before the funeral would begin, many silent and composed, others wailing and weeping and gnashing their teeth. Some controlled themselves until they got to the open casket, and burst into tears.

They came from all walks of life, from immigrants and blue collar workers, to those on the assembly lines at GE and other companies, from leather factories, and from celebrity and fame, Gov. Christian Herter, Red Sox officials, teammates, friends and fans, those who had only seen him play but felt they knew him.

Mrs. Agganis sat still, her lips moving only occasionally. She had been escorted into the church by Louis Thallasites, Harry's friend in the Marines,

Caring for his mother included shoveling the walk at his home after a typical New England snowstorm.

Harry being inducted into the B.U. Hall of Fame along with E. Ray Speare, the captain and star of the 1892 football team.

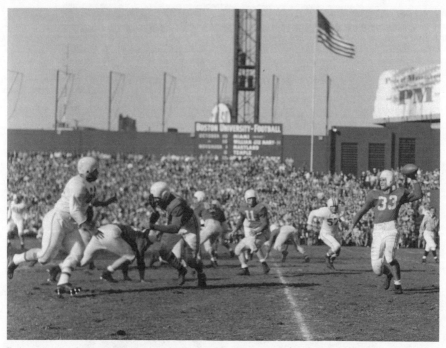

So many people wanted to watch Harry play at B.U. that temporary stands had to be put against Fenway Park's famed left field wall. The Maryland game in 1952 packed more than 35,000 fans to watch him scramble.

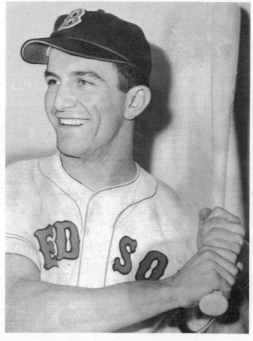

Harry signed with the Boston Red Sox on November 28, 1952, putting on a Sox uniform and his trademark smile.

Harry's mother loved to cook, especially when he brought home his friends and teammates to their home on Waterhill Street in Lynn.

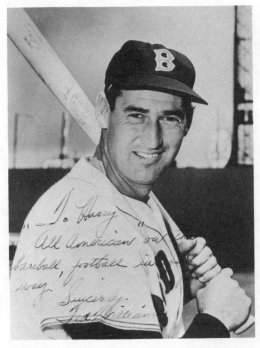

One of those teammates who came to dinner sometimes was Ted Williams, who, like, Harry's other teammates, personalized a photo for him.

Harry visits the Children's Hospital in Peabody with his Red Sox teammates (from left) Sammy White, Jimmy Piersall, Harry, Bill Henry and Johnny Pesky.

In his last photo in a Red Sox uniform, Harry left the hospital to present a scholarship in his name to Cleo Sophios of Medford, which put her through B.U.

In his rookie year of 1954, Harry had his first home run on April 18, against the Philadelphia A's. Waiting to greet him at home plate were Jimmy Piersall (37), Charlie Maxwell (35), Jackie Jensen (30) and the team bat boy. The A's catcher is Joe Astroth and the umpire is Bill McGowan.

In June of 1954, Harry hit a game-winning home run at Fenway against the Detroit Tigers, changed into his cap and gown in the locker room and hustled to B.U. to receive his degree from President Harold Case (r.) and congratulations from coach Buff Donelli.

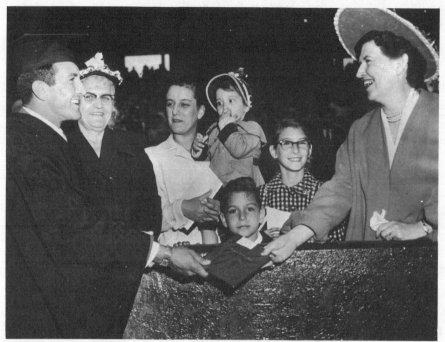

It was a proud moment for the Agganis family when the first college graduate, Harry, showed his diploma to Mrs. Harold Case. Harry's mom was beaming and his sister, Mary, and her children were there.

Harry handled an orange like a baseball on his way to Spring training in Florida in 1954. The players had to wear shirts and ties in those days.

Scenes above show Harry Agganis in the opening game at Fenway Park in 1954. It was a gala occasion. At the left is Harry Agganis kissing his mother with Boston University Coach Buff Donelli looking on. Next is Jimmy Piersall, a great first baseman for the Red Sox, with Harry. Next is Harry with well known radio and television star, Sid Caesar. The final panel shows Harry and Manager Lou Boudreau.

The grim news of Harry's death resounded in headlines across the country.

An estimated 30,000 people passed through St. George Greek Orthodox Church in Lynn to pay their last respects and 20,000 more lined the streets to Pine Grove cemetery the day of the funeral.

WHEN THE GREAT SCORER COMES
TO MARK AGAINST YOUR NAME
HE'LL WRITE NOT "WON" OR "LOST",
BUT HOW YOU PLAYED THE GAME.
GRANTLAND RICE

House Adjourns
Mourn Harry
The Massachusetts House of
resentatives yesterday ad-
rned out of respect to the

News of Tragedy
Stuns Sox Players

him almost every day after I
given permission and to say
nocked hardly tells the st
I had him two of his
seasons in professional ball
he was a real competitor

Artist Jim Dobbins' work symbolized the grief felt with Harry's loss.

A most touching sight at the church was the little leaguers who came to honor the man who loved children.

who was in full dress uniform.

Shortly before the doors opened at 1 p.m. Wednesday, she turned to Harry and said "My young man, my young man, my handsome boy. We're all here with you to get you married."

For the next twenty-five hours, she would go home only once, at 5:30 a.m. She came back and told family and friends, in Greek, "Harry's work is done. He is where he belongs, in the arms of God. God gave me that boy to watch over, but he never really belonged to me. He belongs to the people who loved him and to Christ. God has taken him at this time to bring home to young people everywhere how high they can go from nothing if they work hard and live good lives."

She said Harry was never exclusively hers. "*O Areestos aneeke ston Christo kai ston cosmo pou ton agapoun.*" It meant, "My Harry belongs to Christ and to those people who loved him."

The family stood vigil too. Paul, Harry's brother, didn't sleep for two days, and wouldn't sit. He stood at attention. "Why are you punishing yourself," his wife, Bess, asked.

"That's the least I can do to honor my brother," the ex-boxer said. He never left the church until the funeral was over.

That first night, an estimated 10,000 mourners came, passing through a line of Little Leaguers who stood outside the church. They included virtually all the members of the Class of 1948 from Lynn Classical, who had graduated with Harry. Flowers filled the church, sent by friends and family and admirers and teammates, including Ted Williams, Dom DiMaggio, Bobby Doerr, Norm Zauchin and Johnny Pesky, and from the Brooklyn Dodgers and New York Giants, and from Red Sox owner Tom Yawkey, who did not like funerals and would stay away, despite his attachment to Harry, who had driven him to his mother's home after being signed. There were flowers from the Marines of Camp LeJeune and the Everett Pony League.

At the end of the casket there were three tall candles. Around it stood two honor guards from the Greek-American Amvets, flanking their hero. Most mourners passed by silently, grim-faced and disbelieving. There were cries of grief too, from many of the Greek women, who were dressed in black.

Their keening was unnerving for many who had never seen the suffering tears of Greek women, and their faint sobs were a constant undercurrent of the grief.

The loudest pain couldn't be heard. It was the internal pain of a mother who had lost her youngest son and who didn't want to utter what her heart felt. Her other sons stood guard, Jimmy, Demo, Phil and Paul, and Harry's sisters, Dena and Mary, didn't leave their mother's side. Greeks believed life and death walked hand-in-hand, or *"Zoe ke Charos perpatanei heree me heree."*

Many fainted. Jean Dallaire nearly swooned onto the casket and had to be revived by Mercy Mavris, the funeral director who was also a nurse.

Men wept openly. Several women fainted. Angie Karagianis, the badly crippled man who used a walking device to roam the sidelines and followed Harry everywhere, broke down after being helped to the altar. A most touching moment occurred when several blind people paid their respects by touching their fallen hero.

Mrs. John Pappas of Worcester, whose son was a center at B.U. and died after a game at Syracuse the year before, came although she was ill, because she said Harry had come to her son's wake and funeral as a pallbearer. "I'll go to Harry's even if I have to walk," she said.

Mrs. Agganis put a baseball signed by all the Red Sox in Harry's hand because he had promised it to his nephew, Michael, the son of his brother, Jimmy. Michael was sent to the casket to get it, a photo captured for perpetuity. Then, three Little Leaguers in their uniforms, who had hitchhiked there from Wakefield after playing in a CYO game for St. Florence Church, knelt in prayer before the casket. They were Frank and Thomas McClellan and Mando Cresta. They still had on their hats and cleats and were carrying their gloves. Outside Manning Bowl, a group of Lynn Little Leaguers, lined up in tribute.

Most of Harry's teammates from high school and college, and the sandlots and all-star teams, from Barry Park and the Vrees All-Stars, the Augusta Millionaires and the American Legion and St. George's teams, joined the line, including Lou Tsioropoulos. Lynn Classical teammates included Nils Strom and Vic Pujo. From B.U. came Frank Giuliano, Mario Moriello, Art Boyle, Joe Terrasi, George Spaneas and Bobby Whelan.

And all night they kept coming, through Wednesday into the early morning hours of Thursday, which was breaking hot and sticky and unbearable.

In Washington, the Red Sox were going to play, although they had tried to get the game postponed or cancelled. Washington owner Clark Griffith said it was to benefit the Red Cross and couldn't be changed. The Red Sox players went on the field reluctantly. The stands were almost empty, as they had been the night before when the two teams played a regularly scheduled game that drew only a few thousand people. No one felt like playing that either.

Greek Orthodox ceremonies were conducted before the game by Rev. Thomas J. Daniels, a friend of Harry's, and Rev. Archimandrite Laloussis. A Marine color guard, including some who served with Harry at Camp LeJeune, played taps.

Later, sixty-six-year-old Father Daniels said when Harry came to Washington he went to Sts. Constantine and Helen Church. Daniels said he wasn't interested in sports but he was interested in Harry, who came to visit him on road trips.

"Oh, that boy would have made a fine priest, I know. He was so openly honest about everything." He said Harry used to come into his study after a service and talk. Daniels said he knew Harry was an athlete but that he never saw him perform. He said Harry visited Greek churches on road trips in every city. "We are very proud of Harry in our faith."

He said "He had such a sympathetic face. It was so easy to read just how he felt when I looked at him. And there was never anything of the past. He always looked forward, never behind."

The Thursday game had been scheduled to begin at 2 p.m., precisely at the time Harry's funeral would be starting in Lynn. Red Sox officials got the game pushed back to 3 p.m., but that didn't satisfy many of Harry's teammates, like Lepcio, who wanted to go to the funeral. But the only player who was sent was pitcher Frank Sullivan.

The players lined up along the first and third base lines. There was almost no one in the outfield seats. The stadium seemed entirely empty. Red Sox catcher Sammy White came out to deliver a tribute, an odd choice since he was the one player who seemed immune to Harry's practical joking and sense of humor. White was a most serious man.

"The task that confronts me today is indeed a most difficult one, difficult because it is quite impossible to find the right words to completely express the deep sorrow we all feel for the loss of our teammate," White said."How to tell his mother, his sisters and his brothers just how deep is our sympathy for them presents another difficulty."

"To tell all you people what Harry Agganis meant to me and his teammates really has me groping for appropriate words. Harry was not only a talented athlete with the strength of a Hercules, the competitive spirit and courage of a lion and the possessor of an almost ferocious desire to win—he was a leader and, at the same time, a follower of all that was good," he said.

It was difficult too for the Red Sox to remain composed as White continued. "Harry, you have been and ever will be an inspiration to us. We all sorely miss you, as well as your family and your thousands of friends. We have been lucky to have known you to have been associated with you. We have suffered a tremendous loss and your fellow players all join in a silent prayer of tribute to one of the greatest guys ever to swing a bat, field a ball, or run a base. God be with you."

And then came Harry's old friend and announcer for B.U. and the Red Sox, Curt Gowdy, an eloquent soft-spoken man with a heart-felt soft twang in his voice. Gowdy recounted Harry's life and said "They called him 'The Golden

Greek.' True, his athletic feats were golden and shining, and so was Harry Agganis, personally." Gowdy went on to describe Harry's attributes: "Devoted to his mother and family, extremely loyal to his friends, teammates and coaches ... personal habits which could well be copied by every youngster in the country ... a determined aggressiveness on the field which made him respected by everyone ... these are the things which made Harry Agganis 'Golden' to those who knew him."

The Red Sox would wear black mourning bands on their sleeves for thirty days, and Gowdy would later break down and nearly cry during a sportscast on Boston radio. Yawkey came to Mrs. Agganis and her daughter, Mary, to pledge his support for whatever they wanted to do in Harry's name.

Back in Lynn, the funeral had begun at 2 p.m., to a church filled with sad-faced mourners sweating in hot grief. In another area of the church there were 3,000 more, listening in on speakers. Outside, flowing over the common onto the church steps, were 6,000 more.

From the church to the cemetery, little more than a mile, nearly 20,000 people lined the streets to Pine Grove cemetery waiting to watch the hearse go by, a cortege of silence. It took nine cars alone to transport the flowers.

In the church were the famous and family, friends and admirers and those who wanted to be there to pay last respects. Boston Mayor John Hynes and Massachusetts Gov. Christian Herter were there, with many well-to-do members too of the Greek-American business community. A Boston radio station was broadcasting the funeral for those who couldn't be there. Harry's old B.U. coach Buff Donelli and B.U. President Harold Case came too.

The Red Sox contingent was led by General Manager Joe Cronin, Manager Mike "Pinky" Higgins, who had coached Harry at Louisville too in 1953, Assistant General Manager Dick O'Connell, who had been unhappy at the medical treatment Harry had received, his assistant Mary Trank, who loved Harry, scout Neil Mahoney, who'd followed Harry, and front office personnel.

Mel Massuco, an assistant coach at Holy Cross, and an Arlington high school star who'd played in the great freshman game against Harry, came from his school, as did Boston College coach Mike Holovak, *Boston Herald* reporter James Cariofiles, who'd covered Harry as a *B.U. News* reporter, and Associated Press reporter Dave O'Hara.

Many of his B.U. teammates were in the church, including Frank Giuliano, Joe Terrasi, Len D'Errico, John Simpson, Silvio Cella, Bob Whelan, John O'Neill, Tom Oates, Bob Dunphy, Mario Moriello, John Nunziato, Phil O'Connell, Steve Sobiek, Sam Pino and Pete Sarno, and assistant coach Steve Sinko too.

It was an unnerving event for Sinko, who, with Donelli, had been especially close to Harry. "It was one of the saddest things I ever saw and the Greek tradition made it ten times worse because the casket was open on the altar and the family, as they walked by, the mother and the aunts and the uncles, they would go up there and moan and cry and faint. It was one of the hottest days I'd even been in and I remember sweat just rolling down my legs and to see this parade of old Greeks and immigrants come by, because the Greeks were very close, and to see this sight ... it was beyond description."

The new St. George's church was packed and stifling. Harry's casket had been turned perpendicular to the congregation. His Grace Bishop Athenagoras, wearing a headdress and carrying a staff, led the procession to the Bishop's throne at the right side of the iconostasis.

The priests formed two ranks facing each other from the throne to the mahogany casket. The service began with hymns for the deceased and the reading of the scriptures by Father Bacopulos and concluded with prayers for salvation and eulogies by Father Mihos and Bishop Athenagoras. The choir sang the saddest of funeral songs, *"Ee Zoee En tapho"* (Life in the Tomb) and the dirgeful *"Telefteos Aspamos."* It meant, "The Last Farewell."

Father Mihos started. "His love for God was evident especially to his people, the parishioners of St. George's, who watched him grow from a child into manhood. Our children that idolized him will never again feel the warmth of his handshake and his smile. Yet his spirit will never leave us and his memory will always be an example of the accomplishment of a humble person that,although he reached the pinnacle of success and greatness, he never forgot that humility was the only road to success."

He said several days before his passing, Harry talked with him about how the landscaping was going. "This is the Christian courage and fortitude that a great Christian mother imbued into the heart of a great Christian son. His first question always concerned the progress of the church. When will the church be landscaped? Are we receiving enough donations? He asked that I pray for his recovery and I can still too vividly recall the eagerness and piety with which he received Holy Communion," Father Mihos said.

Bishop Athenagoras gave two eluogies, one in Greek. The first was directed to Mrs. Agganis to whom he offered the sympathy of the Greek Orthodox Church and called her the "Heroic and good mother of Harry Agganis."

"There's no doubt that your sorrow is great but his offering is even greater as an example of our youth of someone who has love and understanding and who knows how to love his mother, his family and church. Believe me, we need more examples like Harry Agganis. He exemplifies the American tradition and the traditions of Christ," His Grace said.

He continued in Greek, the lyrical rhythm of the words like the crushing chorus of a Greek tragedy unfolding. "Not only we, but all those who have gone before, have always sought to solve the problem of death. The ancients asked, but waited in vain for an answer from Jesus. He would only say 'Have faith in me.' Today, I found a grieved but courageous mother who, in all humbleness and with her great faith, has found the answer. 'Your Grace, she said, 'God giveth and God taketh away. Let his will be done.' Is there, then, any need to mourn, when this magnificent lady shows such faith, piousness and understanding? All I could say to her, after listening to such a great lady, was to tell her to pray and God will be merciful."

He walked to Mrs. Agganis' pew and embraced her and the members of the immediate family, as did the other clergy. The family filed by the open casket to say a final goodbye and several broke down. Mrs. Agganis was the last to pass.

She bent over and said, "Good bye Harry. Good bye, my son," leaning over for a brief, tender caress of his cheeks with both her hands as if trying to bring him back. She whispered her private words in his ear, and kissed him goodbye. She was helped back to her seat by her family.

The ordeal was not over for Harry's mother and his family though. They came out of the church into a brutal heat and a surrealistic scene: thousands and thousands of people standing silently. Carrying Harry's casket were the six pallbearers who were among his closest friends, Mike Frangos, Nick Sentas, Jimmy Andrews, Alex Capoulos, and the brothers, George and Socrates Maravelias. Harry's high school teammate, George Bullard, who'd married Harry's high school sweetheart, Joan Fitzgerald, was playing baseball in the minor leagues and said he was so heartsick at Harry's death he'd gone out drinking to drown the pain.

The casket was put into the hearse. Instead of going directly to the cemetery, however, the hearse and the entourage turned toward Harry's home on Waterhill Street in the opposite direction, just so they could stop one final time in front of the home where he had grown up, completing a Greek tradition.

His mother turned to the casket in the hearse and looked. "How can I go back and carry on the way you want me to? But I will," she said.

She added, "*Pethee mou, O pateras sou echei chara, alla ee meetera sou einai leepeemanee.*" "My son, your father is happy, but your mother is sad."

At the church, she had turned to her family and said, "My work is not yet done and that is why I am still here." She was a Spartan mother and Harry had come home with his shield.

There were two hundred limousines and cars traveling in the funeral entourage and they passed by the huge General Electric complex where so many Lynn residents, including Phil Agganis, had worked. Workers stuck their heads out of rows of windows, and some stood on the roof to watch silently. There were long, quiet lines all the way through the city and the neighborhoods to the cemetery, where thousands more waited.

The entourage came to the grave on a slight hillside at the cemetery, not far from Manning Bowl where Harry's play had brought crowds of 20,000 or more to watch his high school games.

There was only a simple stone, an elaborate monument not yet finished. Mrs. Agganis was helped to the graveside by her family, and her brother, Louis Pappas. Harry's brothers, Jim and Demo and Phil and Paul were there too, with their sisters, Mary and Dena. Tony Raimo stood by quietly.

It was a riveting, heart-rending sight. The family by the edge of the grave,the casket open and a silk handkerchief covering Harry's face. Crowds spilled everywhere, pushing up to the sight of a grieving, aching family fearful of the last farewell.

Father Christopher Argyrides presided and poured holy oil and earth on the body in the outline of a cross. Bishop Athenagoras conducted the last service, he too pouring holy oil on Harry before the casket was closed and lowered into the grave. Mourners, including his mother, gently put flowers onto the casket. Others tossed theirs and turned away.

His mother's eyes filled with tears. "Goodbye, Harry," she muttered. "Goodbye, Harry." She had to be helped back to the limousine.

Later, the family invited mourners back to the St. George gymnasium for a traditional meal of fish, feta cheese, unleavened bread and white almond candies.

The next morning, Mrs. Agganis could not be found. She had awakened early and, at seventy-years-old, walked back two miles to the cemetery to simply stand at Harry's grave, and be alone with her son.

She was dressed in the black she had worn since her husband's death nine years earlier, and which she would wear for the rest of her life, most of which she would spend at her daughter Mary's house, unable to be comfortable again in the house where Harry had lived.

DOXA ◆ GLORY ◆ ΔΟΞΑ

The reaction, the aftermath and the tributes and befuddled wonderment at what had happened continued. Ted Williams, who had cried when he heard about Harry's death, delivered a eulogy at the Touchdown Club in Washington, D.C., remembering his lost friend. "Harry was one of the most wonderful boys I ever knew. His loss has left a void in our hearts. His death was a shocking loss," Williams said.

In the St. George Church bulletin, Helen Andrian delivered a touching testament to Harry's life. "To a shocked and grieving community it seemed unbelievable the Invincible Greek has lost a battle. But it has been a long time since Theseus, Hercules, Jason and Leonidas have had a new playmate and they could not wait ... He was every mother's ideal of what her boy should be. He was every young girl's dream of a hero and every little boy's idol."

She talked about how Harry would come in after school and grab an apple or something to eat and shout "Going to the ballpark, Mom'" as he headed for Barry Park to play.

"Why don't you take your bed down there with you," she would say.

Andrian said "His memory will live on forever. He was an American, but he had Greek blood in his veins and he leaves a heritage, for he was an outstanding example of modern American Hellenic youth, proving that 'The Glory that was Greece,' still is."

Cartoons and poems, including a lengthy set of verses written by an admirer, Bill McDonough of Holyoke, Massachusetts, appeared everywhere. McDonough's was sent to the Hall of Fame in Cooperstown. The next-to-last stanza said:

> *"Long live the memory of his integrity so obviously clean*
> *Which death can't destroy, though it shattered his fondest dream.*
> *And, now, he has joined company so select and elite*
> *All-valiant immortals enshrined in their seats.*
> *'The Gipper" and Rockne and Gehrig and Ruth*
> *Will welcome in Heaven this marvelous youth."*

Cartoonist Vic Johnson immortalized Harry with "Gone To Olympus," which showed a mourning man under portraits of Harry in football and baseball uniforms, and Jim Dobbins' work depicting Harry walking into heaven in his baseball uniform, carrying two bats, a football, his football helmet, and his number 33 football jersey. In another cartoon, Bob Coyne stated that "I'll remember how Harry idolized his kid followers from West Lynn, and how he lived that they might follow his fine example." Congressman Thomas Lane read Father Mihos' eulogy into the Congressional record to memorialize Harry.

On July 1, in the *Lynn Daily Item*, Mrs. Agganis reflected that the loss was more than hers. "Harry belonged to the people and to God. I knew when he was very young that he would never fully belong to me. And I prepared myself for it."

She said she wanted his awards encased at St. George's church, where children especially could see them. "I hope the children realize the lesson that God has taught them in Harry's life. Here is a boy who lived a good life, and he achieved glory. He was without a father at an early age. He knew what it was to have to do without things. But it was God's will that he got where he was. And God took him at such an early age to bring home the lesson of his life," she said.

She asked that any donations in his name be made instead to a scholarship fund and that all students be eligible, regardless of race, creed or color. She later donated a stained glass window to the Greek Orthdox Church of the Assumption in Somerville, where Father Anthony, who had stood by her in the hospital, presided.

The encomiums continued. *The Hellenic Chronicle*, the country's largest Greek-American newspaper that had been started by another B.U. alumnus, Peter Agris, had an editorial on the day of the funeral which said "An eternity of youth will look to his deeds for inspiration ... Harry was great but he was humble. Even as fame and fortune smiled on Harry, he never forgot that he owed much to his mother."

A week later, Agris wrote "That Hellenes lost a leader is unmistakable. One of the Greek priests at his funeral said Harry was worth more than a dozen Greek millionaires to Hellenism in America. Yet, let us not selfishly assume Harry was the sole property of Hellenism. As one of the non-Hellenes put it to a sorrowing Greek, 'What do you mean, you lost Harry? Agganis belonged to all of us. He was an All-American.'"

The Jewish Advocate wrote: "All really outstanding men are much more than their achievements in the public limelight. Harry Agganis was such a man. His feats on the athletic field were more than matched by a sweetness of personality, a dedication to religion and strength of character.

Even though his life was short, Harry Agganis set an inspiring example to our youth. He played the games and life hard and to win, but according to the rules. Of the Greek Orthodox faith, he made no foolish distinctions between men on the basis of race, creed or color. His trade was ball-playing; his credo pleasantness, loyalty and righteousness."

After all his athletic triumphs, Harry had reached glory through the weight of his character and integrity, his Christianity, the attributes for which he would best be remembered and the way, the church said, to reach the glory of God.

The Hearst Corporation, which sponsored the high school all-star baseball games in which Harry had played in 1946 and 1947, said two winners of the 1955 *Boston Record-American* sandlot baseball program would receive Harry Agganis Memorial Trophies, and the Red Sox said a similar award would be made to an outstanding player on their team that year.

A few days after the shock started to wear off, Gillooly wrote that Harry had such a sense of fair play, he wouldn't have abided by a rash of claims about spit balls. He said Harry wouldn't have stood for it.

"If he knew a Red Sox pitcher was using a spitter or any other illicit pitch, he would walk right up to him at the risk of ridicule, revilement, a punch on the nose or the condemnatory cackle 'busher' and tell him off."

Columnist Frank Fallaci wrote that "Harry suffered the fate of all epic heroes ... There will be some who ask, 'Can it be. Was he really that good?' They never saw Harry Agganis play."

Austen Lake of the *Evening America*, who had been so critical after Harry was released from the Marines a few years earlier, now rhapsodized that "Young Agganis had something monumental, perhaps a left-over touch from the Age of Pericles. His frame was classic, leanly proportioned, loosely gaunt! He had a coordinated grace, the fluid-flow of motion which bespeaks the natural athlete. For young Harry was dedicated to sport, becoming that athletic rarity, the All-American football candidate who made the major leagues." Lake said Harry's drive to keep his starting job probably killed him by forcing him out of the hospital too soon the first time he became ill in May.

The day after Harry died, Rev. James (Iakovos) Coucouzis, who was now in Geneva, Switzerland as the Bishop of Melita, stood benumbed as he read a cablegram from his friend in Boston, Rev. George Bacopulos. The Bishop's eyes were dimmed by tears. He drew near to the icon of Christ in his room, knelt and prayed. And he recalled Harry in his memory, how he had blessed him before Spring training, and gone to Fenway Park to watch him play, when the Bishop had been assigned to the Cathedral in Boston.

The Bishop saw Harry alive, before him. "With the gilt bronzed brow of his, crowned by his curly, tangled hair, a true Olympic victor's crown." Harry smiled with lips and eyes, he said, "that had the innocent expression of a little child."

In his remembrance, he saw Harry in the office of B.U. President Harold Case, and with throngs of admirers at the Hotel Continental in Cambridge in 1953 where Harry had received the olive crown wreath from Queen Frederika of Greece and been inducted into the school's Hall of Fame.

In August, the Bishop wrote of the time he had seen Harry play for the Red Sox, and, after when Harry came to sit beside him. "I could find no words to congratulate him. My hands were blood red with clapping, my lips were atremble at his triumph, my heart was drunken with pride and joy," he said.

And then he described his image of what had happened to Harry the day he died. "He faced the pitcher again. It was death itself. This time he got ready to hit a home run ... but his bat snapped, it fell out of his hands, his life like a sport missile, flew out of his world sporting-field and he, a Golden Greek, honored the athletic spirit of the people to which he belonged, ran to his home plate a winner, without reproach, for whom the Heavenly manager was waiting, Christ, the great awarder of the prize—waiting to say to him, with gratification, 'Well done, good and faithful servant.'"

Talk started of how to establish a permanent memorial to Harry. Some suggested renaming Fenway Park, but Mrs. Agganis said she hoped there would be scholarships or charitable endeavors in his name.

One of Harry's boosters and admirers was *Herald* sportswriter Bill Cunningham, who wrote of Harry that "He lived a clean life and took excellent care of himself ... I never knew a finer athlete, nor a cleaner young man. When it comes to the persona, however, I find myself groping for words, for Agganis was 'My Boy.' He knew it and seemed to be proud of it.'" He said he had found him an unusual youth in high school, despite his successes, and was impressed by "His modesty, poise and inherent sense of sound values, despite all the publicity and pressure."

The day before Harry died, Cunningham was at Fenway Park covering a game against the White Sox. Zauchin hit a towering home run.

"That was a beauty," Cunningham said to his colleague Henry McKenna. "But it makes me a little sad. He's making it harder for my boy Agganis."

"Yeah," McKenna said, "But don't forget. Your boy Agganis had it made when he fell sick. He'll probably do alright when he gets back."

The day after Harry died, Cunningham remembered the conversation. "That can serve as his epitaph," he wrote.

"Had It Made."

ODEE ◆ ODE ◆ ΩΔΗ

In Germany, Jimmy "Jeep" Kirios, who had been so close to Harry, was serving in the Army, in a special services outfit where he was trying to make use of his singing ability. A few years before, at the end of 1952, Harry had taken him on a ride from Lynn to the neighboring town of Swampscott, to an affluent area called Gallups Point where Harry had wanted to build his mother a house.

They got out of their car and walked up to a precipice overlooking the Atlantic Ocean. It was a breathtaking spot. They looked out over the water and Harry waved his hand. "You see this land," he said, pointing to different areas with a wide sweep, defining his dream.

'I'm going to build a house here, and you're going to build next door," Harry said. "I want our kids to grow up like we did, to play and have fun," he said. Harry was serious, but Kirios wasn't thinking about settling down just yet. He thought they would have plenty of time for families after their long careers had ended.

The day after Harry died, Kirios and his Army buddy, Al Callus, were riding in a bus going through the mountains near Berchtesgarden on their way to an assignment of entertaining. Kirios had not heard the news yet.

He looked over at one of the riders and saw a copy of *Stars and Stripes*, the military newspaper and saw in big, black letters: "AGGANIS DIES AT AGE 26."

He cried out in anguish, "AHHHH! AHHHHH!" The bus driver stopped, thinking someone was hurt or dying. Kirios ran out into the mountains, screaming insanely, hurtling himself into the midst of a beauteous scene, but feeling horrific. He kept running up, higher and higher, until he exhausted his pain.

Callus followed.

Kirios walked and looked at the sky, in a trance. He circled for two hours and finally came down. That night, he went to do his duty and said he would sing only one song. The band knew his best friend had died, but the audience didn't. He sang "With A Song In My Heart,"

He stopped. The band members put down their instruments and walked off the stage.

The song was over.

ZOE ◆ **LIFE** ◆ ZΩH

"As leaves on the trees, such is the life of man" – Homer

Mrs. Georgia Agganis slowly and lovingly pulled down the white cover of the plaque honoring her son, Harry, that hot day of June 19, 1956, at Camp LeJeune, North Carolina, almost a year exactly since his death shocked the sports world, and was still being felt.

An Orthodox chaplain, Alexander Seniavsky, had opened the ceremonies where 2,000 Marines stood at attention and an honor guard was surrounding the base on which the plaque had been placed. The message, under a Marine insignia,was dedicated to his memory. It read:

> "Endowed with peerless talent, Corporal Agganis
> exemplified the finest in competitive spirt and
> sportsmanship. An All-American football player,
> and later a professional baseball player, his
> outstanding accomplishments in the field of ath-
> letics were an inspiration to other Marines who
> served and were teammates with him during his

career in the Marine Corps. His untimely death on
June 29, 1955, after a brief illness, brought sad
ness to his friends in the Marine Corps as well
as in the world of sports."

The date of his death was wrong, but no one was thinking about that. They
hoped the memorial would insure Harry would not be forgotten.

He wasn't. There was life for Harry after his passing, because of the way
he had lived.

In October of 1955, four months after he died, the Agganis Foundation
was established, with a goal of $250,000 to be used for scholarships for youths
of all faiths, and projects which would perpetuate his memory, including construction of a chapel at the Holy Cross Greek Orthodox Theological School in
Brookline, Massachusetts, athletic awards for youths who met his ideals and
image, and for the dedication of the Harry Agganis Memorial gymnasium at
St. George's church in Lynn.

The purpose of the foundation was to create a working fund "That will
serve as a living memorial inspiring the youth of today and tomorrow to emulate
not only the competitive spirit of Harry Agganis, the athlete, but the philosophy
of Harry Agganis, the man. He won the greatest contest of all—the battle of
life."

The first donations came from friends and family, and were followed by
others, large and small, including $25,000 from Red Sox owner Tom Yawkey.
The foundation, which has sponsored a high school all-star football game, has
awarded scholarships in Harry's name to hundreds of scholar-athletes.

Two months after the ceremony at Camp LeJeune, the Harry Agganis
Memorial Game was played at B.U. field, pitting the New York Giants against
the Baltimore Colts. Harry had not lived to play professional football, for the
Colts or anyone else, but was still being honored by the league.

In that game, a young quarterback named Johnny Unitas came off the bench
to replace an injured George Shaw and established himself as one of the greatest
quarterbacks in the history of the National Football League.

Five years earlier, Harry had led B.U. to a 39-7 thrashing of Louisville,
with the freshman, Unitas, watching from the Louisville bench. Unitas, who
had been cut by the Pittsburgh Steelers before being picked up by the Colts, had
gotten his chance right near the campus where Harry had gone to school and
played college football. The game was played again the following year, between
the Giants and the Green Bay Packers.

In 1958, Unitas made a handoff to Alan Ameche in an overtime game for
the NFL championship to beat the Giants, in a game still acknowledged as the

greatest ever played in the league.

Mike Frangos, Harry's boyhood friend, opened the Commodore Restaurant in Beverly, Massachusetts several days before Harry died.

The gymnasium at St. George's was dedicated on December 2, 1956. B.U. President Harold Case was a guest speaker. "There is great wisdom in the plan of St. George's Church to dedicate its gymnasium to the memory of Harry Agganis because he will remain forever enshrined within the heart of Greek youth as a symbol of highest ideals, unique abilities and religious devotion. Young people need such a symbol to give them purpose and motivation for useful living in these confusing days. Harry Agganis will become more than a symbol, he will be a spiritual presence in the years to come," Case said.

Church and religion held a special place in Harry's heart, and he has always been remembered there. In 1955, a forty-day memorial service was held in four hundred Greek Orthodox churches around the United States and in Canada, ceremonies reserved for Greek royalty and statesmen.

More than eight hundred worshipers came to St. George's, and nearly 50,000 turned out across the country and in Canada. In Gary, Indiana, Archbishop Michael told priests to devote their entire sermon to Harry that day. "Harry Agganis was a great personality of our time, and a beloved member of American society. He was especially beloved by American youth. He was young in age, but mature spiritually and mentally."

Harry's awards were given to his church by his family and are permanently housed there. A basketball tournament at the church was also begun in 1956, bringing together Greek-American youths from across the country. The first winner was St. George's Church of Lynn, which also won in 1994. A team representing the Cathedral in Boston, which included Nick Tsiotos, won the tournament five times.

Accolades continued to be written, for years. Shortly after his death, one of his friends among sportswriters—an irascible bunch who rarely got close to athletes—Murray Kramer, wrote that "He was a cinch to have made the grade in professional football. I rank him as the greatest football player I have ever seen and I've seen a lot of them."

His B.U. baseball teammate and chronicler, George Sullivan became a public relations director for the Boston Red Sox and Boston Patriots, a journalism professor at Boston University, and a well-known sportswriter and author of sports books.

Dr. Timothy Lamphier, the Red Sox team physician who treated Harry the first time he was ill, later moved to Florida and lost his license to practice after the deaths of several patients. There was no investigation of Harry's death, although questions remained for decades.

In 1994, Congressman Gerald Solomon of New York, who was a nineteen-year-old Marine in 1951 when he was awed by Harry coming into his barracks and telling the story about how Slippery Rock Teachers College could be considered the winner of a football game against Notre Dame even if they lost 60-2, if they had scored the last two points, used the same story in a debate on the floor of the Congress.

Solomon, a Republican, was debating with Congressman Joe Moakley, a South Boston Democrat and had him befuddled when he mentioned he had first heard the analogy at Camp LeJeune from Harry, and said Harry had played for Boston College or B.U.

Moakley said "It was Boston College." He later said he was confused by Solomon's strategy. "I couldn't understand how Solomon would use a hero from Massachusetts to try to make his point. I apologize to everybody, because everybody knows Agganis went to B.U.," he said.

In December of 1955, an oil portrait showing Harry, without a hat and wearing a Red Sox uniform while holding a football, was presented to the baseball Hall of Fame in Cooperstown, N.Y. It was the gift of William Perdis and Michael Klironomos of Jamaica Plain, and Michael Purdis of Lynn.

On March 9, 1956, a headstone for the grave of Harry and his father, was set and dedicated at Pine Grove Cemetery in Lynn. It shows a sculpture of him in his Red Sox uniform, his gloved left hand outstretched for eternity. On the left side is a football, under which is written: "Dedicated to the glory of God. In prayerful remembrance. May his soul rest in peace. Through Our Lord, Jesus Christ, Amen." On the right side, under a symbol of crossed baseball bats and a ball, is written: Christian. Sportsman. Builder of Character. An inspiration to the youth of America."

The grave still frequently has visitors, some of whom leave behind mementoes. Harry's nephew, George Raimo, found a baseball there in 1991, while he was going to the cemetery to visit the grave of his mother and Harry's sister, Mary. There was an inscription: "In Everlasting Respect."

On June 16, 1956, more than two hundred friends and acquaintances of Harry turned out for the dedication of a square in his name in Lynn, not far from the house where he grew up. The next day there was a memorial service at St. George's, and two days after that, Mrs. Agganis and her entourage went to Camp LeJeune for the dedication of Agganis Field.

In July of 1955, *Newsweek* magazine carried an article about his death which called him "A natural athlete, graceful and versatile ... (who) was idolized in New England circles from his schoolboy days."

Harry was chosen by a panel of writers, announcers and former B.U. coaches as the school's greatest post-World War II athlete, and was the only unanimous pick.

In January of 1995, Otto Graham, the former Cleveland Browns quarterback whom Harry was going to replace, tossed the coin before the kickoff of the Super Bowl game between the San Francisco 49ers and the San Diego Chargers.

Rev. James Coucouzis, the young priest who blessed and befriended Harry before Spring training in 1954, became Archbishop Iakovos, spiritual leader of the Greek Orthodox Church in North and South America.

Ernest Larson, the young airman to whom Harry had written while ill at B.U., died a year after he received the letter.

The little store at the end of Waterhill Street owned by the Demakis family grew into Old Neighborhood, a large meat company.

Dick and Ed Modzelewski of Maryland, the brothers against whom Harry had memorable battles on the field, went on to star in the National Football League. They said Harry was the greatest quarterback they ever faced, in college or the pros.

In 1956, Gum Products put out a special sports card which featured a montage of Harry throwing a football as he was in mid-air, receiving his diploma, and playing baseball, against a backdrop of heavenly clouds, and showing him with his mother.

Years after he retired from baseball, Harry's former Red Sox teammate Billy Consolo received a baseball card at his California home. It showed Consolo's statistics on the back. On the front was the picture of Harry. Consolo doesn't know who made it or from where it came.

Pericles Panos and Manny Voulgaropoulos, the 10-year-old boys who were told to leave the Lowell YMCA in 1942 because they were speaking Greek, had successful careers. Panos became a lawyer and Voulgaropoulos became a doctor who set up clinics in Laos for the Tom Dooley clinic.

John Toner, the man Harry replaced at quarterback, became president of the National Collegiate Athletic Association and was the head football coach at the University of Connecticut for more than two decades.

John Simpson, who played with Harry in 1949, became athletic director at B.U.

Jimmy Kirios, accepting professional advice, changed his name to Jimmy Kerr and signed as a singer with Bob Hope, and made national television appearances and was featured in Las Vegas. He later became a teacher.

George Winkler, Harry's end in 1949, became director of the Harry Agganis football game, following Elmo Benedetto, director of athletics for the Lynn Public Schools.

Lou Gorman, who played against Harry in an all-star high school baseball game in 1946, became general manager of the Boston Red Sox.

John Alevizos, Harry's marketing professor and advisor at B.U., became a developer and vice-president of the Boston Red Sox and Atlanta Braves.

George Bullard, who paired with Harry to form part of the greatest backfield in New England high school football, played more than ten years in the minor leagues and later worked for the district court system in Salem, Mass. He had one at-bat in the major leagues.

Lou Tsioropoulos, who played basketball with Harry at Lynn Classical and St. George's Church, was an All-American basketball player at Kentucky, which won the national championship, and a member of the world champion Boston Celtics of the National Basketball Association from 1956-58, before becoming an educator in Louisville.

Radio Sports Talk show hosts Eddie Andelman and Jim McCarthy, who saw Harry play at B.U., hosted a twenty-fifth anniversary show in 1980 and continued to boost his memory as New England's greatest athlete. Mel Palumbo, one of his coaches, said on the show Harry could have been a professional star in football, baseball and basketball.

New England baseball writers present an annual award in Harry's name.

In 1965, a portrait of an air-bound Harry in his football uniform was used by Alitalia Airlines, under the phrase VOLA ALITALIA, as a symbol of America and a way to attract visitors to the U.S. The same year, *Boston Herald* writer Lou Connelly wrote a tenth anniversary story of Harry's passing, imagining Harry in the twilight of a brilliant baseball career.

In December of 1974, Harry was inducted posthumously into the College Football Foundation Hall of Fame. Another inductee, Elroy "Crazy Legs" Hirsch, came up to Harry's brother, Phil, and said, "Your brother was the greatest."

Harry's death was not the only tragedy on the B.U. teams on which he played. His great end, Bob Capuano, left school early and died shortly thereafter. John Pappas, his center, died after an injury in the Syracuse game of 1953. George Schultz died in an avalanche. Tom Gastall, a quarterback and baseball player who signed with the Baltimore Orioles, died in September of 1956 when the plane he was flying crashed into Chesapeake Bay in Maryland. He had signed five days before Harry died.

The Gridiron Club of Boston presents the Harry Agganis Award to the outstanding football player in New England. Past winners have included Heisman Trophy winner Doug Flutie, Greg Landry of Nashua, New Hampshire, a quarterback with the University of Massachusetts and the Detroit Lions, and Tim Whalen of Tufts University, son of Bobby Whalen, who played with Harry in 1949 and who was named to B.U.'s all-time team with him as a halfback.

The Harry Agganis Award was also established by the National Order of the American Hellenic Education Progressive Association (AHEPA) and Harry was inducted into the AHEPA's athletic Hall of Fame in 1975 with former professional football great Alex Karras and wrestler Jim Londos. Winners of the AHEPA's Agganis Award have included tennis star Pete Sampras.

In 1995, a poll taken by WEEI radio sports talk show host Ted Sarandis found Harry a runaway winner as New England's greatest athlete. Eighteen years earlier, during a rain delay at Fenway Park in 1977, sportswriters took a similar poll, as to who was the greatest athlete ever to play in a Boston uniform, including collegians and pros. That included Ted Williams, Bob Cousy, John Havlicek, and Bill Russell of the Boston Celtics, Carl Yastrzemski of the Red Sox, and Bobby Orr of the Boston Bruins. The winner was Harry.

Art Dunphy, who worked for B.U.'s public affairs office, wrote of that survey and said there was a simple reason for the finding. "Agganis is Agganis is Agganis and to those who saw him play football at Boston University and baseball as a member of the Boston Red Sox, there is no way to convince them that another player was ever, or could ever, be as good."

Harry's portrait hangs in Lynn Classical High School's auditorium and a banner and his number are hanging in the gymnasium. His Red Sox portrait hangs at St. George Church.

Ken Coleman and Curt Gowdy both broadcast B.U. football games in which Harry played and for the Boston Red Sox.

Silvio Cella became football coach and athletic director at Revere High.

Buff Donelli, Harry's coach at B.U., died in Florida in 1994.

Angelo "Junior" Dagres, didn't sign with the Red Sox for a $6,000 bonus. His father took Harry's advice and sent his son to college, where he signed instead with the Baltimore Orioles later for $80,000.

Harry Demeter, the AHEPA president whose chapter honored Harry in 1952, became a judge.

Harry's uncle, Louis Pappas, had a grandson, Eric, who became a catcher for the St. Louis Cardinals in the National League.

Dick Fecteau, Harry's teammate in 1949, and fellow Lynn resident, was shot down over Red China in 1953 while working for the Central Intelligence Agency and spent nineteen years in prison.

Tom McGee, who, as a B.U. student, hitchhiked across the country to watch Harry play, became a state legislator and speaker of the Massachusetts House of Representatives.

Babe Parilli, who beat out Harry for the All-American quarterback spot, eventually became a quarterback for the Boston Patriots.

Joe Paterno, the assistant coach at Penn State in 1951 when Harry gave one of his greatest performances, remained at the school he has taken to national championships. He said Harry could have dominated as a quarterback in any era.

Joe Yukica, a member of that Penn State team, was a successful college coach for many years, including at Boston College.

Cleo Sophios, who received the first Harry Agganis Scholarship at B.U. became a college administrator. The scholarship paid for her four years at B.U.

Ted Williams, perhaps the greatest hitter in baseball history, said he cried in Washington the day of the memorial service for Harry. In his autobigraphy, *My Turn At Bat*, written with John Underwood, he wrote that he was not resentful he had to serve in the military twice. He said he was grateful he had not been permanently injured. He said he thought of Harry, "A guy who wouldn't quit, despite doctor's warnings."

Norm Zauchin, the man Harry competed against for the first base job for the Red Sox in 1955, carried a picture of him in his wallet ever since.

Ted Lepcio had a successful baseball career and went into the trucking business as an administrator and moved to Dedham, Massachusetts.

Jean Dallaire became the host of a popular children's television program, "Miss Jean's Romper Room," which was on Boston TV for fifteen years.

Harold Zimman, Harry's assistant coach at Lynn Classical, died in 1994.

In 1994, more than forty-seven years after they were part of the only high school team to defeat Classical when Harry was at quarterback, former Peabody high quarterback Charley St. Paul, halfback Joe Regis and end Arthur Drivas were presented with an award by Peabody Mayor Peter Torigian, on "The Press Box," a cable television show hosted by Nick Spiliotis.

Perhaps the oddest story about Harry was told by the late actor, Telly Savalas, who briefly had lived in Lynn before Harry came to fame. Savalas said he was a young actor in 1955 and was driving from New York City to New Jersey when his car ran out of gas about 3 a.m. He got out and started to walk down a deserted road.

After a short while, he heard a high-pitched voice coming from a long, black Cadillac which seemed to come out of nowhere. A man dressed in a white suit asked him, "Can I give you a lift?" The man gave him a ride and loaned him money for the gasoline. His name was Bill.

Savalas had him write down his name and address and telephone number. As they drove back to Savalas' car, the man turned to Savalas and said "I know Harry Agganis."

"Who is Harry Agganis?" said Savalas.

The man told him Harry played for the Red Sox.

The next day, Savalas saw a jarring headline in New York newspapers: "HARRY AGGANIS OF RED SOX DIES SUDDENLY."

He called the number the man had given him. It was in Massachusetts. He asked for Bill. A woman answered. When Savalas said why he was calling, she started crying and explained the man he was looking for was her husband—and that he had died three years before, buried in a white suit. He owned a black Cadillac.

They talked more and the woman said she had to see him. She came to New York and showed him a letter her husband had written. Savalas looked at it. He didn't tell her it matched the note the man had given him.

In 1988, Savalas told that story on the Larry King syndicated television show. King asked him for the ending. "I'll tell you that at a later time," Savalas said. He never did, before he died in 1994.

His wife sent a letter to Bessie Agganis, wife of Harry's brother, Paul, in which she said Telly had not told her the ending either. "You may well guess, he's never gotten over it," she wrote.

Savalas had a long and successful career as a television and film actor and was perhaps best known for his portrayal of a tough, Greek-American police detective in New York City in the TV program called "Kojak."

Mrs. Georgia Agganis remained an avid churchgoer who could always be found in the first seat of the last pew on the left, on the aisle, of St. George's Church.

She was philanthropic, and, although she could not write her native language, she sent money through letters written by her niece, Stella Agganis Spyropoulos, to the church Propheti Elias in Logganiko in Greece, and to the monastery there, Ambellaki, in the mountains near there. Harry's name is on a plaque outside the church.

Each Memorial Day, she would go to the grave of Harry and her husband to greet visitors coming to pay their respects to her son. Until her death on January 22, 1968, at age eighty-two, she was often cited in newspaper articles for her humility and strength.

Elmo Benedetto, who spotted Harry's abilities in junior high, would escort Mrs. Agganis onto the field at Manning Bowl and present her with a memento of the Agganis game.

Harry left an estate of $7,500 when he died. He also left behind the gold watch given to him in 1951 as the recipient of the Bulger Lowe award as New England's best college football player, and a wallet which showed how much he cared for his friends and life.

Inside were many business cards and photographs of friends, and notes he had written. His Social Security card was there, as were cards showing his membership in the Association of Professional BallPlayers of America, member number 25684, with dues paid through July 1, 1955, the day after his funeral. Another card showed he was paid through July 1, 1956.

He also kept a small religious card remembering his father, and notes and photos about Jimmy Kirios, columnist Murray Kramer, a picture of Kirios and Vic Pujo together, phone numbers for Johnny Pesky, Harry Demeter, Jr., George Maravelias, B.U. trustee Nick Apalakis, Buff Donelli, a picture of his sister, Mary, on November 26, 1944, a card for his tailor, Stephen Girard of Boston, a Jordan Marsh metal credit card, his student ID card from B.U., his draft card and honorable discharge and Marine identification, and his bank book from the Lynn Institution for Savings, with a balance of $3,023.04.

In 1993 and 1994, a drive was conducted to raise $140,000 to erect a statue of Harry Agganis for the Sports Museum of New England. It was conducted by the newly-established Harry Agganis Team Fund, which included leaders of the Greek-American community.

The drive was successful, and the statue of "The Golden Greek," done by world famous sports sculptor Armand LaMontagne, will stand alongside those of his other works there, Carl Yastrzemski, Larry Bird, and Bobby Orr.

In November of 1993, the Logganiko Society, which gave Harry a going-away party in 1953 before his first Spring training in 1953, raised $25,000 in one night for the Harry Agganis Team Fund, to help erect a statue in his honor. More than three hundred fifty people attended. William Markos, a member of the Harry Agganis Team Fund, was master of ceremonies.

In May of 1994, the Greek-American community of greater-Lowell raised more than $73,000 in one night for the same cause. The event was held at a restaurant owned by George Spaneas, who was coached by Harry at B.U. in 1954. Nearly five hundred fifty people attended. The keynote speaker was Ken Coleman. The master of ceremonies was George Behrakis.

On May 9, 1995, a uniform worn by Ted Williams was sold at auction for $57,500 in San Francisco. It was the uniform with the sewn-in black armband that the Red Sox players wore in memory of Harry.

Dick Johnson, the museum's curator, said Harry is the athlete they have most wanted there, as the greatest all-around athlete to ever come out of New England. There was already a small exhibit about Harry, including the first baseman's mitt he had given to Joe Stoico, who donated it back.

The first statue visitors will see is Harry Agganis, in his red B.U. jersey with Number 33, poised to pass, his face stern, his hair curled, his left arm cocked behind his left ear, his right arm pointed slightly up, the fingers aimed at the heavens.

TIME ◆ **HONOR** ◆ TIMH

by Steve Kiorpes Bulpett

On June 28, 1955, the day after Harry Agganis died, *Boston Daily Record* sports columnist John Gillooly reminisced about the day he was in the Boston Red Sox locker room after a game and was marveling at the sight of so many well-toned athletes, and yet how Harry stood out even in that group, which included the great Ted Williams.

"Agganis was something to see," he wrote. "A Greek god for sure, all thew and sinew and shoulders. Some real Atlases in that particular nudists colony, towelling and relaxing and cooling out after a ballgame. Williams, for one, a hunk of handsome man. And blond Jackie Jensen, golden boy from the Golden State. But if a sculptor walked in and wanted someone to take discus in hand and pose in the classical fashion, most likely the artist would select Agganis for his model."

In 1993, a drive was begun by the newly-formed Harry Agganis Team Fund to raise money to erect a statue of Harry for the Sports Museum of New England. It culminated with a night in May of 1994 in which more than five hundred fifty people, primarily from the strong Greek-American community came together to honor and remember him, almost four decades after he had passed away. The legend of Harry Agganis was continued with the commissioning of world famous sports sculptor Armand LaMontagne.

The group included *Boston Herald* sportswriter Steve Kiorpes Bulpett, also a television and radio personality, who covered the Boston Celtics. He found out on one road trip just how dear Harry's memory was to so many people and wrote about it for *The Hellenic Chronicle*. The article, reprinted here by permission, is called "The Warmth Of Harry's Legacy."

United Flight 293 had just begun to push away from the gate at Denver's Stapleton Airport. It was painfully early in the morning and the last thing on a writer's sleep-deprived mind was friendly conversation with the chap two seats away. There had been a Celtic loss the previous night to the Nuggets and a defeat the night before that in Sacramento. A few days earlier, there had been losses in Portland, Oregon and Oakland, California. The next game/loss was scheduled for Seattle. There had, in sum, been too many early flights and too much bad basketball and too many miles between wherever we were and home.

Pushing through some notes on my carry-on bag, I inadvertently exposed to view some literature on Harry Agganis. I had been carrying it with me everywhere, just in case I encountered a potential contributor to the statue drive. The gentleman two seats away spoke up.

"Harry Agganis," he said. "I haven't seen that name in years."

In short order, he explained that he was originally from New York and had been a fan of Harry in the early 50s, following his career from football at Boston University to major league baseball and the Red Sox. "Every time I hear someone talk about Bo Jackson or Deion Sanders, I laugh to myself. I know better," he said. "I just think about Harry Agganis."

Feeling more awake as he spoke, I asked the man if he was Greek. His reply began with a laugh. I don't recall his name specifically, but it had several syllables and ended in –ski. "Polish," he said. "Very Polish ... hey, I hope you don't think Harry Agganis was a hero only to the Greeks."

If I hadn't been aware of that fact before the Harry Agganis Team began its work, I certainly was now. I was not surprised in the least to find tremendous support for the effort in the Greek community; his story had been faithfully passed through church and home to all generations. Harry Agganis is a part of who we are. But to learn the depth and emotion that exists for Harry outside our community is to get a true measure of his legacy.

On a cold morning as flight 293 made its way toward Seattle, that legacy produced a very warm feeling.

The warmth has been very much a part of the drive to commission the statue of Harry Agganis. It has been there in the graciousness of the media outlets that provided radio and television time to get the word to the people. And it has been there in the eyes of all who contributed amounts both great and small.

Harry will take his place in the museum alongside Larry Bird, Bobby Orr and Carl Yastrzemski, who have been immortalized by sculptor Armand LaMontagne. As an athlete, there is no question Harry belongs. As a person, however, there is perhaps no earthly place worthy of the man. Harry Agganis raised common decency to uncommon heights. His modesty in the face of incalculable fame, his humility and his dedication to family stand as the greatest monuments to his being. When the subject at home would turn to Harry Agganis' achievements, my mother would always add that Harry was an even better person than player.

Indeed, no mere athlete could have accomplished what Harry Agganis did.

There have been additional chapters written into the Harry Agganis legend. The effort that produced $140,000 is remarkable on several fronts. To begin with, understand that the statues of Bird, Orr, and Yastrzemski were financed through business subsidy. The funding was produced both generously and quickly by a sponsoring corporation. But it is "The People" who are sculpting Harry's statue. This was a wholly grass roots campaign, encompassing all economic strata. From the Greek picnics to the fraternal organizations to the foundations, the people stepped forward.

And that is as it should be, for Harry Agganis was a man of the people.

For all of time, as well. We live in an age of instant gratification, but the enduring nature of Harry Agganis is a warm and comforting reminder that character survives. His life spanned a tragically brief twenty-six years, making it nothing less than incredible that forty years after his passing, the torch still burns brightly. Throughout this statue drive, we never had to explain; we had only to mention the name.

My life didn't begin until two years after Harry's death, but in a very personal sense, he has always been there. My passion for basketball was born and nurtured at the tournament at St. George that bears his name. When it came my turn to play in his gym, each trophy our team earned was placed with pride in a case beneath a large painting of Harry in his Red Sox uniform. He was there for all of us.

I suspect it was no different for a lot of people, and not just those from St. George. Harry Agganis was a beacon ahead guiding us toward greater accomplishment—the latest being the statue that will illuminate his memory for future generations.

The feeling is warm, indeed. And it rises from the spirit and legacy of Harry Agganis.

Epigraph

That you were handsome, our clippings offer proof;
And highlight films and statistics forever record
An athlete ahead of his time, a field outdistanced.
But a solid character can't be displayed
On a pedestal: your good deeds depend on us.

Only armchair quarterbacks like to boast
They knew the game was really never in doubt;
But that the chiseled features of Harry Agganis
Could be taken at twenty-six, remains,
For many, a very hard thing to believe.

George Kalogeris

◆ BIBLIOGRAPHY ◆

"10,000 Console Mother At Harry Agganis' Bier," *Boston Daily Globe*, June 29, 1955.

"20,000 Say Farewell To Lynn's Beloved Harry Agganis," *Lynn Telegram-News*, July 1, 1955.

"500 Cheer Award To B.U. Star," *Boston Post*, December 6, 1951.

"Abp. Cushing Offers Tribute To Agganis At Mayor's Field Day," *Boston Daily Globe*, June 29, 1955.

"Agganis And Scarbath Named To Senior Bowl," *Mobile Press Register*, November 30, 1952.

"Agganis Body To Lie In State Until Rites," *Boston Evening American*, June 28, 1955.

"Agganis Field Dedication," *Camp Lejeune Globe*, June 22, 1956.

"Agganis Memorial Rites Held In Greek Churches," *The Hellenic Chronicle*, August 4, 1955.

"Athletic Injury Probably Caused Death Of Agganis," *Boston Post*, June 28, 1955.

"Boston Univ. Gets Star Lynn Athlete," *Lynn Telegram-News*, June 10, 1948.

"Death Of Agganis Shocks Red Sox," *Springfield Union* (Massachusetts), June 28, 1955.

"Donelli Applauds Agganis," *Boston Daily Globe*, October 18, 1949.

"Grieving Throngs At Agganis Bier," *Lynn Telegram-News*, June 29, 1955.

"Harry Agganis Dead," *Boston Evening Globe,* June 27, 1955.

"Harry Agganis Is Key To 'T,'" *Lynn Telegram-News*, November 24, 1946.

"Harry Agganis of Boston Red Sox Dies," *New York Times*, June 28, 1955.

"Harry Agganis Repeats As 'Athlete Of Year,'" *Boston University News*, April 29, 1952.

"Harry's Last Words To Mom," *Boston Evening American*, June 29, 1955.

"Is He College Football's Greatest Passer?" *Saturday Evening Post*, October 18, 1952.

"Maryland Breaks B.U. String, 14-13," *Boston Sunday Post*, October 13, 1949.

"Mrs. Agganis in 25-Hour Vigil," *Boston Traveler*, June 29, 1955.

"Obituary," *New York Times*, June 28, 1955.

"Obituary," *Stars and Stripes*. June 29, 1955.

"Red Sox Notables, Little Leaguers At Agganis Rites," *Boston Daily Record*, July 1, 1955.

"Sgt. Sam Recalls Agganis As All-Around Athlete, Gentleman While Stationed Here," *Camp Lejeune Globe*, June 8, 1956.

"Sports Greats Attend Funeral Services For Agganis," *Boston Daily Record*, July 1, 1955.

"The Spirit Lives On," *The Hellenic Chronicle*, July 7, 1955.

"Thousands Mourn Agganis" *Lynn Daily Evening Item*, June 30, 1955.

"Tributes Endless For Agganis," *The Hellenic Chronicle*, June 30, 1955.

"Why They All Pick Agganis," *Football Stars*, 1952.

Ahern, John, "Agganis, Classical's Great Passer," *Boston Daily Globe*, October 20, 1947.

Carens, George C., "As Agganis Goes, So Goes B.U. Fortune," *Boston Traveler*, September 9, 1949.

Cashman, Joe, "Passing Of Agganis Top Sport Shocker," *Boston Daily Record*, June 28, 1955.

-----., "Passing of Agganis Top Sport Shocker," *Boston Daily Record*, June 28, 1995.

Claflin, Larry, "Joyce Like A Dad To Agganis," *Boston Evening American*, June 28, 1955.

-----., "Lynn's Greatest Athlete," *Agganis Memorial Game Program*, August 20, 1956.

Cloney, Will, "Death Of Harry Agganis At Age 25 Traced To Old Sports Injury," *Boston Post*, June 28, 1995.

-----., "Walked Out As A Champion," *Agganis Memorial Game Program*, August 20, 1956.

-----., *Boston University Program*, November 12, 1955.

Collins, John, "10,000 File Past Agganis Bier," *Boston Herald*, June 29, 1955.

Conway, Jr., Jack, "Hearst Sandlot Final," *Boston Daily Record*, August 13, 1948.

Costello, Ed, "A Big Leaguer," *Agganis Memorial Game Program*, August 20, 1956.

Coyne, Bob, "Harry Deserved That Award!" (cartoon) *Boston Post*, December 5, 1951.

Cunningham, Bill, "Game Goes On, Despite Tragedy," *Boston Herald*, June 29, 1955.

-----., "Harry 'My Boy' To Sportswriters," *Boston Herald*, June 28, 1955.

Daley, Arthur, "The Golden Greek," *Newsweek*, June 29, 1955.

Dalton, Ernest, "Classical Rallies In Ninth to Overhaul Newton For Title, 7-6," *Boston Sunday Globe*, June 8, 1947.

-----., "Lynn Classical Thumps Ludlow, 14-2, For State Diamond Title," *Boston Sunday Globe*, June 22, 1947.

Drohan, John, "GM Cronin Eager To See Rookies Agganis, Consolo," *Boston Traveler*, February 19, 1953.

-----., "Stobbs Has Cause To Recall Agganis," Boston Traveler, May 27, 1949.

Dunphy, Art, "Sports Yesterday," *Boston University Today*, June/July 1978.

Egan, Dave, "Agganis Greatest Of His Generation," *Boston Sunday Advertiser*, 1951.

-----., "Agganis To Make It Despite Criticism," *Boston Daily Record*, March 9, 1954.

Fitzgerald, Ed, "Agganis of Boston U.," *Sport Magazine*, December, 1952. p. 28.

-----., "One Man Team Hits The Big Time," *Sport Magazine*, December, 1952.

Frost, Jack (UPI), "Agganis Rated Tops Among Nation's Touchdown Passers," *Lynn Telegram-News*, October 26, 1949.

Garber, Jess, "Chronicling Sports," *The News-Chronicle* (Shippensburg, PA). November 7, 1952, p. 1-B.

Gilooly, John, "Friends Of Agganis Refuse To Forget," *Boston Daily Record*, October 18, 1955.

-----., "Sox Apollo Ruled Own Olympus," *Boston Daily Record*, June 28, 1995.

-----., "Sox Scout 'Shadowed' Harry At 16," *Boston Daily Record*, April 28, 1954.

-----., "Strong Men In Tears At Agganis' Bier," *Boston Daily Record*, June 29, 1955.

Gilooly, Mike, "Players, Fans Honor Harry At Washington" *Boston Evening American*, June 30, 1955.

-----., "Sox Still Stunned By Agganis' Death," *Boston Evening American*, June 28, 1955.

-----., "Ted Pays Tribute To Harry," *Boston Evening American*, June 29, 1955.

Golenbock, Peter. *Fenway: An Unexpurgated History of the Boston Red Sox* . New York, 1992.

Goodenough, Tap, "Agganis Could Have Become Track Star," *Boston Evening American*, July 2, 1955.

-----., "Grid Or Diamond," *Boston Evening American*, September 1, 1953.

-----., "Sgt. Agganis' Grid Duel With LeBaron Sellout," *Boston Evening American*, October 24, 1950.

Hartley, Frank, "Agganis Sharing Apartment With Rookie From Texas U." *Lynn Item*, May 20, 1953.

Hern, Gerry, "Buff Donelli Claims Loyalty Only Word To Describe Agganis," *Boston Post*, June 28, 1995.

Hines, Jr., Paul, "Classical Has Romp," *Boston Post*, October 28, 1946.

-----., "Funeral Of Agganis Will Be Held Today," *Boston Post*, June 30, 1955.

Hirshberg, Al, "Boston's Golden Greek," *Sport Magazine*, November, 1950.

-----., "Is He College Football's Greatest Passer," *Saturday Evening Post*, October 18, 1952

Holbrook, Bob, "Agganis Rites Thursday; May Cancel Sox Game," *Boston Daily Globe*, June 28, 1955.

-----., "Thought It Was Home Run—Agganis," *Boston Daily Globe*, April 16, 1954.

Johnson, Anne, "Most Alert, Most Alive," *Agganis Memorial Game Program*, August 20, 1956.

Kaese, Harold, "Mother First Concern, So Agganis Chose B.U. and Red Sox," *Boston Daily Globe*, June 28, 1955.

Keane, Clif, "Agganis Would Have Made Good Priest" *The Boston Globe*, June 29, 1955.

-----., "Higgins Lauds Star, Death Shocks Mates," *Boston Daily Globe*, June 28, 1955.

Kennedy, Tom, "Agganis Better Than Most Pros," *Boston Evening American*, October 25, 1952.

Kramer, Murray, "Last Visit To Harry One To Remember," *Boston Daily Record*, June 29, 1955.

-----., "Sudden End For Sox Star," *Boston Daily Record*, June 28, 1995.

-----., "Embolism Wipes Out Agganis' Great Career," *Boston Daily Record*, June 28, 1955.

Lake, Austen, "Agganis Was A Victim Of His Own Tenacity," *Boston Evening American*, June 29, 1955.

-----., "Conversation Piece Among The Red Sox," *Boston Evening American*, March 8, 1955.

-----., "Word To Harry About Turning Professional," *Boston Evening American,* January 29, 1952.

-----., "Zauchin Blows Hot Breath On Agganis' Neck," *Boston Evening American*, March 10,1955.

Mahoney, Frank, "B.U. Degree," *Boston Daily Globe*, June 28, 1955.

Moore, Gerry, "Agganis Won't Quit Baseball For Pro Football," *Boston Sunday Post*, January 24, 1954.

Morse, Web, "Highest Tributes Paid Athlete Harry Agganis," *Christian Science Monitor*, June 28, 1955.

Nason, Jerry, "35,000 To See B.U., Maryland," *Boston Daily Globe*, November 1, 1952.

-----., "Agganis Greatest Footbal Player Donelli Has Seen," *Boston Daily Globe*, June 28, 1955.

-----., "Agganis Greatest Football Player Donelli Has Seen," *Boston Daily Globe*, June 28, 1955.

-----., "The Best Campus Football Player," *Agganis Memorial Game Program*, August 20, 1956.

Pave, Marvin, "Agganis Was Model For Young Unitas," *Boston Globe*, August 11, 1972.

Ralby, Herb, "Agganis Gets Offense Call in BU Opener," *Boston Daily Globe*, September 22, 1951.

Roberts, Ernie, "Agganis Would Like To Play Against Wm. and Mary," *Boston Daily Globe*, September 20, 1951.

Sampson, Arthur, "Agganis Signs With Red Sox For Reported $60,000 Bonus," *Boston Herald*, November 29, 1952.

-----., "Lynn Rites Thursday For Athlete," *Boston Herald*, June 28, 1955.

Siegel, Art, "This Is Where He Belonged," *Agganis Memorial Game Program*, August 20, 1956.

-----., "Kazmaier Great, Agganis, O'Rourke, Better," *Boston Traveler*, November 7, 1951.

-----., "Sox Job First With Agganis," *Boston Traveler*, February 23, 1954.

Smith, Red, "Views of Sport," *New York Times*, November, 1952.

Stiles, Maxwell, "Pacific Boosters Hail Agganis," *Los Angeles Mirror*, August 23, 1952.

Stout, Vic, "Inspiration To The Marines," *Agganis Memorial Game Program*, August 20, 1956.

Sullivan, George, "Break Gave Agganis Grid Start," *Boston Traveler*, June 29, 1955.

-----., "Harry Began Sports Life on Lynn Lot," *Boston Traveler*, June 28, 1955.

Walsh, Bob, "Agganis Death Stuns City, Nation," *Lynn Telegram-News*, June 28, 1955

Wheeler, Ralph, "Harry Top School Athlete in 25 Years," *Boston Herald*, June 28, 1955.

◆ INDEX OF NAMES ◆

Wilbur, Del, 171
Wilkie, Wendall, 18
Williams, J.F., 31
Williams, Ted, 5, 6, 7, 8, 70, 91, 99, 126,
   141, 152, 154, 155, 160,163, 167,
   168, 169, 174, 183, 184, 186, 190,
   211, 224
Williams, Wally, 89
Winkler, George, 71, 72, 73, 75, 79, 82,
   221
Woodling, Gene. 175
Woodward, Stanley, 115, 135
Wynn, Early, 172

-Y-
Yawkey, Tom, 56, 95, 201, 218
Yellin, Rabbi, 146
Yukica, Joe, 102, 103, 224

-Z-
Zauchin, Janet, 181
Zauchin, Norm, 6, 166, 177, 179, 180, 181,
   182, 185, 189, 192, 198, 202, 224
Zimman, Harold, 28, 29, 54, 55, 65, 191,
   224
Zimman, Helen, 191
Zimmer, Don, 145, 148
Zingus, Chris, 101
Zingus, Evanthia, 101
Zingus, Harry, 76, 100, 101, 110

ABOUT THE AUTHORS

Nick Tsiotos is a public school teacher in Boston. He graduated from Winthrop, Mass. High School where he was captain of one of the school's greatest basketball teams. He was also graduated from Suffolk University, where he played on a team that participated in two NCAA small college basketball tournaments. He received his master's degree in education from Boston State College, and was the spokesman for the Harry Agganis Team Fund. He still lives in Winthrop.

Andy Dabilis is a reporter for The Boston Globe, where he has written about politics and sports, including Harry Agganis. He also worked for United Press International in Boston as a political reporter, and Massachusetts and New England editor. He was an Air Force officer and was graduated from Chelmsford, Mass. High School, Northeastern University in Boston, and received his master's degree from Boston University. He lives in Boston.

George Sullivan was a Boston University teammate of Harry Agganis. A longtime Boston sportswriter and columnist, Sullivan later was a B.U. professor before returning across Kenmore Square to Fenway Park as the Red Sox' public relations director. Like Agganis, an ex-Marine, Sullivan has lectured at a variety of colleges, including Harvard. He is working on his tenth book.

Steve Kiorpes Bulpett is a columnist for *The Boston Herald*. He covers the Boston Celtics and the N.B.A. He is the eastern correspondent for *Sports Illustrated*, covering professional basketball's Atlantic Division. He was twice selected "Best Sportswriter" by *Boston Magazine*.